IF MONEY TALKS, WHAT DOES IT SAY?

COMPARATIVE POLITICS

Comparative Politics is a series for students, teachers, and researchers of political science that deals with contemporary government and politics. Global in scope, books in the series are characterized by a stress on comparative analysis and strong methodological rigour. The series is published in association with the European Consortium for Political Research. For more information visit www.ecprnet.eu

The Comparative Politics series is edited by Professor David M. Farrell, School of Politics and International Relations, University College Dublin, and Kenneth Carty, Professor of Political Science, University of British Columbia.

OTHER TITLES IN THIS SERIES

If Money Talks, What Does it Say?

Corruption and Business Financing of Political Parties

IAIN MCMENAMIN

OXFORD
UNIVERSITY PRESS

OXFORD
UNIVERSITY PRESS

Great Clarendon Street, Oxford OX2 6DP,
United Kingdom

Oxford University Press is a department of the University of Oxford.
It furthers the University's objective of excellence in research, scholarship,
and education by publishing worldwide. Oxford is a registered trade mark of
Oxford University Press in the UK and in certain other countries

© Iain McMenamin 2013

First Edition published in 2013

Impression: 1

British Library Cataloguing in Publication Data
Data available

Library of Congress Cataloging in Publication Data
Data available

ISBN 978–0–19–966570–9

Printed in Great Britain by
MPG Books Group, Bodmin and King's Lynn

Dom' mhuintir

Contents

Acknowledgments

Ben Reilly encouraged me to visit Australia, so he is the first person I must thank. I am very grateful indeed to the Political Science Programme and the National Europe Centre of the Australian National University (ANU) for hosting me in 2007. Keith Dowding, Ian McAllister, and Paul t'Hart, all from ANU, generously read my first paper on this topic. Richard Eccleston volunteered to look over a draft of my Australia chapter. Earlier versions of the argument of this book were presented at the Joint Sessions of the European Consortium for Political Research (ECPR) in Lisbon, April 2009; the World Congress of the International Political Science Association in Santiago, Chile, July 2009; the Centre for International Studies, Dublin City University (DCU), September 2009; and the Annual Conference of the Political Studies Association of Ireland, October 2010. I am grateful to all who provided comments, especially my ECPR discussant, Kaare Strøm. I would also like to thank the anonymous referees of the various journals in which earlier versions of these ideas have been published. I began the Canadian and German research while a Government of Ireland Research Fellow in the Humanities and Social Sciences. The DCU School of Law and Government provided travel funding and granted leave to spend six months in Australia. I am indebted to Conor McGrath for references and to Agnès Joannisse and Elections Canada, Monika Schlenger and the Goethe Institute, Ellin Allern, Eric Bélanger, Flemming Juul Christiansen, Charlie Lees, Eoin O'Malley, and Karsten Ronit for assistance in pursuing data. I am very grateful to David Farrell for encouraging me to submit my work to the ECPR series at Oxford University Press. At OUP Dominic Byatt, Jo North, Sarah Parker, and Lizzy Suffling helped me through a long process with exemplary professionalism. Finally, I would like to thank my beloved wife Virpi. Without her efficient typing of my illegible manuscript this book would not have been published.

List of Tables

List of Figures

1

Introduction

Corruption is the abuse of the political system. It is both a behavioural phenom-enon and a normative concern. Many debates about corruption in democratic countries occur at cross-purposes, as behavioural and normative claims interact with, and bypass, each other. This problem is particularly evident in the discussion of the subject of this book: business financing of political parties. There is often great controversy as to whether business funding corrupts politics. These disputes relate to a behavioural issue of whether and how parties and businesses benefit and a normative issue of what types of benefits and exchanges constitute an abuse of the political system. This is a disagreement about both facts and values. It is very difficult to structure a normative debate about a behaviour, the very existence of which is in doubt. This book seeks to identify the motivation behind business contributions to political parties, and the benefit, or lack thereof, to both sides. It dispels some of the mystery about putatively corrupt behaviour, so that democratic societies can concentrate on deciding whether the behaviour violates their norms.

Corruption as the abuse of politics is a wide contestable definition. By contrast, in recent decades scholars have preferred narrower legalistic definitions (Rose-Ackerman 1999, 9), which have the important advantage of conceptual clarity and concrete empirical expression. However, such definitions are less useful when there is a disconnect between legal standards and popular norms, and between the view of the political and business elite and the rest of society (Johnston 1996, 290). Many ordinary people view the constant interaction between business and politics with suspicion, and perceive the volume of corporate lobbying with suspicion. Business financing of parties is considered even more dubious and often as *prima facie* evidence of corruption. 'Money talks' is a good summary of this attitude. Those who work at the interface of business and politics tend to see things differently. Politicians and businesspeople argue that corporate lobbying is inevitable for business and helpful for good public policy. They also tend to accept business financing of parties as valid participation in democratic politics.

'Money talks' is a hypothesis, not an axiom. If money talks, what does it say? Why do businesses contribute to political parties? Is money a universal language? Do business contributions to political parties convey different messages in differ-ent countries? The relationship between money and politics is usually regarded as very difficult to study, consisting of the 'stuff of detective stories' (Loesche 1993,

219). However, as the following examples show, this depends very much on the distribution of business money and the distribution of political power.

In 2001 Stuart Wheeler gave five million pounds to the Conservative party, the largest political donation in British history (Jones 2001). Mr Wheeler made his millions from a betting business. At the time of his donation, Wheeler's own company was forecasting that Labour would win a clear victory over the Conservatives. Wheeler claimed that he was motivated by his belief that the Conservatives' William Hague would make a better prime minister than Labour's Tony Blair. He also supported the Conservatives' strong opposition to the replacement of the British Pound with the Euro. Since the Conservatives were not in power, and not likely to exercise power for some time, Mr Wheeler's decision would have been a strange one for a pragmatic donor. In the circumstances, it is reasonable to accept that his donation was ideological.

Between 1989 and 2010, the American telecommunications giant, AT&T donated over $41 million to politicians. The company's business has been famously politicized. It was broken up in a landmark anti-trust case in the mid-1980s, but managed to re-form in 2005. Its mergers and attempts to enter new markets continue to be controversial. In 2010, AT&T reportedly spent $15 million on lobbying and was mentioned in relation to 225 bills. The company has given 45 per cent of its donations to the Democrats and 54 per cent to the Republicans, with the split varying little from year to year (Center for Responsive Politics 2011a). It is safe to infer a pragmatic motivation when a corporation hedges impartially between the two dominant political parties. AT&T seems concerned to look after its business interests and cares little, or not at all, about the ideological positions of the competitors.

The small and picturesque Irish city of Galway holds a horse racing festival every summer. In the 1990s, it became especially popular with politicians and property developers. Ireland's biggest political party, Fianna Fáil, had its own tent at the festival (Ross 2009, 112–17). The horse-racing festival was a key opportunity for the party to network with potential financial supporters and also an opportunity for businesspeople to get to know senior politicians. Property developers were particularly associated with the Fianna Fáil party and its tent at the Galway races. Many of the developers who frequented the tent were personal friends of Fianna Fáil politicians. Some received appointments to state boards. Many in the property industry made financial contributions to the Fianna Fáil party and its candidates. Was their money speaking ideologically or pragmatically? Did developers believe that Fianna Fáil would provide the best government for Ireland? Or did they frequent the tent and contribute money in the hope of securing benefits that would help their property development businesses? It is very hard to tell because Fianna Fáil had been in government for all but three years of a twenty-three year period. In those years, ideological and pragmatic payments to Fianna Fáil were observationally equivalent. The Galway Races continues to excite political controversy in Ireland, because there are incompatible interpretations that are compatible with the facts.

This book does not just add up the business money sloshing around in the political system and sound a warning that money talks. It uses hard evidence to find out what the money has to say. It is able to identify the motivations behind business contributions to political parties. Essentially, the method of inference in the British and American examples is applied systematically to thousands of payments by hundreds of companies in three different countries. In other words, it associates the distribution of business money with the distribution of power.

Political and legal debate about business financing of politics tends to elide the differences in motivation and consequence between contributions. For example, in the USA, business involvement in political finance is defended by the right of freedom to speech and denounced as the privileging of special interests over the equality of citizens. In January 2010, the US Supreme Court overturned a ban on 'electioneering communications' by corporations. The Constitution, wrote Justice Anthony Kennedy, 'prohibits Congress from fining or jailing citizens, or associations of citizens, for simply engaging in political speech' (Liptak 2010). President Obama called the decision 'a major victory for big oil, Wall Street banks, health insurance companies and the other powerful interests that marshal their power every day in Washington to drown out the voices of everyday Americans' (The White House, Office of the Press Secretary 2010). 'Powerful interests ... [drowning] out the voice of everyday Americans' is compatible with both pragmatic and ideological contributions, but the two interpretations have very different normative implications.

Large volumes of pragmatic payments will be channelled relatively impartially to governing parties regardless of their ideology, as well as to prospective governing parties in opposition. Therefore, pragmatism should stabilize the political system by increasing the likelihood of the re-election of governments and giving an advantage to established parties over potential new entrants. Pragmatic payments also give an advantage to parties in powerful positions, whether to Fianna Fáil in Ireland or the duopoly of Democrats and Republicans in the USA. In terms of political competition, powerful interests drown out popular preferences and ensure stability. In relation to the economy, widespread pragmatism encourages constant interaction between politicians and firms. It should tend to favour private goods targeted at particular firms, over public goods, as pragmatic firms seek competitive advantages in exchange for political finance. If the Irish developers' and AT&T's payments were pragmatic, this gave an important economic advantage to AT&T's telecommunications business and to property interests contributing to the Irish governing party. There seems to be a trade-off between public policy that is engaged with, and informed by, the concrete concerns of firms, but tends to produce private goods, and public policy conducted at a distance from business, but more focused on broader, clearer public goods.

Ideological payments do not treat parties equally. They constitute a bias towards parties embracing a pro-business ideology, probably of the free-market variety, but possibly corporatist. Ideological payments should not necessarily favour established parties if new entrants are ideologically attractive. Ideological payments promote public policy driven by a more or less coherent philosophy of overall social welfare. Instead of producing private goods, defined and sought by firms, it should focus on defining and producing public goods. If the Irish developers' and Wheeler's payments were ideological this gave an important political advantage to Fianna Fáil and the Conservatives, but no economic advantage to the businesses in question.

This book concentrates on Australia, Canada, and Germany. Their unusually permissive and transparent systems of political finance regulation have special advantages for an analysis of the motivation of business payments to political parties. Moreover, there were turnovers of power in the period studied in each country. This avoids the problem encountered in the Irish example above. Added leverage is gained from Denmark, New Zealand, Norway, the UK, and the USA. The principal source of quantitative evidence is a new database of all the payments made by 960 firms to the principal political parties in the three countries over periods of between seven and seventeen years. The key source of qualitative evidence is over two decades of newspaper reports on political finance from each country.

In Canada, until the ban on corporate donations, money tended to speak pragmatically. A large number of firms sought to make a reciprocal exchange: an unlikely but potentially large benefit for the firm in exchange for a certain but small benefit for a party. In Germany, money tends to speak ideologically. A small number of companies grant a certain but small benefit to a party as an expression of a political preference. In Australia, pragmatism dominates, but there is also an ideological preference for the right. These patterns are associated with fundamental differences in political economy and party system. Pragmatic Canada and Australia are liberal market economies, while Germany is a co-ordinated market economy. Canada's two traditional principal parties were almost ideologically indistinguishable, but Australia's parties compete on a left–right basis.

In liberal market economies, the highly competitive, short-term focus of firms generates substantial demand for private goods that help firms develop an advantage over their rivals. Pragmatism is an important motivation for business financing of parties and since pragmatism is embedded in the basic profit-seeking mission of the firm the contribution rate is high. The preference for less state intervention, and the awareness of the state's power to disrupt the business environment, engenders a widespread awareness of the importance of public policy goods to the overall business sector. This results in a relatively important ideological motivation in business contributions to parties. However, this depends on the policy risk. In a polarized political system, the political risk should be greater. If there is a little difference between parties' economic policies and reputations, as in Canada, the ideological motivation is marginal.

In a co-ordinated market economy, the most important policies for firms tend to be the public goods defined, championed, and, to a substantial extent, actually delivered by their business associations. In this context, the pragmatic motivation for contributions to political parties is very weak. The combination of consensual political institutions and constrained parties means there is a very low risk of major policy change from election to election. So, there is a low interest in ideological financing of political parties. Since both motivations are undermined by the political economy, the contribution rate is very low.

It is sometimes suggested that business financing of politics is problematic only because of a perception of corruption (Chrétien 2007, 398). Others argue that the passing of money from businesses to politicians is a social ritual, without political or economic ramifications (Milyo 2002). It has also been defended as a form of good citizenship that underwrites democracy itself (Shecter 2002; Elliott 2003). This book refutes each of these arguments by showing clear associations between the pattern of business contributions and political power and/or ideological position. It is hoped that such empirical clarifications can help set the terms for debate about what corruption means in contemporary democracies.

The book is organized straightforwardly. The next chapter introduces the key concepts of the argument and methods used in the research. Then succeeding chapters weave together statistical and qualitative evidence from Canada, Australia, and Germany. The penultimate chapter adds evidence from five other countries. The conclusion discusses the empirical results in the framework of the neo-classical conception of corruption. It also offers some advice to reformers in the area of political finance.

2

Theory and Research Design

1. INTRODUCTION

The interface between business and politics is widely studied. While popular debate and academic research often advert to the importance of business financing of politics, it has rarely been the subject of systematic cross-national study. Indeed, this book is a pioneering study of cross-national study of firm behaviour in political finance. The paucity of research in this area surely reflects its theoretical and empirical difficulty. Much of the literature uses concepts that are difficult to apply to actual behaviour and much of the relevant behaviour is difficult to observe. Politicians and businesspeople have very strong incentives to avoid candour in discussing the motivations for business financing of parties. The aim of this chapter is to outline a strategy for overcoming many of these difficulties. It begins by assessing the relevance of the literature on business–government relations to this book. The next section introduces the two basic motivations for business contributions to political parties and shows how they can be inferred from behaviour. An application of exchange theory follows, with an emphasis on access, a word that is central to practitioner and academic discourse on this subject. Then, several cross-national hypotheses are developed. The case selection section includes a global classification of legal regimes for business financing of politics. The last section reviews the quantitative and qualitative methods used in the empirical chapters.

2. BUSINESS AND DEMOCRACY

This research contributes to the massive literature on the uneasy but vital relationship between capitalism and democracy (Mills 1959; Frye and Shleifer 1997; Dahl 1998, 179; Kaufmann, Kraay, and Zoido-Lobatón 1999; Olson 2000). The tension between the currencies of the market and democracy, between money and votes, is an inherent one (Lindblom 1977, 189–200; Vogel 1996). The political influence of big business is usually divided into intentional and structural categories (Lindblom

1977, 193–4; Offe 1985, 170–220). A useful way of thinking about intentional business behaviour is to distinguish between different actors (Wilson 1990; Hillman, Keim, and Schuler 2004; McMenamin 2009, 212–14). The firm can approach politics directly (Salisbury 1984; Useem 1984; Coen 1997; Martin 2000), or through intermediaries such as business associations (Schmitter and Streeck 1981; Bennett 1999; Greenwood and Jacek 2000) or political consultants (Heinz *et al.* 1993). On the political side, there are huge differences between the bureaucracy, the executive, and the legislature. As a further complication, business may make contact with one type of political actor in order to influence a different political actor. For example, parties can influence the legislature and the legislature can influence the executive. Pragmatic firms can pursue their interests with political parties through two principal channels, lobbying and cash contributions. These are often, but far from necessarily, related. Other methods of relating to parties are sometimes proposed, such as charitable giving (Hansen and Mitchell 2000) and various types of networking. However, these activities fit under political finance and lobbying. The connection between these two is vital to the approach taken here. This book understands pragmatic business financing of parties as part of the lobbying process. The benefit of financial contributions for business is an increased likelihood of successful lobbying.

While this research is easy to locate within the wider study of business and politics, it does not fit so easily into an existing research programme. Many of the above permutations of business and political actors have been intensely studied, but there is a very sparse literature on the relationship between firms and political parties. Beyond Grant's discussions of the 'party state' (Grant, Martinelli, and Paterson 1989; Grant 1993, 13–18), only a handful of systematic treatments are to be found (Hopkin 1997; Della Porta 2004; McMenamin 2012b). Thus, inspiration has to be somewhat indirect. There is a well-established literature on comparative political finance. However, it tends to be very much party-centred and tabulates sources of party income and expenditure in broad categories (Williams 2000; Nassmacher 2001; Scarrow 2007; Smilov and Toplak 2007; Nassmacher 2010, 26; Koss 2011, 18, 78). There is a handful of interesting country studies based on firms (Stanbury 1993, 291–318; Fisher 1994; Ramsay, Stapledon, and Vernon 2002; Bond 2007; McMenamin 2008). Scarrow draws some interesting comparative conclusions from the absolute and relative size of corporate and individual contributions to parties in Germany and the UK (Scarrow 2006). Nonetheless, her study does not focus on the firm's motivations as is done here.

There is a voluminous and impressive literature on US political finance that has much in common with the approach taken here. It is dominated by a tradition of quantitative studies of political donations. The American system of political finance tends to constrain and warp flows of money, such that they are difficult to interpret as indicators of firms' motivations. America's disclosure of business money in politics is relatively transparent, but it is not permissive. Moreover, the USA's candidate-centred presidential political system is very different to the party-centred parliamentary systems of other long-established democracies. Therefore, the next section introduces a general framework for understanding business funding of political parties.

3. IDEOLOGICAL AND PRAGMATIC MOTIVATIONS

This book aims to measure and explain variation in the pragmatic and ideological motivations for business contributions to political parties. The pragmatic motivation seeks private goods from the political system. In other words, pragmatic money is interested money. Another popular, but very different, explanation is that business contributions to parties are ideological. Ideological payments promote a public good. They express a preference for government based on a particular set of values and assumptions. Businesses often support a free-market ideology, but can also support other views of government and business, such as a developmental state. These very different motivations should have important consequences for politics and the economy. Pragmatism's effects on public policy should be disorganizing and distorting. In the language of American politics, the more important is pragmatic business financing of politics, the more important is 'corporate pork'. Pragmatism's effect on political competition is conservative, in the sense that pragmatic firms will finance those in power and those most likely to win power, disadvantaging newer or weaker competitors. Ideological payments are aimed at influencing political competition. They usually bolster right-wing parties and thus represent a different sort of conservatism to pragmatism. However, they should not have any direct effect on public policy, and only influence it by acting as a right-wing bias in the political system more generally.

This section generalizes the approach introduced in the book's opening examples. It shows how an association between the distribution of payments and the distribution of power can be used to infer the motivations of business contributors to political parties. The distribution of ideological donations should be relatively stable over time. Party ideologies change slowly. Even if parties tack to the left or the right for tactical reasons, it is very rare for the left–right ranking of parties to change. In contrast, the distribution of pragmatic donations should follow short-term changes in the distribution of political power. These two motivations may interact in a single decision about the distribution of political contributions. For example, take a firm that has an ideological preference for the right. Under a left-wing government it may be prepared to contribute to the left, while also continuing to express its ideological preference by funding the right-wing opposition. More generally, imagine an index of political power that runs from zero, when the right holds all power, to one hundred, when the left has a power monopoly. Also, let there be a measure of ideology: zero for a position at which any funding to the left is unacceptable and one for no ideological preference between left and right. The product of these two is the percentage of a firm's political contributions donated to the left. So, a firm, which assesses all power to be held by the left, will contribute exclusively to the left if its ideological score is one, that is, if its motivation is purely pragmatic. It will contribute zero to the left if its motivation is a purely ideological commitment to the right. A firm, the right-wing preference of which is tempered by pragmatism, might split its contributions equally between left and right. To summarize, a firm's distribution of cash to parties is a strategic decision taking into account political power and the firm's ideological position, if it has one.

At a point in time, the distribution of a firm's money can be to the left, to the right, a hedge between left and right, and, of course, a firm can decide not to contribute. If we consider two time points, shifts between the four basic distributions give us the sixteen cells in Table 2.1. If the two time points are divided by a change of government we can identify some of the strategies as clear indicators of ideological (colour-coded white) and pragmatic motivations (colour-coded black). In this example, a left-wing government has replaced a right-wing government. It can be inferred that firms that gave to the left in opposition, as well as in government, are ideologically committed to the left. Similarly, firms that continue to give to the right, even after its ejection from government, are committed to a right-wing ideology. Firms that shift from right to left, as power shifts from right to left, are classified as pragmatic. Those that hedge before and after the election, have no ideological preference, and are pursuing a pragmatic, low-risk strategy. Other strategies suggest an interaction of ideological and pragmatic motivations (colour-coded grey). Those that did not contribute while the right were in power, but contribute to the left when in power, combine an ideological preference for the left with a pragmatic desire not to signal hostility to a right-wing government. Firms that hedge under the right but, under a left-wing government, contribute exclusively to the left, suggest a similar mix of pragmatism towards right-wing governments and a preference for the left. The same logic applies to those that contributed to a right-wing government but abstain from political finance under the left and firms that plumped for the right in government but hedge after a turnover. The other seven cells do not have implications for the underlying

TABLE 2.1 *Classification of turnover strategies*

Right in power	Left in power			
	NON-CONTRIBUTOR	HEDGE	LEFT	RIGHT
NON-CONTRIBUTOR			Interaction	
HEDGE		Pragmatism	Interaction	
LEFT			Ideology	
RIGHT	Interaction	Interaction	Pragmatism	Ideology

Source: Iain McMenamin (2012), "If Money Talks, What Does it Say? Varieties of Capitalism and Business Financing of Parties", *World Politics*, volume 64(1), pp 1–38, Cambridge University Press.

motivations of the firms. This table is the basic means by which motivation can be inferred from the flow of cash. Thus, the problematic endeavour of asking firms and politicians about their motivation is unnecessary.

Different motivations should influence the contribution rate as well as the pattern of payments. Pragmatic payments to parties seek to increase a firm's profits. Therefore, a system dominated by pragmatism is likely to see a much greater proportion of firms contribute to parties than one where contributions are an ideological indulgence. The next section delves more deeply into the pragmatic motivation.

4. DISCRETE AND RECIPROCAL EXCHANGES

Pragmatic payments seek benefits. In the USA, there is a well-established body of research on the benefits to firms of financing politicians. However, this research programme has produced some conclusions, which suggest benefits are minimal or non-existent and others, which suggest that benefits are substantial. This section resolves this paradox by emphasizing the political costs of accepting business money and the distinction between discrete and reciprocal exchanges. The concept of access dominates practitioner discourse on this topic. Access is reinterpreted in light of the importance of political costs and reciprocal exchange.

4.1 The Paradox of US Political Finance Research

Business payments have tended to be tiny in relation to the value of government decisions. Undoubtedly, there is a supply of political benefits, which can be hugely valuable to firms (Stigler 1971, 4–6). Furthermore, these benefits can be targeted at particular firms (Clawson, Neustadtl, and Weller 1998, 68–71). In some polities, such as the USA and the EU, a huge lobbying industry has developed to help businesses win these political benefits. Thus, it seems that politicians have something business wants. Political finance comes cheaply to businesses. It is extremely rare, even in the case of the most outrageous scandal, for the amounts of money involved to constitute a major expense for the firm in question. It is also very unusual for the amounts involved to approach the value of the policy benefit. Gordon Tullock observed a long time ago that, when compared to the potential value of benefits, business spends very little on political donations (Tullock 1972; Ansolabehere, de Figueiredo, and Snyder 2003, 110). In the American legislative systems, legislators can add 'earmarks', or highly targeted spending commitments, to more general bills. Many of these earmarks benefit individual firms. According to the Center for Responsive Politics, for the vast majority of members of

Congress, the total value of contributions received rarely exceed 0.5 per cent of the total value of earmarks they have sponsored (Center for Responsive Politics 2011b). In recent decades, American businesses have not even spent up to the low maxima set by legislation (Ansolabehere, de Figueiredo, and Snyder 2003, 108–9). Experts are fond of contrasting the small cost of political campaigns with other types of advertising (Sorauf 1992, 187). For example, former Federal Electoral Commission member and Republican, Bradley Smith, recently said, 'Political spending needs to be kept in perspective. Americans will spend about $12 billion on potato chips this year; Coca Cola will spend more on advertising this year than will be spent by all the candidates who have run for president. It costs money to communicate, whether you are talking about cars, cola or politicians' (Smith 2008). The amounts given on behalf of individual businesses are too small for politicians to be worried about the withdrawal of support (Sorauf 1992, 172). And crucially, the marginal contributors are individuals, not businesses (Ansolabehere, de Figueiredo, and Snyder 2003, 124–5).

An enormous effort by American political scientists has failed to show a consistently convincing link between donations and political decisions. In particular, a sophisticated literature tries to relate campaign donations to legislative voting. A key methodological challenge has been the simultaneity problem: just as donations may influence votes, votes may influence donations. A large minority of studies deals with this issue by using instrumental variables. Many of the articles also exploit the analytical advantages of variation over time or variation within a specific policy area (Stratmann 2005, 143–4). In three-quarters of the thirty-six articles reviewed by Ansolabehere *et al.* 'campaign contributions had no statistically significant effects on legislation or had the "wrong sign"'(Ansolabehere, de Figueiredo, and Snyder 2003, 113–14). Stratmann's meta-analysis of the same sample of articles reverses the interpretation. He consistently finds that contributions are statistically significant, although he does not provide an estimate of magnitude (Stratmann 2005, 145–6).

Business money has been targeted at those politicians best placed to influence decisions. Also, some studies, such as those on stock market values, have demonstrated that financing of politicians adds value to firms. Business money is spent strategically on those who are most likely to be able to provide benefits: likely winners, incumbents, and those in powerful positions (Ansolabehere, de Figueiredo, and Snyder 2003, 110; Krozner and Stratmann 2005; Stratmann 2005, 147–8). A handful of articles use an indirect approach to demonstrate the value of business contributions to politicians. Jayachandran exploits the natural experiment created by the unexpected defection of James Jeffords, which shifted control of the Senate from the Republicans to the Democrats (Jayachandran 2006). Knight successfully interacts campaign contributions and the probability of a Bush win over Gore, as predicted by the Iowa Electronic Market in 2000, to explain stock market changes (Knight 2007, 406–8). The conclusions of this literature are paradoxical. In the USA, business financing of politics has some clear features that seem to indicate that no benefit is sought or received and others that indicate that benefits are sought and received. The problem is that this literature does not pay enough attention to the political costs of selling influence and tends to assume discrete, rather than reciprocal exchanges.

Business cash has very substantial costs. Politicians must be seen to represent their constituency in order to gain re-election. They cannot afford a perception that their political support can be bought. In a democracy, politicians need to emphasize that the currency of votes trumps that of money. Politicians have to manage their relationship with business supporters in such a way as to minimize this cost. In terms of fundraising, politicians can try to raise money from non-business sources, in particular, ordinary voters. To the extent that business funding in aggregate is important to them, they can reduce their reliance on any individual business by raising small amounts from a large number of firms. The funding of American politics generally fits this pattern. Funding linked with business is high in cross-national perspective but is smaller than other sources (Sorauf 1992, 172; Ansolabehere, de Figueiredo, and Snyder 2003, 124–5). Not only do politicians avoid financial dependence on businesses, they also avoid discrete exchanges.

4.2 Reciprocal versus discrete exchanges

A discrete exchange is explicit and simultaneous. By contrast, in a reciprocal exchange, each actor's part of the exchange is separately performed and the terms are unstated and uncertain (Molm 2000, 261–2). Reciprocal exchanges are likely to involve more and smaller payments. Politicians are supposed to represent votes, not dollars and are accountable to voters, not corporations. Therefore, a discrete exchange of cash for decisions is not worthwhile. However, reciprocal exchanges, which make it hard to associate a payment with a decision, reduce political costs sufficiently to allow politicians to accept, and seek, useful funding from business.

This emphasis on reciprocal exchange has much in common with a promising strand of the US literature. Clawson *et al.* think of campaign contributions as interested gifts, 'which create a generalized sense of obligation and an expectation of mutual back-scratching' (Clawson, Neustadtl, and Weller 1998, 19). In other words, nothing is demanded directly in return for a contribution but a contribution is expected to increase the probability of policy benefit being provided under some circumstances at some point in time. Gordon has managed to produce systematic evidence of the benefits provided by interested gifts in the committees of the Californian Senate (Gordon 2005). Businesses contribute to legislators in return for access. When a vote is likely to be close, lobbyists increase the pressure on behalf of contributing businesses. In such circumstances, legislators will change their vote because of their relationship with a contributing business. In other words, they see a good opportunity to reciprocate a gift given in the past. When their vote is not crucial, politicians will often vote against the preferences of their contributors. It is only when their vote is crucial that they see an opportunity to provide a gift in return for their campaign funds. Since these opportunities are rare the politicians incur only a minimal cost. Gordon herself explicitly distinguishes this gift relationship from a 'market relationship, where one is traded explicitly for the other' (Gordon 2005, 21; Clawson, Neustadtl, and Weller 1998, 34). This looks very like the more fundamental distinction between reciprocal and discrete exchanges. She rightly says that the above process can occur without participants' awareness of the nature of the relationship and does seem to believe that this is actually the case (Gordon 2005, 140–1). There is at least one accepted observation that sits uncomfortably with the self-deception account. If political contributions were always, or usually, unsolicited, albeit expected, self-deception would be more credible. Instead, we know that American politicians fundraise incessantly and solicit contributions from businesses, sometimes very aggressively (Clawson, Neustadtl, and Weller 1998, 36–8). This calculated behaviour on the part of extremely busy people suggests that they have, at least in a general sense, an awareness of the links between funding and public policy. Taking account of political costs and reciprocal exchanges reconciles the small amounts, strategic distribution, and difficult-to-observe benefits of business financing of politics. Reciprocity is developed through the access system.

4.3 Access as reciprocal exchange

Practitioners and many academics talk of the sale of access, not the sale of decisions. In a basic sense, the sale of access is a discrete exchange of cash for the chance to meet decision-makers or those close to decision-makers. In a much more important sense, that of a lucrative benefit to contributing businesses, the sale of access is a reciprocal exchange. Most access does not constitute an opportunity to lobby, never mind an opportunity to lobby with the expectation of a favourable outcome. Instead, the access businesses can usually buy offers a chance to develop a relationship, which if maintained and improved, might eventually be reciprocated in an opportunity to lobby or even a valuable decision. This is usually evident both from the low quality of the access and the low price at which it is sold. Access ranges from a chance to shake a politician's hand to an opportunity to lobby one-on-one. It is useful to think of the latter as a discrete exchange and the former as a reciprocal exchange. Obviously, there is always discrete exchange in the limited sense that a political contribution can buy an invitation to an event.

A range of factors influences the quality of access. Firstly, the situation matters. If the ratio of political contributors to politicians is large, it is unlikely that business representatives will have a chance to lobby the politicians. However, if the ratio is smaller, politicians may have enough time to hear contributors state their case. The duration of an event works in a similar way. The longer the event the more likely it is that businesses will have an opportunity to lobby. Publicity is another important variable. As already mentioned, the perception that decisions can be bought is costly to democratic politicians. Therefore, they are much more likely to allow themselves to be lobbied in a relatively secret situation.

These variables can be used to analyse the quality of access available at fundraising events, as shown in Table 2.2. An important institution in Canadian politics has been the leader's dinner. This was a highly public occasion with a set-piece speech and often thousands of attendees, many at tables paid for by businesses. This sort of event only rarely provides an opportunity for real lobbying. Businesspeople would often find themselves with only one politician at their table, and, unless they were seated together, no privacy. Of course, contributors can dine behind closed doors with politicians. These events can also cater for large numbers, such as dinners or receptions for regular or large contributors' clubs. The most obvious long, public, large event with opportunities for lobbying is the annual party conference, which is important for many European parties. Companies can often gain access by sponsoring some aspect of the conference or even by buying a stand at which they can promote their interests. The closest secret equivalent of the conference is an extended policy seminar or workshop. In Australia, such workshops can last longer than a day and are a benefit offered to members of donors' clubs. Meetings between small numbers of donors are rarely long or public due to the potential costs to the politicians. However, pre-dinner receptions at large events such as conferences and leaders' dinners might fit into the category of a short public event with few people. The final category is that of high quality access—a short, secret one-to-one meeting at which a representative of a donor business receives an opportunity to lobby a decision-maker.

Secondly, some features of the firm influence the quality of access. Clearly, the bigger the donation, the more useful it will be to the politician. However, this is a complicated issue, because the larger a donation the more visible it will be and the greater political cost it will impose on a politician. In Canada, the size of contributions was conventionally capped in order to avoid the perception and reality that politicians could not refuse favours. Indeed, politicians quite often pointed out how they can and do refuse to make decisions in favour of political contributors. The size of a firm also decreases the likelihood that the contribution has bought the lobbying opportunity, as the sheer economic weight of large firms usually gives them good access to decision-makers. The particularity of the policy

TABLE 2.2 *Fundraising events and access*

	Many people		Few people	
	Public	Secret	Public	Secret
Short	Leader's annual dinner	Club dinner	Pre-dinner reception	One-to-one meeting
Long	Party conference	Club seminar	–	–

at issue increases the cost for politicians. Therefore, the narrower the issue the less likely politicians are to allow themselves to be lobbied. For example, if a decision benefits only one firm, the politician may be open to allegations of favouritism or corruption. On the other hand, if a policy benefits a wide range of firms and others, it is easier to claim that the decision was unconnected to donations and lobbying. The visibility of an issue also reduces opportunities for lobbying by increasing the politician's costs. Areas under close public scrutiny are ones where politicians are more likely to resist the claims of special interests and party funders. Thirdly, some politicians are easier to access than others. More powerful politicians should have more money from more sources than less powerful politicians. Contributions will be less valuable to them and they will be less likely to trade them for high-quality access. Also, the more visible the politician the higher will be her costs of granting lobbying opportunities to businesses. Table 2.3 summarizes these influences on the quality of access.

Considering the different circumstances that influence levels of access suggests that most fundraising events provide, at their most useful, only a fleeting, risky, and low-quality opportunity to lobby. The 'language of access may serve to symbolically launder the money going from' business to policy benefit (Hall and Wayman 1990, 800), but, ironically, it also may serve to taint meetings between businesspeople and politicians, where there is no opportunity to receive a hearing and state a case.

High quality access, in the sense of receiving an opportunity to influence a politician, requires a minimum amount of time, a maximum number of participants, and a minimum level of secrecy. Any degree of publicity increases the politicians' costs so much that no lobbying opportunity is likely to be granted. On

TABLE 2.3 *Influences on quality of access*

Situation	Ratio of contributors to political actors	Decrease improves access (by improving prob. of benefit to firm)
	Publicity	Decrease improves access (by lowering political cost)
	Duration	Increase improves access (by improving probability of benefit to firm)
Business	Size of contribution	Improves access (by increasing political benefit)
	Size of firm	Decreases value of access (by decreasing probability that payment is reason for access)
	Particularity of issue	Decreases quality of access (by increasing political cost)
	Visibility of issue	Decreases quality of access (by increasing political cost)
Politician	Power	Decreases quality of access (as likely to decrease value of contribution)
	Visibility	Decreases quality of access (by increasing political cost)

many social occasions, there will be too many people, and too little time, to even mention an important and sensitive issue, which is of particular concern to a firm. So, for example, the annual leaders' dinners, and other large fundraising dinners starring cabinet ministers, are likely to have provided low quality to businesses that invested in tickets.

However, many access opportunities are consistent with reciprocal exchanges between businesses and parties. Such events serve to build and maintain relationships that might, on a later occasion, increase the chances of a real lobbying opportunity and the chances that such access achieves its aim of influencing a decision. High quality access consists of an often brief, but secret, one-to-one meeting or communication with a decision-maker, as well as some real expectation that the 'pitch' will be considered favourably. This sort of access is more likely to be provided through a broker such as a member of a minister's staff office, one of the party's 'bagmen', an MP, or a provincial politician, who not only realizes that the firm is a regular and substantial political contributor, but may well remember a name and a face and have some understanding of the needs and problems of the firm. In other words, the decision-maker would need to be convinced, often through his trust of the broker, that he and his party are obliged to reciprocate the firm's financial contributions.

In practice, the distinction between discrete and reciprocal exchanges can be subtle. Indeed, businesspeople that mistake discrete for reciprocal exchanges can be disappointed. A ticket purchased as a lobbying opportunity can turn out to be a social occasion, at which lobbying is neither possible nor welcome. Instead, the rationale is that a sequence of such payments and meetings can develop a relationship, which will put politicians under an obligation to try to reciprocate when lobbied in the future. Moreover, such meetings contain elements of both a reciprocal and a discrete exchange. There has been a discrete exchange of cash for the in-itself unimportant opportunity to share a social occasion with some politicians and a reciprocal exchange of cash for the important opportunity to receive a policy benefit. Since the political decision is the ultimate benefit sought, in this book, discrete exchanges will refer to exchanges of cash for immediate lobbying opportunities and reciprocal exchanges will refer to exchanges of cash for possible lobbying opportunities in the future.

4.4 Pragmatism and benefits

Pragmatic payments seek to increase business profits through government decisions. Business payments have tended to be tiny in relation to the value of government decisions. Moreover, a heroic effort by American political scientists has failed to show a link between donations and voting. However, business money has been targeted at those politicians best placed to influence decisions, and some studies, such as those on stock market values, have demonstrated that financing of politicians adds value to firms. Taking account of political costs and reciprocal exchanges reconciles the small amounts, strategic distribution, and difficult-to-observe benefits of business financing of politics that have made the American literature frustratingly paradoxical. Discrete exchanges risk substantial political costs, but reciprocal exchanges have a much lower cost because the absence of simultaneity and clarity make it difficult to associate payments and decisions. The access purchased by business is an opportunity to develop a relationship, which if carefully nurtured, might be reciprocated in a valuable policy benefit. The motivation for payments and the nature of exchanges form the dependent variables for the analysis of this book. Does the relative importance of ideology and pragmatism vary across countries, and, if so, why? This vital question has hardly been asked, never mind answered. The next section considers what might explain such cross-national variation.

5. CROSS-NATIONAL VARIATION

Variations in motivation for business payments to political parties might represent fundamentally different economic and political systems (McMenamin 2012a). Political, economic, and political economy perspectives are considered in turn. As mentioned earlier, the literature on political finance usually considers business funding from a party perspective. Nassmacher (2010, 265–6) does not state, but hints at, a plausible theory relevant to this book's subject. Along with other authors (Katz and Mair 1995, 2009; Casas-Zamora 2005, 4), he notes the rise of public funding of political parties in recent decades. This funding may have replaced business funding of political parties. Perhaps public funding has freed political parties from the often time-consuming and political costly process of raising money from business. Koss (2011) has been the first to systematically tackle the rise of state funding. He argues that, in countries with many veto points, parties tend to prioritize the pursuit of policy and office over vote-seeking. Such parties have an incentive to seek a consensus on state funding. Even absent these conditions, a discourse on political corruption can bring about a consensus in favour of state funding. These arguments are explicitly targeted at the mix of funding for political parties, rather than the motivation for business funding of parties. Nonetheless, they have an implication for the importance of business funding.

Secondly, political institutions can inspire a theory on the pragmatic business financing of parties. Pragmatic contributions should follow the distribution of power, with hedging where parties share power, and all contributions going to the governing party, where power is concentrated. So, there should be more hedging in consensus democracies, which 'instead of being satisfied with narrow decision-making majorities . . . seeks to maximize the size of these majorities'

(Lijphart 1999, 2). Thirdly, the nature of party competition could drive business motivations. The more polarized a party system, the more ideological contributions should be expected. In countries where parties are ideologically divided between left and right, ideological payments should be more likely. Where ideology does not separate the principal political parties, ideological payments should be less prevalent. Finally, the institutional and party system logics should interact. Polarization should be neutralized by consensual institutions. Therefore, the relatively polarized and majoritarian polities should have a greater predominance of ideological motivations than less polarized and majoritarian systems. Institutions should have a greater effect if polarization is held more or less constant. Polarized consensus democracies should have more hedging than polarized majoritarian states. Similarly, less polarized consensual countries should have more hedging than less polarized majoritarian systems. All these hypotheses focus on the nature of the political system, but do not consider the firms that spend money on political parties.

The most relevant economic theories focus on the number of firms seeking a benefit and the size of benefits. In groups, individuals tend to free-ride on the efforts of others. If a public good, such as a tax benefit for a particular sector, is provided firms in that sector will benefit whether they contributed to the political effort to win the political benefit or not. This leads to the collective action problem. It is often not rational for the individuals in a group to pursue their common interest. The larger the group the less likely its members will participate in politics (Olson 1971, 28). This insight is important to the ideas of pragmatic and ideological motivations. Pragmatic payments seek private goods and are therefore not subject to collective action problems. Ideological payments seek public goods and are subject to massive collective action problems. This collective action problem means that they are not likely to be motivated by a pragmatic concern to maximize profits. The size of the benefits should be a function of the extent and nature of government involvement in a sector (Stigler 1971). Some types of business are more regulated than others. In some sectors, the government can be a large customer or competitor of private firms. Studying either or both the number of benefit-seeking firms or the nature of the benefit focuses on particular economic sectors, which will have a certain level of government involvement and a certain number of firms. As a theory of business political action, economic theories usefully identify some of the fundamental incentives facing firms. However, they offer no theory of the political system itself.

Business financing of political parties happens at the interface of politics and the economy. Indeed, this is exactly what makes it interesting and controversial. So, a political economy approach would appear to be more promising, as it can consider the firm and the political system together. The varieties-of-capitalism approach to political economy takes seriously the position of individual firms and how they relate to the rest of the economy and political system. This makes it a good place to look for a plausible theory of the motivations of business financing of parties.

Moreover, this school incorporates many of the insights of the political and economic literature cited above, while generating different implications.

The varieties-of-capitalism school stresses the 'complementarity' (Hall and Soskice 2001, 17; Iversen 2005, 164), 'elective affinity' (Kitschelt *et al.* 1999, 430), or 'equilibrium' (Iversen 2005, 148) between a whole range of institutions at the political, legal, social, and economic levels. Liberal and co-ordinated market economies are the two dominant types amongst the long-established rich democracies. The varieties-of-capitalism approach has also been used to identify a dependent market economy in post-communist Europe (see Nölke and Vliegenthart 2009) and a rather different type of co-ordination in East Asia (see Hall and Soskice 2001, 34–5). Some authors distinguish between two types of national and sector co-ordinated economies in Western Europe (Kitschelt *et al.* 1999, 429–30). There are also mixed types displaying important characteristics of the co-ordinated and liberal models (Soskice 1999, 112–15; Iversen 2005, 58; Hall and Gingerich 2009, 145–6; Hancké, Rhodes, and Thatcher 2009, 281–2).

Hall and Soskice's canonical presentation highlights institutions that impact on the immediate environment of firms. This section combines Hall and Soskice's analysis of the firm with Iversen's (2005, 122–82) and Wood's (2001) emphasis on the political system's ability to credibly commit. These fundamental differences in political economy should result in very different levels of ideology and pragmatism in business financing of parties. The following institutional complementarities define the liberal market economy. Firstly, the stock exchange dominates the market for corporate governance. Firms need to attend to their share price and current profitability. Secondly, in industrial relations, companies rely on the market to govern relations with their employees. This means firms have the flexibility to chase the short-term results that the stock market demands. Thirdly, liberal market economies emphasize generalist training and education, rather than industry-specific apprenticeships (Culpepper 2007). Thus, workers can adapt to changing firm strategies and, more importantly, to a number of jobs over their career. Fourthly, contracts and competition tend to define inter-firm relations. Crucially, business associations play little or no role in the basic economic strategy of the firm. Instead, associations offer lobbying functions or sell marketing and public relations services that could be, and often are, also offered by other firms. Once again, this fits into the relatively short-term focus of the firm in a liberal economy.

Fifthly, liberal countries have majoritarian political systems. Their executives are relatively unconstrained by the legislatures. Majoritarian polities cannot credibly commit to providing the support and co-ordination that a co-ordinated market economy requires. In this political context, it is to be expected that firms will have a more short-term focus, greater flexibility, and more potential for radical innovation. Firms tend to advocate less state intervention, as this reduces the policy risk and most firms in liberal economies do not need the range of state-provided or state-supported institutions that are important in co-ordinated economies. Sixthly, liberal political systems tend to be based on a simple left–right divide (Kitschelt *et al.* 1999, 431, 434; Iversen 2005), in which the centre-right has tended to be more successful (Iversen 2005, 160). The majoritarian electoral system tends to give the right an advantage because the median voter is not attracted to long-term social insurance and means-tested benefits for the poor (Iversen 2005, 124–6, 142). Also, more flexible centre-right right parties have an advantage in targeting their electoral campaigns at the shifting concerns of the median voter.

The intensely competitive short-term focus of firms in liberal market economies generates substantial demand for private goods that could help firms develop an advantage over their rivals. Pragmatism should be an important motivation for business financing of parties and, since pragmatism is embedded in the basic profit-seeking mission of the firm, the contribution rate should be high. The preference for less state intervention, and the awareness of the state's power to disrupt the business environment, generates a widespread awareness of the importance of public policy goods to the business community. This should result in a relatively important ideological motivation in business contributions to parties.

Co-ordinated market economies contrast with liberal countries in all six spheres. In the market for corporate governance, the stock exchange is complemented by networks of firms and banks that provide other opportunities for finance (Vitols 2001, 342–3). They allow firms to pursue long-term strategies that do not necessarily maximize short-term share price and profitability. Secondly, employment security is very high and the institutionalized equalization of wages within sectors reduces incentives for workers to move from employer to employer. This encourages firms to commit to long-term specializations and incremental innovation. Thirdly, training and education is often highly specific to a particular company or industry. Of course, this system matches employees' qualifications and incentives to the relatively long-term and niche strategies of firms. Fourthly, inter-company relations exhibit institutionalized and informal co-operation, as well the market relationships of competition and contract. Associations are powerful organizations, which tend to speak authoritatively for the interest they represent (Streeck 1983). Their importance depends on, and reflects, their indispensability to the basic strategies of member firms. Business associations often play a crucial role by facilitating the diffusion of technology across firms, and ensuring that the state plays an effective role in supporting and subsidizing research and training, sector by sector (Streeck 1992).

Fifthly, the executive in a co-ordinated economy is much more constrained than its liberal counterpart. This consensual system underpins the highly credible commitment of the political economy to stable public policy to support the long-term investment and co-operation needed for incremental innovation, in which co-ordinated market economies have comparative advantage (Streeck 1992, 36). Sixthly, and finally, political parties in co-ordinated economies have less ideological flexibility and a weaker right-wing bias than their counterparts in liberal market economies. Parties tend to have relatively weak capacities and incentives to manoeuvre ideologically in pursuit of the median voter. However, leaders' dependence on left-wing or broadly consensual party structures means their parties can credibly commit to policies that support individuals' and firms' investment in highly specialized skills and markets.

In co-ordinated economies the most important policies for firms tend to be the public goods defined, championed, and, to a substantial extent, actually delivered by their business associations. In this context, the pragmatic motivation for contributions to political parties is likely to be weak. The combination of consensual political institutions and constrained parties means there is a very low risk of major policy change from election to election. So, there is also likely to be low interest in ideological financing of political parties. Overall, contributions should be rare. The remaining sections set out how these concepts will be used to study business financing of parties in the selected countries.

6. RESEARCH DESIGN

Good research is a sequence of carefully considered choices. The next two sub-sections set out the decisions that were made at various stages of the research process, so the advantages and disadvantages of the research design can be assessed. The first sub-section outlines the case selection. The next section explains how the country cases will be analysed and how they will be combined to study cross-national variation in firm motivation.

The book's argument takes the form of a two-level analysis, within country cases and across them. This two-level design involves some shifts in the identification of dependent variables (the variation of which we seek to explain) and independent variables (with which we seek to explain variation in the dependent variables). The dependent variable of the quantitative country case studies is the distribution of business payments to parties. This dependent variable has already been introduced: contribute to the left, contribute to the right, hedge between the two sides of politics, and decline to contribute at all. Firm motivation is then inferred by trying to explain variations in the distribution of payments by reference to the distribution of power, or simply which party is in government, while controlling for alternative explanations such as firm size and sector. The results of this analysis take the form of an aggregate firm motivation, pragmatic or ideological, or a mix of the two motivations. The next dependent variable is the type of pragmatic exchange, discrete or reciprocal. This aggregate firm motivation becomes the dependent variable for the cross-national analysis, which examines whether varieties of capitalism, party systems, or political institutions best account for the differences across country cases.

6.1 Country case selection

Business donor motivation can be inferred by comparing the distribution of payments to the distribution of power. Therefore, measuring the dependent variable requires tracking business payments to parties over time and political parties' control of government over time. For such a study to be possible, a potential country case must meet a number of regulatory and political criteria. This section begins with the population of 113 countries for which basic regulatory information is available. Then it applies seven criteria, one by one, until all but three countries are eliminated. The first three criteria are regulatory. These criteria are applied to each country in Appendix 1. The payments cannot be tracked if they are secret, so transparency is a necessary condition for inclusion. Also, since the intention is to infer firm motivation from the payments, those payments must be an indicator of the firm's calculations. For this to be true, the payments need to be permissive. A political finance regime is permissive if it allows business contributions to politicians and parties and does not limit their size. If a system is not permissive, any reported payments will have been warped and constrained by the law and will not be clean measures of business motivation. Transparent and permissive regulations allow the identification of distribution of business money in the political system. However, these patterns cannot be used to infer motivation unless they can be associated with clear variations in political competition, which is ensured by the last four criteria. They are a population of over one million, the existence of an electoral democracy, a stable party system, and at least one full legislative term of reported payments while each of the principal parties have been in government.

The first, and most obvious, criterion is transparency. The American system of political finance regulation has been impressively transparent for a long time. Candidates must disclose all donations from Political Action Committees, through which legal persons, although they are banned from donating directly, can co-ordinate the donations of individuals. Also, candidates are required to disclose all donations of $200 or greater from individuals. However, during the 1980s, the lack of disclosure of so-called 'soft money' was a major limitation to this transparency. Sorauf's celebration of the US as a beacon of transparency is now seriously out of date (Sorauf 1992, 203, 229). The 'law of available data' (Sorauf 1992, 164) no longer prevents students of business donor motivation from travelling beyond the USA, as political disclosure requirements swept across the world in the late twentieth and early twenty-first centuries (Pinto-Duschinsky 2002; Scarrow 2007). The International IDEA Political Finance Database, which reports political finance rules as of 2002 (International Institute for Democracy and Electoral Assistance 2002) indicates that 53 per cent of respondent countries (sixty countries) required disclosure by parties. Moreover, there are several respects in which some countries are more transparent than America. In Australia, all payments (and in-kind contributions) to political parties have to be reported, whether they are political donations or not. In Britain, the sources of loans to political parties now have to be disclosed.

The second and third criteria establish the permissiveness of the regulatory regime for political finance. The study of the motivations of business contributors to political campaigns has hitherto largely been restricted to America. This literature grew up in the aftermath of legislative change, which required the disclosure of political contributions. The ensuing research tended to assume, at least implicitly, that transparency was a sufficient condition for valid inferences about business payments to politicians. Of course, this was largely implicit because the vast majority of the scholars in this research programme were not just Americans, but 'Americanists', or specialists in the politics of the USA. Therefore, they, very understandably, did not consider whether the USA was a good case with which to test, or from which to develop, theories about firm behaviour in political finance.

The permissiveness of regulations affects whether, and how, we can study the motivations of business contributions to political parties. The 'bizarre and incongruous regulations' pertaining to political finance in America (Persily 2006, 219) are far from permissive. Businesses cannot directly contribute to election campaigns. Instead, they can only engage in political finance through the unique institution of the Political Action Committee (PAC). A business can coordinate voluntary political contributions from individuals in the form of a PAC, which is, in turn, subject to contribution limits to party committees and candidates. Individuals are also subject to contribution limits, which include any money channelled through PACs. Until the Bipartisan Campaign Reform Act of 2002, businesses could evade this structure by making 'soft money' contributions. These were contributions to parties that were spent on 'party-building' activities, as opposed to contributions to election campaigns. Two judicial decisions in 2010 have lead to 'Super PACs', which can spend unlimited amounts on political advocacy, but cannot contribute directly to candidates or explicitly co-ordinate their efforts with a candidate's campaign. While these new entities have been important in the 2012 electoral cycle, they have drawn their funds from rich individuals, not firms (Palmer and Phillip 2012). Even though all American studies take into account the precise regulations creating the measures they use in their models, they rarely question whether the measures are good indicators of the logic of business political behaviour. Perhaps contributions are smaller than the maxima because businesses have not been allowed to make direct contributions? Perhaps contributions are smaller than the maxima because the limits are so low that it does not matter whether a contribution is trivial or less than trivial? Irrespective of the answers to these questions, there is little doubt that we would observe very different behaviour if there were no regulation.

It might be argued that soft money provided a more permissive and still relatively transparent indicator of business calculations (Appollonio and La Raja 2004, 1136). There were no limits on the amounts and, for elections in the 1990s, the amounts were reported relatively efficiently. However, soft money was supposed to support 'party-building' activities, not candidates' election campaigns. A lot is known about the sources and destinations of soft money. There were significant differences in the identity of soft and hard money contributors, as well as the distribution of their contributions (Appollonio and La Raja 2004, 1144, 1151–2). Moreover, parties, the only recipients of soft money, spend their money very differently to candidates, the main recipients of hard money (Ansolabehere and Snyder 2000). Undoubtedly, some of the soft money went to fund congressional candidates (Dwyre 1996; Magleby and Smith 2003, 43). Nonetheless, in general, '[w]hat is not known is to whom this money [went] and why' (Drope and Hansen 2004, 29). Therefore, soft money does not provide a clear indicator of business calculations and, like hard money, has major limitations as a data source from which to infer firm motivation. To the extent that pragmatism exists in America, it is difficult to observe because of the way in which the complicated system masks the value business puts on any potential benefit from funding politicians.

According to the IDEA database, over 80 per cent of respondent countries, that is ninety-three states, reported no ban on corporate donations. Furthermore, thirty-eight transparent countries allow corporate donations and twenty-four transparent countries place no limits on corporate donations. The IDEA database correctly identifies the Netherlands as a legally permissive and transparent system of political finance. However, there is a comprehensive customary ban on business donations in Dutch politics (Gidlund and Koole 2001, 118). Therefore, the Netherlands is excluded before proceeding further.

This research aims to infer the motivation of business donors from the relationship between their pattern of payments and the distribution of political power. Thus, the next task is to select countries have that clearly observable variations in political competition, as well as transparent and permissive political finance regulations (see Table 2.4). In doing so, the first step is to exclude the two micro-states (with populations under one million) of Cape Verde and the Seychelles and the non-democracy of Singapore.[1] Party system stability is a more demanding criterion. If the identities of the principal competitors change, it is not possible to attribute changes in the flow of money to ideology or pragmatism (McMenamin and Schoenman 2007, 156–7). A party system was judged stable if the same two parties had occupied the first two places in three out of the four last elections to the lower house of the national legislature (including constituent assemblies). If there have been only three elections since a transition to democracy, the standard is two out of three. If there have been less than three elections, the party system is classed as unstable. This excluded eleven countries. More

---

[1] This is according to Freedom House's list of electoral democracies from 2004, the same date as the regulatory data.

TABLE 2.4 *Political criteria applied to transparent and permissive regimes*

	Population over 1m	Democracy	Party system stability	At least one term per competitor under transparency
Australia	Yes	Yes	Yes	Yes
Canada (pre-2004)	Yes	Yes	Yes	Yes
Germany	Yes	Yes	Yes	Yes
Colombia	Yes	Yes	Yes	No
Denmark	Yes	Yes	Yes	No
Ghana	Yes	Yes	Yes	No
New Zealand	Yes	Yes	Yes	No
Norway	Yes	Yes	Yes	No
United Kingdom	Yes	Yes	Yes	No
Ecuador	Yes	Yes	No	
Georgia	Yes	Yes	No	
Latvia	Yes	Yes	No	
Lesotho	Yes	Yes	No	
Moldova, Republic of	Yes	Yes	No	
Namibia	Yes	Yes	No	
Nicaragua	Yes	Yes	No	
Papua New Guinea	Yes	Yes	No	
Peru	Yes	Yes	No	
Thailand	Yes	Yes	No	
Venezuela	Yes	Yes	No	
Singapore	Yes	No		
Cape Verde	No			
Seychelles	No			

detailed investigation revealed obstacles in six of the nine remaining countries. In practice, the authorities in Colombia have not disclosed payments (Cepeda Ulloa 2005, 134, 137). Danish records do not specify the size of donations (personal communication from Flemming Juul Christiansen, 6 September 2010). Norway's records do not go back far enough and its party system is too complicated (Statistics Norway 2010a, 2010b). New Zealand's on-line records only provide a full parliamentary term's data under a Labour government (Elections New Zealand 2008). Similarly, a full term's data only exists for Labour governments in Britain. Ghana also lacks sufficient variation under a transparent regime. Thus, the regulatory and political criteria eliminate all countries other than Australia, Canada, and Germany. These countries constitute the core case studies of the book. However, the penultimate chapter leverages extra data from Denmark, Norway, New Zealand, the UK, and the USA. The next sub-section proceeds to explain how motivations will be inferred in the coming chapters.

6.2 Inferring firm motivation

In all three countries, political donations by businesses had to be reported. The limit above which disclosure was required varied. In Canada it was only C$100, in Australia A$1,500, and in Germany €10,000. The Australian system reports all payments to political parties, whether they are donations or not. In practice, many, and probably most, political contributions are reported as 'other payments'. The Australian data also take into account payments to 'associated entities' that raise funds for parties. In all three countries, the figures include in-kind donations, such as cars, alcohol, and hotel accommodation. Neither were there restrictions on the purposes for which it could be used. The only significant restriction on source was a ban on foreign donations. Thus, reported payments represent a relatively pure indicator of the political calculations of businesses, rather than flows of money that have been channelled and limited by a regulatory system.

With the important exception of the USA, scholars have been very reluctant to exploit the detailed data generated by official disclosure regimes. One possible reason is that doing so is very labour-intensive. More importantly, there is also some scepticism as to the usefulness of the data themselves. The literature tends to fasten upon loopholes and enforcement, which can provide opportunities to make secret payments to parties (Landfried 1994; Saalfeld 2000; Tham 2003; Orr 2006, 2007; Young and Tham 2006; Ewing 2007). It also reports instances of unreported payments that were publicized in the wake of journalistic or official investigations. Of course, any undisclosed payments weaken arguments based on disclosed payments. However, it is not clear what proportion of payments is unreported. The volume of payments in Australian and Canada, and the outcry that accompanies reports of evasion of disclosure in all three countries suggests that reported payments dwarf unreported payments. Moreover, it is not the extent of unreported payments that really matters, but whether they exhibit a systematically different pattern to reported payments, and, therefore, yield substantially different inferences about motivation. No such argument is made explicitly in the literature. Nonetheless, there does seem to be a relatively consistent and quite reasonable implication that secret payments are somehow bribes, even if in many scandals there is little or no evidence of a benefit. These concerns present two different threats to the conclusions of this study. Firstly, they may systematically bias the results for each country away from pragmatism and towards ideology by under-reporting a large number of bribes. Secondly, variations in the accuracy of disclosure may bias conclusions about the differences between the three countries.

The extent of non-disclosure, by its very nature, cannot be known. Similarly, and relatedly, corruption, using a legal definition, is famously hard to study and even harder to measure at a systemic level, because of the secret nature of corrupt exchanges. The most popular way around this problem has been to measure perceptions of corruption. Transparency International's Corruption Perception Index (CPI) combines rigour and comprehensiveness. The three countries' scores on the 2009 CPI are very close (Transparency International 2009). Canada and Australia are the joint eighth least corrupt states, while Germany is fourteenth least corrupt. The difference between Germany and Australia is statistically insignificant, with only a very small statistically significant difference between Germany and Canada. These data suggest that both threats mentioned above are probably quite small. Since these three countries are judged to be amongst the least corrupt in the world, it seems unlikely that there are corrupt payments so massive in size that they would indicate a substantially greater amount of pragmatism in each country. The three countries' similarly low levels of corruption suggest that disclosure variations have not systematically biased conclusions about the differences between the countries.

Disclosure is not a major threat to validity, but it does set a limit to generalization. Earlier it was argued that the political costs of business funding are important to understanding this subject and that the visibility of payments increases political costs. Obviously, business financing of parties in general should be much more politically costly under transparent political finance regimes. Also, the proportion of pragmatic payments should decrease and within pragmatic payments, the balance should shift away from discrete exchanges and towards reciprocal exchanges. So, it should be difficult to apply the analysis of this book to opaque systems of political finance, including the less transparent past of the main case study countries. Nonetheless, this is a relatively minor caveat. As the case selection process showed, twenty-four countries have permissive and transparent regulations. Also, this research should be useful those interested in less transparent contexts, and confined to much more fragmentary and anecdotal evidence. The magnitude of bias in generalization beyond the regulatory case selection criteria is unknown and unknowable, but the direction is surely as indicated above.

In all three countries, samples have been drawn from published lists of large firms. Only those with less than 50 per cent state ownership have been included. The research design avoids the potential sample selection bias (Munger 1988; Kim 2008) that is sometimes evident in the study of the distribution of contributions (Fisher 1994; Burris 2001). In other words, it includes non-contributors as well as contributors. The Australian data set exploits the essentially uniform political finance regulations and party systems at the federal level and in the six states, but excludes the territories. The Northern Territory has a different party system, while only one poll of voting intentions had been held in the Australian Capital Territory during the sample period. Moreover, the territories are outliers on several other measures of party competition (Sharman and Moon 2003). The territories represent a tiny proportion of both the Australian population and business contributions to parties. The period of the Australian sample is 1999 to 2005. 1999 is the first year from which disclosed payments are available on-line, while a major upward change in disclosure limits precludes the inclusion of later data. The firms are the 450 firms included in the *Business Review Weekly* Top 1000 in both 1999 and 2005, minus firms registered in New Zealand and Papua New Guinea.

The sample contains 22,050 observations: 450 businesses by seven years by seven jurisdictions. There were fourteen elections and one turnover.

The Canadian sample is restricted to the federal level. Canadian party systems are regionalized with different sets of parties competing in different provinces. Moreover, the provinces have varied significantly in the transparency and permissiveness of their political finance regulation. The Canadian data run from 1984 to 2000. The end-date once again marks a regulatory change, while the start-date was limited by the necessity of manually gathering data from the period before 1993. The 195 firms all featured in the *Globe and Mail Report on Business* Top 1000 in both 1983 and 1998. Thus, there are 3,315 observations, with four elections and two turnovers. The German sample also relates to the federal level only, but for different reasons. Germany has a national party system and similar regulations at the state (*Land*) level to the federal level. However, the law does not require parties to disclose at which level they received contributions. At any rate, it is widely assumed that large contributions are intended for the federal parties (Clemens 2000, 28). The German sample begins in 1992, after a reduction in the disclosure threshold. *Die Welt* listed all 315 firms in its Top 500 in both 1997 and 2002. There are 4,415 observations in the German sample, with four elections and one turnover. There are some differences in national database construction due to practical considerations relating to regulatory uniformity, data availability, and the time-consuming work of data entry. Nonetheless, they represent essentially comparable groups of consistently very large firms. Table 2.5 summarizes this basic information about the samples. Descriptive statistics for all three countries can be found in Appendix 2 and the data themselves can be downloaded from http://webpages. dcu.ie/~mcmenami.

TABLE 2.5 *Characteristics of the samples*

	Firms	Years	Jurisdictions	Observations	Elections	Turnovers
Australia	450	7 (1999–2005)	7	22 050	14	1
Canada	195	17 (1984–2000)	1	3315	4	2
Germany	315	14 (1992–2005)	1	4410	3	1

In all countries, firms with over 50 per cent direct state ownership have been excluded. The Australian sample is defined by membership of the *Business Review Weekly* Top 1000 in both 1999 and 2005. The start-date is set by the availability of electronic records, while the end-date is set by a major regulatory change, which moved the threshold for reporting from A$1,500 to $10,000 per annum. The Canadian sample is defined by membership of the *Globe and Mail Report on Business* Top 1000 in both 1983 and 1998 (accessible via http://www.lib.uwo.ca). The Canadian start-date is due to the time-consuming nature of data entry. The end-date marks a break in the continuity of records. The German sample is defined by membership of *Die Welt* Top 500 in both 1997 and 2002 (see http://top500.welt.de). 1992 is the beginning of the German sample because of a large reduction in the threshold for reporting introduced in that year and 1997 is the earliest year for which the *Die Welt* list is available. 2005 is the last year for which data are available. The formation of a grand coalition in Germany in 2005 is not counted as turnover.

Source: Iain McMenamin (2012), "If Money Talks, What Does it Say? Varieties of Capitalism and Business Financing of Parties", *World Politics*, volume 64(1), pp 1–38, Cambridge University Press.

The Canadian sample counts payments to the Liberal and Progressive Conservative parties. The German and Australian samples are slightly more complicated. For most purposes, the German figures treat the Christian Democratic Union (CDU) and the Christian Social Union (CSU) as one party. The CSU is the Bavarian conservative party, while the CDU represents conservatives across the rest of Germany. These two parties are a permanent electoral alliance; do not compete on each other's territory; agree on a 'chancellor candidate' going into each general election; have always governed together; and, finally, have, on at least one occasion, subsidized each other. Their competitor is the clearly unitary Social Democratic Party (SPD). There is a somewhat similar situation in Australia. The Liberal Party is the conservative free-market party in most of Australia. However, the National Party is the conservative option in some rural areas. They operate as an electoral coalition; agree on a prime ministerial candidate; govern together; and transfer money between the two parties. They face the Australian Labor Party (ALP). The country chapters also engage with sources of potential bias from different reporting requirements and party systems in the three countries.

Essentially, the data analysis consists of using variations in party control of government to predict whether a given firm will not contribute, contribute to the left, contribute to the right, or hedge. The data also contain information on the sector of each firm, thereby testing the economic perspective on business financing of political parties. The statistical technique can fill the sixteen cells of Table 2.1 with predicted probabilities. These figures are clearly interpretable in terms of the relative importance of pragmatism and ideology in motivating business financing of political parties.

As already mentioned, the notion of pragmatically motivated payments to parties leaves more questions unanswered than the notion of ideological motivation. The distinction between discrete and reciprocal exchanges can be very illuminating. The association between the distribution of payments and the distribution of power provides a strong basis for inferring motivation, but, although it provides some hints, it does less well in specifying the nature of pragmatic exchanges. Thus, the case study chapters use qualitative material, chiefly newspaper reports, to investigate the pragmatic exchanges between firms and parties. The newspaper reports were obtained from key word searches in the LEXIS-NEXIS database. This generated a corpus of 475 documents and 202,000 words for Australia; 641 documents and 365,000 words for Canada; and 320 documents and 303,000 words for Germany. The media sources provide information about the finances of the parties, the regulation of party finance, and the motivations of the business contributors. These sources are at their most useful in trying to distinguish between different types of exchange. Many of the newspaper articles are focused on our research question. They seek to identify the benefit gained by businesses that contribute to political parties. Sometimes they review the law and summary statistics generated by the disclosure regimen. However, much of their material is hearsay and anecdote. While these are journalistic staples, neither has great prestige in academic circles, to put it mildly. Nonetheless, given the cost of visible exchanges to both firms and politicians, it is difficult to obtain more direct evidence. Moreover, anecdotes tell a story, or in the words of contemporary academic jargon, they trace the causal mechanism. It is, of course, very dangerous to generalize from such sources. Here, I never generalize from an anecdote, but rather from a series of overwhelmingly similar anecdotes from different sources. Also, it is important to emphasize that all the qualitative interpretations are consistent with the rigorously collected and analysed quantitative data. It is intended that the two types of evidence support each other.

The country chapters also outline in some detail the basic political economy, political institutions, party system, and political finance regime in each country, and thus establish the values of each country on the variables hypothesized to explain cross-national variation. There is useful variation for each hypothesis. Germany has a high level of public funding; Australia a substantial level; and public funding was negligible in Canada. Canada's federal polity is remarkably majoritarian, but Australia's Commonwealth and six states are constrained by more influential upper houses. Germany is a consensus democracy. Canada has the least polarized party system, Germany the most, and Australia is in between. Their economies vary in size and sectoral profile. Germany's economy is far the largest and is dominated by manufacturing. Both Canada and Australia have large natural resources sectors, but in our sample there is a larger proportion of natural resources firms in the Canadian data set. Finally, Germany is a co-ordinated economy and Australia and Canada are both liberal economies. However, policy risk is much lower in Canada, because the two principal parties were pro-business and usually had relatively minor differences in relation to economic policy.

7. CONCLUSIONS

The concept of triangulation provides a good insight into the purpose, challenge, and method of much social science research. In mathematics, triangulation refers to the process of determining the location of a point by measuring it from known points at either end of fixed baseline, rather than measuring the distances to the point directly. Similarly, the social sciences often rely on indirect methods of measurement because the behaviour is difficult to directly observe or because the theoretical concept is unobservable. This clearly applies to the subject of firm motivation for financing political parties, as disclosure of the true motivation is very likely to impose a substantial cost on both firm and politicians. This consideration counts against the relatively direct methods of interviews or surveys asking firms why they contribute to political parties. Instead, the following chapters infer motivation indirectly from the relationship between the distribution of payments and distribution of power. In addition to this logical triangulation, this chapter has described a series of procedures, which also include data and method triangulation. Data triangulation is especially suited to qualitative research, in which any one source may suffer from substantial measurement error. Therefore, agreement is required amongst multiple media sources before their interpretation is used in the argument. This book also employs method triangulation by cross-checking conclusions across quantitative and qualitative sources. So, it is not just the quality and quantity of data in any one method, but their combination through which it is hoped to generate highly credible conclusions about the unrevealed, but politically and economically important, motivations behind business contributions to political parties.

Research is an iterative and social process. It can be thought of as a number of stages such as the suggestion of an idea, the formalization of a theory, an initial empirical plausibility probe, followed by a series of rigorous tests. A research article is often relatively clearly located at one of these stages, but this book, like many others, combines earlier and later stages of theory development. This is relatively clear considering its relationship to the existing literature and the types and quantities of data with which it approaches different questions. The statistical analyses of the three countries use the language of theory testing. They have much in common with the longstanding American literature and they meet the standards of that research programme. The conclusions on types of exchange build on theoretical developments in American politics and receive substantial assistance from the quantitative results. Nonetheless, they rely on newspaper reports, even if they are numerous and conservatively interpreted. Thus, these conclusions may be closer to a successful plausibility probe than a fully-fledged theory test. In other words, the conclusions of this research, like all research, are subject to uncertainty. The principles, methods, and techniques overviewed in this chapter will be applied to the three country cases in the next three chapters, beginning with Canada.

3

Canada: Pragmatism and Centrism

1. INTRODUCTION

In Canadian political finance, money spoke the language of pragmatism. Each year, an average of over 50 per cent of firms in the sample gave money to one or both of the two big parties. The distribution of money clearly tracked changes in government. Business contributors treated the two dominant competitors equally. Whatever individual firms may have said or intended, in aggregate, Canadian business was remarkably frank about its pursuit of business interests through political finance. The clarity and simplicity of the basic motivation contrasts with the subtle way in which the political system delivered benefits to its business donors. Most payments seem to have been predicated on reciprocal, rather than discrete, exchange. Straightforward bribery was rare. The purchase of access to politicians dominated media coverage of business financing of parties. However, in the sense of a real opportunity to lobby a politician, the sale of access was not the main benefit accruing to business contributors. Instead, their money served to build a maintain relationships. Canadian business money said, softly and subtly, but insistently, that, in exchange for small but certain financial benefits, contributing businesses expect to receive special consideration of their lobbying efforts. This expectation was relatively firmly embedded in a long-established and well-known, if far from predictable, system of party–firm relations. Special consideration was delivered through personal and organizational relationships that would not have existed, or would have been of inferior quality, had financial contributions not been made.

This chapter starts with an introduction to Canada's political economy. It then goes on to review the regulation of political finance and the overall finances of the principal political parties. The next section is a quantitative analysis of the motivations of business contributors to Canadian parties. Thereafter, a series of sections evaluate interpretations of the Canadian system of party–firm relations. These begin with 'supporting the democratic process', the stock answer when businesses are asked about the purpose of their payments to parties. Next is ideology, which includes a case study of the 'free trade' election of 1988. I then move on to a case study of the 'earthquake election' of 1993 to illustrate the dominant pragmatic motivation for business financing of Canadian parties. The next section investigates the nature of pragmatic exchanges in terms of illegal transactions, and discrete and reciprocal exchanges. I exploit a case study of the reunification of the Canadian centre-right to show how business donations served to build networks of interest rather than reflect networks of loyalty. The conclusion summarizes briefly and considers the end of business financing of Canadian political parties and the subsequent evolution of the party system.

2. THE CANADIAN POLITICAL ECONOMY

Canada is universally regarded as a liberal market economy (Kitschelt et al. 1999, 435–6; Rueda and Pontusson 2000, 365; Hall and Soskice 2001, 19–20, 59; Bernard 2008; Hall and Gingerich 2009, 138). It exhibits each of the institutional complementarities that underpin the comparative advantage of liberal market economies. Firstly, the stock exchange, not banks or other stakeholders, dominates the market for corporate governance. The value of domestic publicly listed firms is over 100 per cent of GDP, a value very similar to that of the USA. Relative to its population and economic weight, Canada also has one of the highest levels of venture capital in the world (Carpentier, L'Her, and Suret 2010, 406) with particularly strong growth since 1994 (Cumming and MacIntosh 2006, 575). About one-third of Canadians own financial securities (Li, Iscan, and Xu 2010, 877). In contrast to other liberal market economies, the ownership of Canadian firms is quite concentrated (Ben Amar and André 2006, 518). However, Canada is close to the archetypically liberal USA in the unusual strength of its legal protections for investors (Ben Amar and André 2006, 521). This system means that firms need to attend to their share price and quarter-to-quarter profitability.

Secondly, in industrial relations, companies rely on the market to govern relations with their staff. Employee relations in Canada have always been diverse, reflecting different legal systems in the provinces and different balances of power between capital and labour in workplaces. Unsurprisingly, Canada's wage-setting arrangements are much more decentralized than even other liberal market economies. As part of this diversity, multifirm agreements were never common (Jacek 1986, 420), but collective bargaining at the firm level increased in importance until the 1980s. At the same time, union membership peaked at 40 per cent of the labour force (Fudge and Tucker 2000, 293). As in many other countries, the contraction of manufacturing drove the drop in unionization (Fudge and Tucker 2000, 299). Canada's union density is slightly above the average, and its collective bargaining coverage below the average, for a liberal market economy. Canadian unions have rarely pursued an agenda of transforming society. Instead, they have concentrated on the narrow interests of their members. While many unions have traditionally supported the National Democratic Party, they have never had the close relationships with national political parties typical of countries with important labour or social democratic parties. Employment protection is slightly above the mean for a liberal market economy and unemployment protection is well above average (Iversen 2005, 47, 50). Overall, firms have the flexibility to chase the short-term results that the stock market demands.

Thirdly, Canada emphasizes generalist training and education, rather than industry-specific apprenticeships (Culpepper 2007, 618–21). Thus, workers can adapt to evolving company strategies and to several jobs over their working life. Canada appears to have low levels of on-the-job training compared to other liberal market economies, never mind co-ordinated economies (Zeytinoglu and Cooke 2009, 96). Only 5 per cent of Canadians have vocational qualifications, even fewer than the average for liberal market economies. Nonetheless, Canada has a remarkably high rate of participation in non-university third-level education (Boothby and Drewes 2006, 2). The returns to vocational qualifications are small in comparison to more academic credentials (Boothby and Drewes 2006, 17). Another classically liberal trait of the Canadian education system is that, while overall spending levels are close to other rich countries, Canada's investment, like that of the United States, is very much skewed towards third level. Like the USA and Australia, it attracts large numbers of highly skilled immigrants, including PhDs (Gera and Songsakul 2007, 65).

Fourthly, relationships between companies are defined by contracts and competition. Business associations play little or no role in the fundamental economic strategy of the firm. Instead, they provide lobbying functions or sell marketing and public relations services that are also frequently offered by other firms. Once again, this fits into the comparatively short-term focus of the firm in a liberal economy. Canadian business associations have tended to be competitive (Jacek 1986, 434). Attempts to give them a substantial institutionalized role in policy-making and implementation have failed at both national and, to a lesser extent, at sectoral levels. 'Labour is relatively weak, business interests predominate over them and business-labour relations are adversarial' (Haddow 2002, 71). These structural problems contributed to the failure of negotiations between government, business, and labour in the 1970s and 1980s under both Trudeau's Liberals and Mulroney's Progressive Conservatives (Jacek 1986, 431; Haddow 2002, 72–3). The weakness of business and labour organizations meant that government bolstered the composition of Canadian Labour Force Development Boards with representatives of women's and ethnic groups (Haddow 2002, 74). 'Used to benefiting from privileged access to government through informal lobbying in a setting where organized labour is relatively weak in both the industrial and political arenas . . . business could see no reason to share influence with labour and equity interests' (Haddow 2002, 74). The Quebec board was somewhat more successful, at least partly because of the stronger business associations and trade unions in that province. Sectoral councils have had to 'soothe the traditional concern among firms about sharing proprietary information . . . with competitors'

(Haddow 2002, 77). Lobbying by individual firms has been an important and generally legitimate part of politics in Canada since the Second World War (Schneider 2006, 115). The public affairs units and senior management of large firms, as well as specialized consultants and law firms, lobby the government (Rush 1998, 516–19).

Fifthly, Canada is a federation of majoritarian Westminster governments. Elections are run according to the first-past-the-post electoral system. The electoral system has usually provided one-party majority federal government, but in its absence Canadian parties have always opted for minority government rather than coalitions (Paun and Hazell 2010, 216–17). Canada has recently returned to majority government after a triumphant election for the incumbent Conservatives under Stephen Harper. The electoral system has also occasionally magnified changes in voting patterns and thereby contributed to party system instability. Relatedly, the system often exaggerates the regional bases of support for parties. For example, the Liberals gained an anti-western image after 1957 because they rarely elected MPs west of Ontario, even though they regularly received about 20 per cent of the vote in the west. This has fed into cabinet representation. Between 1962 and 1984 either largely francophone Quebec or the west was effectively excluded from cabinet representation.

The Canadian prime minister is a remarkably powerful figure. An international expert survey ranked Canada's prime minister as the most powerful in the world and found little difference between the influence of prime ministers Mulroney and Chrétien (O'Malley 2007, 17, 20), whose tenure dominates the period under examination in this book. Some of this power can be explained by reference to general characteristics of Westminster systems such the power of appointment; the right to decide on the timing of elections; strict party discipline; the focus of the electronic media (Savoie 1999a, 74, 79–80, 94–7; Savoie 1999b); and the use of polling to provide information on popular opinion. However, much of the prime minister's pre-eminence derives from the nature of Canadian political parties, which exist mainly to contest elections and do not constrain policy-making (Savoie 1999a, 77, 91–4). Moreover, the fact that Canadian party leaders are elected by members, often as relative political outsiders, reduces prime ministers' dependence on their cabinet colleagues. Liberal Pierre Trudeau initiated centralized power through a great expansion of the Prime Minister's Office in 1968, and succeeding prime ministers have also operated within that framework.

While Canadian parties are organizationally weak, the Canadian parliament is true to its Westminster origins in terms of party discipline. This rigid discipline and the absence of a substantial party structure mean that party leaders and prime ministers dominate legislative politics. There is a strong consensus that parliament has 'a marginal role in lawmaking' (Atkinson and Thomas 1993, 426). Members of Parliament have little influence over legislation, but can use parliamentary questions to represent constituency interests (Soroka, Penner, and Blidook 2009). Canadian MPs do not seek to pursue distinctive legislative careers. Instead, they virtually all aspire to serve in government (Kerby 2009, 593–4). The upper house, the Senate, is a weak revisionary chamber (Luzstig 1995; Simeon 2004, 100). The government appoints Senators to represent the provinces until the age of seventy-five. Governments make these appointments on a partisan basis and the Senate does little to represent provincial interests. In spite of its usual marginality, the Senate was the scene of a major political conflict over the Goods and Services Tax introduced by the Mulroney government. The Canadian Supreme Court became more important with the introduction of the Charter of Rights and Freedoms in 1982. Interest groups have exploited the Charter to challenge the parties' dominance of policy-making. The Supreme Court, and before it the Judicial Committee of the Privy Council, sitting in London, have influenced the evolution of Canadian federalism. Canada's founders intended it to be a relatively centralized political system, but a series of court decisions, together with the sheer scale and complexity of the country, have exerted a powerful pressure to decentralize.

Constitutionally, Canadian federalism is symmetrical. Each province has a unicameral legislature, which also operates on the Westminster model. While the Constitution envisages a clear division of labour, the two levels of government have become intertwined. As in Australia, the federal level exercises much of its influence through fiscal power, in the principal forms of taxation, conditional and block grants, and equalization payments. The provinces are primarily responsible for the education and health services that citizens value most. They have consider-able revenue-raising powers of their own, not least through their control of natural resources, which are abundant in some provinces. Indeed, provincial and munici-pal governments outspend and out-tax the federal government.

This is a study of payments to the federal parties in Canada. At this level, it is one of the most majoritarian systems of government in the world. In some respects, like the power of the prime minister and the passivity of parliamentary parties, it may be the most concentrated system of democratic government in the world. The Canadian federal government clearly cannot commit to providing the support and co-ordination that a co-ordinated market economy requires. In this political context, it is to be expected that firms will have a more short-term focus, greater flexibility, and a greater potential for radical innovation. Firms should also tend to advocate less state intervention as this reduces the policy risk. Moreover, most Canadian firms do not need the range of state-provided or state-supported institutions that are important in sustaining incremental innovation in a co-ordi-nated market economy.

In terms of the sixth and final set of institutions, the party system, Canada is highly unusual, but seems particularly congruent with a liberal market economy. The Liberals and the (Progressive) Conservatives are Canada's two traditional political parties, dating back to the mid-nineteenth century. They are also the only parties ever to have formed governments. For over a century, Canadian politics has been characterized by long periods of Liberal hegemony and shorter terms of

Conservative government. Since the Second World War the Conservatives have been in power from 1957 to 1963, as a minority government from 1979 to 1980, in the sample period, under Brian Mulroney, from 1984 to 1993, and returning under Stephen Harper in 2006. All Canadian parties, including the traditional big parties, have retained the nineteenth-century form of the cadre party (Carty 2003, 358–60). Party bureaucracy hardly exists. Instead, constituency organizations tend to comprise a relatively personal, ephemeral, and amateur support for the local candidate. The national party is dominated by personal appointees of the leader, who are often public affairs specialists. The central party tended to employ about ten to twenty-five during the 1990s (Dyck 2004, 314). At both levels, the party is relatively dormant until an election is called. The parties are 'as much vehicles for the politically ambitious as they are disciplined recruitment agencies' (Carty 2003, 368). There is a high turnover of Canadian politicians (Savoie 1999a, 344) and candidates, even for the party leadership, often come from outside the party (Whitaker 1977, 197–8). Enterprising Liberal politicians recruited their leader for the 2011 general election, Michael Ignatieff, from Harvard University. The cadre party organizational form has given parties the flexibility to deal with economic and social heterogeneity of Canada. It has also enabled the parties to operate with minimal ideological restrictions. The two have had very similar profiles on economic matters, with the Progressive Conservatives having a somewhat stricter reputation in relation to budgetary management (Bélanger 2003, 544). Nonetheless, the centrist Liberal party operated on the basis that 'the business of Canada was business' (Whitaker 1977, 167). Instead of ideological competition, the national parties brokered deals amongst diverse interests (Carty 2002, 726) and managed a franchising operation, with an image marketed professionally at the national level, which could be adapted and managed according to the varying conditions of individual constituencies (Carty 2002, 730).

The Canadian party system is volatile and has undergone major change every few decades. One way of classifying these eras is to look at the main competitors of the two old parties. Prior to 1993, their principal competitor was the New Democratic Party, the 'social conscience of Canada'. In 1993, the PC's parliamentary representation was almost eliminated by the emergence of the Reform Party and the Bloc Québécois. The Bloc Québécois was the federal electoral wing of the nationalist Parti Québécois, which has dominated its own province's domestic politics in recent decades. The other insurgent party was partly motivated by discontent with the old parties' preoccupation with Quebec. The Reform Party's original slogan was 'The West Wants In'. In later elections it tried to break away from its regionalist image by stressing populist and individualist themes.

The PC government from 1984 to 1993 under Brian Mulroney implemented a relatively right-wing pro-business agenda and opened up some ideological space between the two big parties. Its Liberal successor under Jean Chrétien moved to the right, adopting many of the Mulroney government policies it had criticized during the 1993 election. The new ideological and regional environment made it very difficult for the Progressive Conservatives to recover from the 1993 disaster. Moreover, the rise of the Bloc excluded them from the naturally conservative Québécois constituency to which Mulroney, the PC leader from 1983 to 1993, had successfully appealed.

As the Quebec example shows, the federal party system can interact with the party systems of the provinces. However, party competition at the two levels has become increasingly separate over the last few decades. Canadians have come to live in two 'two political worlds' (Blake 1985, quoted in Carty 2003, 349). In some provinces, the principal parties are different at the provincial and federal levels. In British Columbia, provincial elections offer a choice between the New Democrats and Social Credit, but federal elections pit Liberals against Conservatives. In other provinces, the parties are nominally the same at the two levels, but are entirely separate or even opposed to each other. In 1998 the leader of the federal PC, Jean Charest, resigned to become leader of Quebec's Liberals. A remarkable indication of the independence of the two levels of party competition is that the federal party system earthquake of 1993 had little or no discernible effect on provincial party competition. The official structure of the Progressive Conservative party reflected this situation. There was no formal organizational or financial link between federal and provincial parties, even though many are members at both levels. The Liberals maintained a similar split in Quebec, Ontario, Alberta, and British Columbia but had joint federal and provincial parties in the other, less populous, provinces.

In summary, Canada's party system has a greater political bias against the left and greater short-term policy flexibility than most other liberal political economies, including Australia. The party system represented little or no threat to pro-market policies, and so provided a very weak basis for ideological behaviour. However, before studying the motivations of business contributors to Canadian parties, it is necessary to consider the overall system of political finance.

3. CANADIAN POLITICAL FINANCE

3.1 Regulation

Until the reform of 1974, both parties relied, almost exclusively, on big business for their income. They failed in repeated attempts to broaden their financial base (Paltiel 1970, 20, 32–3, 37, 42). After the First World War, party leaders began to remove themselves from fundraising. In addition to specialization, the division of labour insulated the leadership from scandal (Paltiel 1970, 26–7). The secretive system was based on 'bagmen', who solicited funds from chief executives of firms, especially those headquartered on Toronto's Bay Street. In the 1940s, the methods of collection broadened out to social occasions, such as fundraising dinners (Paltiel 1970, 32). The legal regime, if it can be so called, for it hardly existed, was based on the traditional Westminster reluctance to legally acknowledge political parties. In the British style, there was a requirement that candidates disclose election expenses and prohibitions on bribery, but very little enforcement. After each election between 1962 and 1974, at least 20 per cent of candidates did not file returns (Stanbury 1993, 30).

Intellectually, the new political finance regime of 1974 could be traced to the Barbeau Committee of 1964 to 1966. Politically, it was enabled by the minority status of a Liberal government, under pressure from the New Democrats, and mindful of the contemporaneous Watergate affair in the United States and rumours of a scandal in Quebec. It essentially aimed to diversify and disclose the income of political parties. A tax credit facilitated an explosion in individual political contributions. The credit offered no marginal gain over $1,150 and, thus, most businesses did not even bother to claim it. The reform also capped election expenses for parties and candidates, while reimbursing some of those expenses. In the sample period, this amounted to 22.5 per cent of the total election expenses for a party (Stanbury 1993, 42). In addition, parties gained a statutory entitlement to free broadcasting time and a guaranteed amount of broadcasting time, charged at normal commercial rates. However, there was no limit on 'operating expenses' for parties. The definition of operating expenses could be expanded to election-oriented expenditure outside the official campaign period. Therefore, in practice, parties were not subject to spending limits. The fact that the Progressive Conservatives could spend a remarkably accurate 99.96 per cent of their limit in 1984 suggested that the definition was very manipulable indeed (Stanbury 1993, 66). The act did not ban or cap corporate contributions; however, it did require disclosure. While this may have discouraged some donors (Trumbull 1975; Trueman 1978), business contributions continued to play a major role in Canadian political finance.

Of course, it was possible to evade the disclosure regime, for example, by using an intermediary trust fund to hide the ultimate source of donations. While provincial parties did employ this ruse on a substantial scale (Allen 1989h; Canadian Press Newswire 1995; Western Report 1996), it does not appear to have been so important at the federal level. At the national level, some of the more prominent examples related to trusts to supplement the income of party leaders (Laver and Wallace 1988). More seriously, two major sources of political funds were not included in the act. It did not regulate the very large amounts of money contributed to candidates for the leadership of the two leading parties. In the years they took place, the leadership campaigns accounted for large proportions of overall political fundraising (Paltiel 1970, 40), with seven figures seemingly required to win control of either the Liberal or the Conservative party. The Tories introduced a disclosure rule in the midst of the 1976 leadership campaign and abandoned it in 1983. While six candidates disclosed details of contributions in 1976, Brian

Mulroney, unsuccessful in 1976, and triumphant in 1983, who was perceived to have spent lavishly in the earlier contest, did not reveal the sources of his money (Sallot 1983). In the contest to replace Mulroney, the two leading candidates, Jean Charest and Kim Campbell, massively outspent the $900,000 limit set by the outgoing leader. By the end of the era, former Liberal finance minister, Paul Martin, was said to have raised €10 million for his leadership bid (Willis 2003).

The other major loophole in the system related to the finances of riding (constituency) associations, the obligations of which related only to the five-week period of a general election campaign. Perhaps because of this relative secrecy, some corporate donations may have migrated from the central party treasuries to the ridings (Free Press Parliamentary Bureau 2001) and the sums spent at this level began to rival those spent by the federal party itself. The opacity of riding association finances infected the campaign finances of candidates, who often disclosed large contributions from their riding associations, the ultimate sources of which remained unknown (Geddes 2000). Moreover, the ridings did not have to disclose what they did with the frequently large surpluses they raised in excess of the maximum permitted campaign expenditure (Matas 1994).

There were no major changes to the regime between the years 1984 and 2000. Nonetheless, there were some notable amendments. As of 1993, foreign contributions of any sort were banned. In 1997, the election period was shortened and access to the permanent voters' list, which was useful for fundraising, was legalized. Unsurprisingly, this post-1974 era of political finance had a massive effect on the finances of the parties.

3.2 The finances of the Canadian parties

The opposition Progressive Conservatives immediately and vigorously adapted to the new regulations. The Conservatives adopted direct mailing techniques from the US Republicans (Globe and Mail 1980) to encourage small donors, both individuals and businesses, to take advantage of the tax credit. This gave the Tories a large base of reliable donors. By the mid-1980s they were sending out several mailings a year to 90,000 regular supporters, as well as occasional mailings of 50,000 soliciting new supporters (Clark 1986). Using another standard US technique, they sought to cultivate a group of wealthy committed donors known as 'The 500' (Stanbury 1993, 87). Moreover, the Conservatives continued to solicit regular donations from big business. From 1978, the Conservatives began to pull ahead of the Liberals (Trueman 1979; Sheppard 1980). Indeed, after the first year under the act, the Liberals' dependence on corporate contributions began to increase (Gray 1980). The relative complacency of the 'natural governing party' of Liberals ceded a financial advantage to the Conservatives that lasted almost twenty years (McQuaig 1988a). Liberal attempts to emulate their rivals' fundraising prowess were hampered by the structure of the party, and, for much of the 1980s, by the embattled position of leader, John Turner. The federal Liberal party was literally a federation. It was impossible for individuals to join the party. Its 'members' were the provincial or territorial associations. The party did not have a list of members and, in spite of its best efforts, the federal party was not able to gain access to records at the constituency level (Henderson 1986; Winsor 1987; Stanbury 1993, 108). Moreover, the party's money was fragmented into a large number of accounts (Paltiel 1970, 36). Some riding (constituency) associations were rumoured to have very healthy balances, but the party's headquarters could not verify how much money they had, never mind get it transferred to the centre (Sallot 1986). Furthermore, eight of the twelve associations were 'dual purpose' organizations, which sought to contest elections at both the provincial and federal levels. The federal party's failure to return a portion of money contributed by the provinces during the 1980s bolstered resistance to a restructuring of the Liberals' finances (Geddes 1990). In contrast, the clear separation of federal and provincial Progressive Conservative parties allowed the centralization and professionalization of fundraising (Stanbury 1993, 80–3). Finally, the Liberals' fundraising suffered from infighting and, at times, from sheer incompetence (Maclean's 1989).

Figure 3.1 shows that the parties allowed massive deficits and achieved large surpluses. Unsurprisingly, the deficits are associated with election years. The

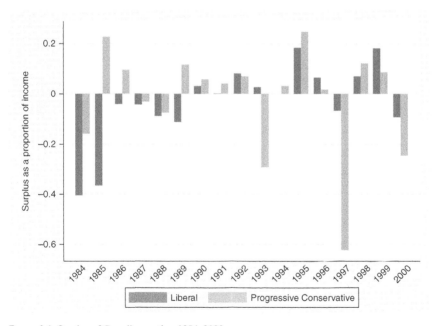

FIGURE 3.1 Surplus of Canadian parties, 1984–2000

Source: Elections Canada.

Progressive Conservatives survived a deficit of over 60 per cent of income in 1997. The Liberals' inability to control their finances is evident from their six straight deficits from 1984 to 1989. During this time, the Liberals' annual income often came in considerably below that of the New Democrats (CP 1983). In addition to attempting to reform their regular fundraising sources, the Liberals embarked on 'Project 200', which aimed to eliminate their deficit with contributions of $25,000 from two hundred large firms. While it brought in a substantial income, it fell well short of its target (Sallot 1986). The Conservatives, even during their time in the political wilderness in the 1990s, have managed useful surpluses in non-election years.

In contrast to the very different fiscal fortunes of the two parties over the sample period, dependence on the corporate sector remained more or less constant (see Figure 3.2). Corporate contributions represent about half of the income for both parties from 1984 to 2000. Even though the income of the parties fluctuated, a substantial difference in dependence on corporate contributions between the two parties was never sustained for more than a year. The only year in which there was a very large difference is 1990, when the governing Progressive Conservatives received over 56 per cent of their income from corporate contributions, but the Liberals received only 33 per cent. In the preceding three years, the Liberals had been more dependent on the corporate sector.

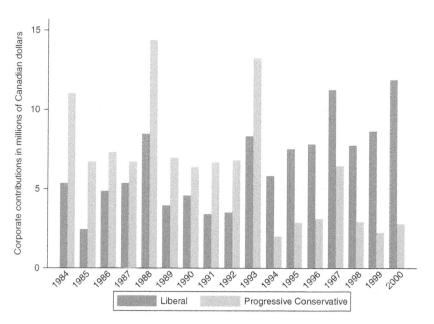

FIGURE 3.2 Corporate contributions to Canadian parties, 1984–2000

Source: Elections Canada.

The electoral disaster of 1993 precipitated an immediate and sustained collapse in the corporate income of the Progressive Conservatives, along with a less spectacular, but nonetheless very large, increase in the business revenues of the Liberals.

As Figure 3.3 illustrates, the sample of large contributors moves in the same direction as overall business contributions, and with the same turning points, but the swings are less extreme. This means that opposition parties, even those that seem to have little prospect of winning power, are more dependent on big business funding. In this sense, in spite of their strategic behaviour, big businesses do 'support the democratic system' by enabling an unpopular opposition to survive financially and attempt to regain political competitiveness. The newly elected Progressive Conservatives obtained less than 10 per cent of their income from the sample big businesses in 1985 but relied on them for 30 per cent of their income in 1998, after a second electoral rout by Chrétien's Liberals. Large businesses accounted for a relatively stable proportion of overall business funding. The range varied for the two parties, again reflecting the PC's desperate situation after 1993. For the Liberals big business accounted for 12–25 per cent of business income. However, the Progressive Conservatives ranged from 9 per cent in 1985, in the aftermath of regaining power, to 30 per cent in 1998, facing a second parliamentary term as a minor party. The next section investigates the motivations behind these swings in business donations.

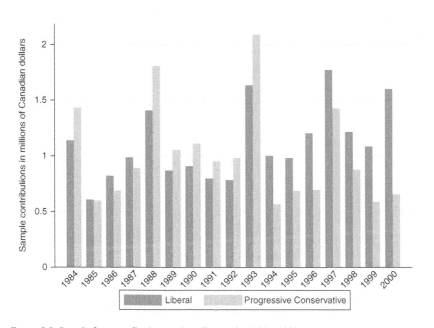

FIGURE 3.3 Sample firm contributions to Canadian parties, 1984–2000

4. MOTIVATIONS FOR CONTRIBUTIONS
TO CANADIAN PARTIES

This section presents a quantitative analysis of large firm strategy in political finance in Canada from 1984 to 2000, using the data and methods described in detail in Chapter 2. The Canadian contribution rate was impressively high. In a given year, an average of 51 per cent of firms contributed to at least one of the parties. Such a high contribution rate is surely suggestive of pragmatic rather than ideological payments. The timing and distribution of payments has much more potential to shed light on the motivations behind business financing of Canadian political parties. To begin the analysis of firm strategy, a measure of *Bias* is calculated, defined as payments to the Liberals as a proportion of payments to both parties. Figure 3.4 shows the distribution of Bias in the Canadian data. Canadian firms choose between the three strategies introduced in the theoretical framework. More subtle distributions are rare. Twenty per cent of annual payments are exclusively to the PC, with 22 per cent going exclusively to the Liberals. Fifteen per cent clearly hedge by dividing annual payments equally between the two big parties.

Since the firms so clearly structure around these strategies, the dependent variable is constructed as follows: no contribution; *Left* (bias $> = 0.67$); *Hedge* (bias between 0.34 and 0.66 and *Right* (bias $< = 0.33$). The following variables are

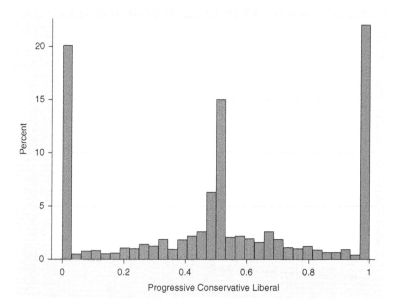

FIGURE 3.4 Distribution of bias in Canada

Note: 1,696 observations; 167 firms. Bias is proportion of reported contributions to the Progressive Conservatives and Liberals paid to the Liberals in a given year.

Source: Iain McMenamin (2012), "If Money Talks, What Does it Say? Varieties of Capitalism and Business Financing of Parties", *World Politics*, volume 64(1), pp1–38, Cambridge University Press.

used to explain variation in the firm's contribution strategies. First, there is a dummy for *Left* Government. The Progressive Conservatives were in power until 1993 and the Liberals thereafter. Next is *Years*, which counts the number of years until the next legally required election. There is also an interaction of Years and Left. *Poll* uses monthly opinion polls from Gallup to compute the probability of the Liberals winning more votes than the Progressive Conservatives in the event of an immediate election. Figure 3.5 illustrates that after 1988 the Liberals managed to maintain a huge lead over the Progressive Conservatives in opinion polls. The first economic variable is *Income* (logged to reduce the impact of outliers). Large firms should be more likely to hedge because of the lower costs of payments relative to their income. Finally, the firms have been classified into seven sectors, based on amalgamations of the UN ISIC classification.

The multinomial logit models in Table 3.1 use these variables to explain variations in firm strategy. The separate equations predict the logged odds of each of the contribution categories by reference to non-contribution. Standard errors are clustered by firm to account for heteroskedasticity. Year dummies are included in model two to deal with time dependence.[1] The Poll variable was severely collinear with Left and was dropped. The first model is a basic equation to facilitate comparison with the other two country studies. Model two, which corrects for time dependence and includes an interaction of Years and Left, is the most statistically accurate equation for the Canadian sample. The nature of multinomial logit coefficients makes their substantive implications difficult to discern and this is, of course, a greater problem with lots of variables and interactions. However, the models can be used to produce predictions in the form of the sixteen-cell table of strategies presented earlier. The simulation is derived from the most complex model. All variables were left at sample values, except for Left and its interaction. The rank-order of predicted strategies is identical for the basic and complex models.

The predictions in Table 3.2 illustrate the dominance of pragmatism. Over three-quarters of firms are expected to make a payment to one of the big parties over a two-parliament period. The pure ideological strategies are less popular than all pure pragmatic or interactive strategies. The interactive strategies do not exhibit a bias towards either left or right. The sums of the interactive categories that lean towards the left or the right are almost exactly equal. The models predict a massive advantage for the government. If the Progressive Conservatives are in power there should be 3.8 times as many PC-only contributors as Liberal-only contributors. If the Liberals form the government, the equations predict 5.3 times as many Liberal-only as PC-only contributors. Firms are less likely to hedge under a Liberal government. Canadian firms react decisively and dispassionately to changes of

---

[1] Beck, Katz, and Tucker (1998) prefer using cubic splines rather than year dummies, but there was insufficient variation in the data sets to compute the cubic splines. There were some collinearity problems, which were alleviated by the additional omission of the last year.

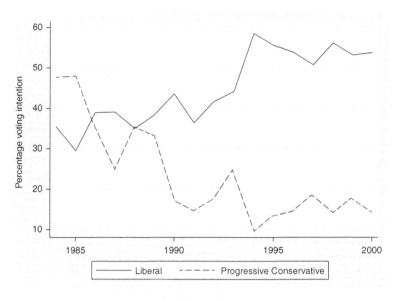

FIGURE 3.5 Popularity of the parties in Gallup polls

TABLE 3.1 *Multinomial logit estimates of firm strategy in Canada*

	Model 1	Model 2
	HEDGE	HEDGE
LEFT	−0.597 [.0.15]***	−2.087 [0.39]***
YEARS	−0.277 [0.031]***	−0.326 [0.06]***
LEFT*YEARS	–	0.252 [0.092]***
Constant	−11.473 [1.27]***	−11.2 [1.28]***
	RIGHT	RIGHT
LEFT	−1.196 [0.147]***	−3.72 [0.8]***
YEARS	−0.214 [0.034]***	−0.17 [0.06]***
LEFT*YEARS	–	0.46 [0.18]**
Constant	−4.619 [0.874]***	−4.86 [0.9]***
	LEFT	LEFT
LEFT	0.849 [0.162]***	0.385 [0.39]
YEARS	−0.066 [0.0278]**	−0.242 [0.1]**
LEFT*YEARS	–	0.19 [0.115]*
Constant	−6.873 [0.858]***	−6.47 [0.88]***
Year Dummies	No	Yes
Observations	3315	3315

Note: Robust standard errors clustered by firm in brackets. *** = significant at 1%; ** = significant at 5% * = significant at 10%. Income figures imputed from data for 1983, 1987, 1994 and 1998 using Amelia II (King et al. 2001). Income and sectoral controls are included in both equations.

TABLE 3.2 *Predicted turnover strategies: Canada*

Right in power	Left in power			
	NON-CONTRIBUTOR	HEDGE	LEFT	RIGHT
NON-CONTRIBUTOR	0.22		0.12	
HEDGE		0.029	0.067	
LEFT			0.02	
RIGHT	0.15	0.035	0.08	0.015

power. The effect of Liberal government has a much larger negative effect on PC contributions than it has a positive effect on Liberal contributions. Also, the effect of Liberal government on hedging is considerably smaller than its influence on exclusive contributions to either of the parties. Each of these results makes sense in terms of pragmatic contributions and the political context of the time. Hedging maintains good relationships with the government and the opposition and there-fore, as the equation shows, should be less sensitive to changes in government. While the Liberals had serious problems in opposition to Mulroney's PC govern-ment, they were always a much more plausible alternative government than the Progressive Conservatives were during the Liberal's time in power under Chré-tien. The Progressive Conservatives' years in opposition began with the disastrous election of 1993, which reduced them to only two MPs. Their failure to regain their status as a major party in 1997 was almost more demoralizing. So, pragmatic firms had greater reason to fund the opposition Liberals than they had to bankroll the Progressive Conservatives in opposition. Canadian business money spoke the language of pragmatism.

In addition to changes in the distribution of political power, the electoral schedule also has an implication for pragmatic firms. The closeness of an election has a much larger effect on the hedging category than the other two contribution patterns. In other words, firms react rationally to increasing political uncertainty. Larger firms are more likely to adopt each of the contribution strategies in all equations. Moreover, as predicted, size is most strongly associated with hedging. By contrast, sectoral dummies perform weakly. The only significant result is that financial firms are more likely to hedge. The Canadian party system was, of course, more complex than the two-party framework of this analysis. The New Democrats to the left of the Liberals have never attracted serious numbers of business donations. After 1993, the Progressive Conservatives lost much of their parliamentary representation to the upstart right-wing Reform Party. However, the Reformers did not attract enough business funding to seriously modify the results reported here (Curtis, 1999; Elections Canada 1997, 2000).

Having established the basic motivation for business financing of Canadian parties the chapter proceeds to build on the statistical analysis by conducting largely qualitative assessments of various interpretations of Canadian party–firm relations.

5. INTERPRETING BUSINESS FINANCING
OF PARTIES IN CANADA

5.1 Supporting the democratic process

'Supporting the democratic process' was the stock answer of firms asked to explain why they gave money to the Liberal and Conservative parties (Shecter 2002). This phrase was crafted to rule out pragmatic and ideological motivations. Business funding was portrayed as playing a role similar to that of public funding in Canada and other jurisdictions. 'Supporting the democratic process' was often closely preceded or followed by references to 'good corporate citizenship' (Matas 1987) or some such phrase, in order to emphasize altruistic motives. Reference to the democratic process was sometimes meant to rule out any desire to influence the outcome of elections in the favour of ideologically preferred parties. Instead, business contributions sought to maintain healthy competition within a set of democratic rules. For example, a Bank of Montreal spokesman said, 'The philosophy behind giving is to support the political process. You don't give to receive a benefit' (McFarland 2000).

Sometimes the democratic motivation was construed as a sort of wide ideological commitment, as illustrated by an industrialist who justified fundraising for the Conservatives in 1941 as 'for the purpose of considering what [could be done] to assist the Party to resume the important part it has played in the maintenance of constitutional government in Canada' (Paltiel 1970, 32). More recently a Gulf Oil spokesman articulated similar concerns: 'We do contribute, at least to major parties in the federal and provincial arena who do support the free-enterprise system, and we have done so in past years. Our view is that someone has to help support the political process' (Palango 1978). This statement can be construed as signalling a preference for the Liberals and Conservatives over the NDP and no preference as to which of the two traditionally pro-business parties should rule. It was during the Tory party's long decade in the political wilderness that business money did, in a very real sense, support the democratic system. It played a vital role in preserving the Tory party, unifying the right and restoring competitiveness to a party system that the Liberals had dominated. Indeed, Conservative fundraisers claim to have emphasized the health of the democratic system in their approaches to potential donors during this period. The party's national director said, 'Corporate Canada believes in a healthy political process (and) demands a competitive environment. We have marketed ourselves that way' (Geddes 1996). In 1986, Liberal fundraiser Leo Kolber made the same plea, 'This is an appeal to foster a two-party system—no more, no less' (Naumetz 1986b). Of course, democratic arguments could also be used to denounce payments, which ensured the survival, and resurgence in a new form, of a party that could not garner many votes and could not attract substantial funding from citizens.

However, the overall pattern of payments does not suit the thesis of support for the democratic process. If this were the case, results would be linked to votes, or maybe legislative seats. Indeed, this is the case with public financing of political parties, in Canada and elsewhere, which is much more plausibly presented as a support for democracy itself. The reward for governing parties is very difficult to construe as support for the process. Governing parties are very rarely treated differently by public finance systems. When they are, as in the United Kingdom (Ewing 2007, 184–5), they receive less money than opposition parties, which do not have the considerable advantage of controlling the resources of government. This is not to say that support for democracy was not wholly or partially an explanation for some Canadian business donations. Nonetheless, support for democracy is not a convincing interpretation of the general pattern of payments to Canadian parties.

5.2 Ideology and the free trade election of 1988

Ideology has not been an important motivation for business contributions to Canadian political parties. Traditionally, power alternated between two pro-business parties. Nonetheless, at times, such as during the Trudeau era, and most of Turner's period of leadership, the Liberals could have been described as centre-left. However, these were examples of a centrist party tacking to the left, rather than a leftist party seeking the support of the median voter in the centre of political spectrum. As the data show, the vast majority of business donors ignored such differences, treating the two big parties more or less equally, by consistently hedging or pragmatically giving more to the government than to the opposition.

Sometimes, the right made ideological appeals to businesses, but this was usually a vain attempt to try to change established pragmatic strategies. Reform leader, Preston Manning, emphasized the party's tax-cutting agenda when speaking to businesspeople (Curtis 1999). A Reform fundraiser was probably correct when he said, 'They may not have given us money, but ninety per cent of them preferred Reform's policies' (Curtis 1999). Some Tories also credited ideology with a role in gaining business donations. In 1996, the party president solicited donations on the basis of the pro-business policies of the Mulroney governments, but thought that this was proving difficult since the Liberal government, and especially the famously conservative finance minister Paul Martin, had adopted many of their policies. By contrast, the party's national director played down the importance of ideology in gaining support from business. Instead, he emphasized the need to have an alternative to the Liberals that did not threaten regional splintering and the undoubted damage that would do to business prospects (Geddes 1996).

The election of 1988 was an exception to the pattern of minimal ideological differences between the parties. Turner began his leadership on the right, advocating policies very like those eventually implemented by the Mulroney government. However, under pressure from his party, he moved to the left, proposing full employment and guaranteed income policies in the run-up to the 1988 election. His position on free trade began as qualified approval for closer trade links with the USA and ended as a promise to rip up the free trade agreement if elected (Goar 1988). In an after-dinner speech to a ballroom of businesspeople, Turner asked that Canadian business sacrifice profit for national independence by rejecting the free-trade deal (McQuaig 1988b). The Tory Prime Minister, Brian Mulroney, chose to treat the 1988 election as a referendum on the free trade agreement he had signed with the United States. The free trade agreement was 'the most dramatic shift in the country's economic direction [for] more than a century' (Taylor and Baskerville 1994, 471). The election polarized around this issue, with the Progressive Conservatives on one side and the Liberals and New Democrats on the other (Luzstig 2004, 119). The business sector was almost completely united in favour of the Free Trade Agreement (Woodside 1989, 166; Taylor and Baskerville 1994, 471). Indeed, business leaders had put the idea on the political agenda in the first place (Luzstig 2004, 122–3). Progressive Conservative Prime Minister Mulroney took it on board as a potential side payment to Western Canada in return for acquiescence to a new constitutional deal for Quebec (Luzstig 1996, 82). Thus, the election of 1988 is surely a 'crucial case' for the theory that ideology mattered to business donors to Canadian political parties.

If businesses had been ideologically motivated, they should have favoured the Progressive Conservatives to an extent that went significantly beyond a pragmatic bonus for the incumbent government. A large number of newspaper articles suggested that the Liberals' stance on free trade was going to reduce the amount of money they got from corporate fundraising. Indeed, these articles were faithfully reporting what some political actors thought. The Liberals feared that their free-trade position hit corporate contributions in the west (Carlisle 1988). This was a shock to Liberals, who were not used to a distinction between the two parties being made on anything other than incumbency. 'It's tantamount to political intimidation', said one western Liberal, who claimed businesses that previously gave to the party were refusing to do so unless the party or candidate supports the deal. 'We've been frozen out' (Ferguson 1988). The free trade issue was also reported to be a problem for corporate fundraising by provincial Liberals (Walkom 1988). Stanbury, the authority on Canadian political finance in this period, endorsed this view (Stanbury 1993, 139–40).

However, other senior Liberals denied that free trade affected the amounts of money coming in from business. The Liberals' secretary general admitted that some business donors had expressed concern about the party's position on free trade. However, she said that this had not affected donations and was partly due to a misperception that the Liberals were actually against free trade (CP 1988). In spite of concern and even hostility, business donations were strong, while the level of individual contributions continued to disappoint (Goar 1988). The party's chief financial officer said, 'I'm not denying that there were some companies who felt so strongly about the issue that they closed their cheque books . . . But they were the exception.' His impression was that firms, which supported free trade, continued to give equally to both parties but also contributed to advocacy groups such as the Canadian Alliance for Trade and Job Opportunities. He reported that the Liberals would not be prioritizing business in their fundraising efforts for the year after the election and denied that this decision was linked to the fee trade controversy (Delacourt 1989).

The data clearly support the second interpretation; there is no evidence of a significant ideological effect in 1988. The Progressive Conservatives' share of business contributions (either in total or in the sample) is not noticeably higher than in 1993, by which time the Tory government was facing a Liberal party that had accepted free trade. Nonetheless, businesses did feel motivated to contribute substantial finances of approximately $13 million on advertising to support the free trade agreement. Other expenses incurred in support of the deal included company inserts of free trade promotional material in employees' pay slips and mailings to shareholders, and meetings with employees on company time to lecture them on the benefits of the deal (Vancouver Sun 1997). It is possible that, had this independent political advertising not been available, businesses would have contributed more to the Progressive Conservatives. Nonetheless, it is important to remember that Canadian businesses made an unequivocal decision not to punish the Liberals, nor reward the Tories, when there was no legal impediment to so doing.

Ideology may have influenced some Canadian businesses' decisions on how to distribute political donations. However, an awareness of ideology contributes only a little to our understanding of the flows of business money to Canadian parties. This is evident from the overall data and from the instructive case of the 1988 election. Pragmatic motivations can also be studied instructively by focusing on a famous election.

5.3 Pragmatism and the earthquake election of 1993

Business contributions to Canadian parties were largely the product of conscious, if not necessarily intense or ongoing, pragmatic political calculations. Very large companies delegated the distribution of political contributions to a public affairs division (Curtis 1999) or even to a special political finance committee. Even if such dedicated units existed their brief was usually to administer a set policy, rather than to react to political events (McFarland 2000). For example, in 1999 the head of public affairs at a very large Canadian firm said, 'We have a very fluid federal situation right now and, frankly, we don't know how to respond to it' (Curtis 1999). This is in contrast, for example, to the boards of American corporate Political Action Committees, which constantly make decisions about which individual candidates to fund (Clawson, Neustadtl, and Weller 1998, 39–42). One of the most popular policies was to give the same to both big parties (Simpson 1978; Poirier 1987), and to double the amounts in election years. Other firms gave more, again, often double, to the governing party (McIntosh 1986). Yet another variant was to give half as much to the official opposition as to the government, and half as much again to other national parties. Patterns in provincial politics were very similar (Stead 1980; Sheppard 1984; Ferguson 1989). For older firms, these were well-established policies, which may well have pre-dated the introduction of disclosure in 1974. Fragmentary evidence suggests that a sixty–forty split between the government and the official opposition had become common amongst banks and other large, regular contributors by the 1950s (Whitaker 1977, 201) and hedging was widely acknowledged even earlier (Paltiel 1970, 29). These automatic policies came under increasing strain after 1993, as the old Tory party became increasingly unlikely to re-establish the traditional alternation of governments. For example, after the 1993 election, the Royal Bank of Canada violated its formal policy and decided to continue to treat the Progressive Conservatives as if they were the official opposition (McFarland 2000). For newer firms, the policies were often formed in reaction to requests for funding from parties and in imitation of what they saw as standard practice amongst other firms. Outside the biggest firms, there was no official policy, even if there was often a traditional distribution of funds. Even if a policy was in place, large firms would wait for a letter from the party and a visit from one of its 'bagmen', the senior fundraisers who were often current or former business executives. Smaller firms would receive, or seek out, invitations to collective fundraising events.

The aggregate effect of such strategies is clear from the data. The volume of business contributions increases in election years and governing parties enjoy a large bonus, while opposition parties receive continuing support. Nonetheless, losing power is a huge financial shock and in the twentieth century the official opposition, whether Liberal or Conservative, often battled to avoid bankruptcy (Paltiel 1970, 31, 37). Pragmatic calculations could also be made prospectively by contributing to a party that seemed likely to win or maintain power at the next electoral test (Paltiel 1970, 41). There were some reports that business contributions tracked opinion polls (Howard 1993). Business contributions do seem to broadly follow the poll ratings of the two big parties. However, popularity does not have a significant effect after controlling for which party was in government. The Progressive Conservatives began their drastic drop in popularity before leaving government, but it was not until after 1993 that their income from business fell.

Popularity was one of several factors that fed into business analysis of the pragmatism of contributing to an opposition party. There is good evidence that many businesses only wished to contribute to an opposition party that was united and had a coherent leadership. Some businesses expressed a reluctance to contribute to the Liberals, because of the infighting and policy swings during John Turner's leadership (Naumetz 1986b). In particular, some businesses found themselves subject to multiple, uncoordinated requests for funding from different representatives of the party (Laver and Wallace 1988). Understandably, this made a very bad impression. Also, businesses were reluctant to make payments that would be swallowed up by the party's seemingly uncontrollable deficit (MacKenzie 1988). The refusal of businesses to donate to either the Reform (and its successor the Alliance) or Progressive Conservative parties in 2000, unless they merged, was undoubtedly a major factor behind their subsequent unification. Relatedly, after the disastrous election of 2000, businesses did not view either Day of the Alliance or Clark of the Tories as plausible alternative prime ministers (McNish and Laghi 2002; Pedersen 2001). Earlier in the twentieth century, business donors also withheld funding from weak or uncooperative leaders (Paltiel 1970, 28, 30, 41–2).

Our sample period contains one turnover. It illustrates eloquently how business strategies operated in the context of a change of power. The Progressive Conservatives began the election year of 1993 as an extremely unpopular party that had been in power since 1984. They chose a new and inexperienced, but initially very popular, leader, Kim Campbell, to fight the election. The election results were difficult to predict for many reasons, including small poll differences between the PC and the Liberals and the rise of two new regionally focused parties as serious contenders, the Reform Party and the Bloc Québécois (Cairns 1994, 221). Regardless of serious economic problems, constitutional and cultural issues played a major part in the campaign. There was an implicit consensus between the PC and Liberals that the welfare state would suffer in the struggle to control the public finances. Thus, there was little ideological basis on which businesses could choose between the two parties. The changes in vote shares were dramatic and the votes were grossly distorted by the interaction between the first-past-the-post electoral system and contrasts in the regional distribution of party votes. The governing PC was reduced to two members, while the Liberals received a huge bonus.

Table 3.3, again in the sixteen-cell format, summarizes how the sample firms reacted to the turnover. The largest category, at 18 per cent, consists of those who hedged irrespective of the government. The blatantly pragmatic strategy of shifting from Progressive Conservatives to Liberals is well represented at over 10 per cent. The second largest category is to hedge under the PC and then commit to the Liberals. This is by far the largest of the categories, which suggest an interaction of pragmatic and ideological logics. Small numbers of companies seem to be ideological, cleaving to the PC or the Liberals, whether in government or not.

Pragmatism was undoubtedly the dominant motivation for business contributions to Canadian parties. It was a conservative pragmatism with widespread hedging and a clear bias towards governing parties. In other words, most Canadian businesses did not try to second-guess political competition by focusing funds on the party most likely to win the next election. However, some businesses were reluctant to contribute to chaotic divided opposition parties and a few businesses did pay some attention to opinion polls. The numbers suggest pragmatism, but

TABLE 3.3 *Turnover strategies: Canada, 1993*

Right in power	Left in power			
	NON-CONTRIBUTOR	HEDGE	LEFT	RIGHT
NON-CONTRIBUTOR	0.22		0.062	
HEDGE		0.0184	0.144	
LEFT			0.056	
RIGHT	0.041	0.041	0.103	0.067

Notes: N = 191. 169 companies contributed in the period 1989–1997. 1988–1993 counted as the Progressive Conservatives' period in government, even though the 1993 election was in October. 1994–1997 counted as the Liberals period in government. The Liberals continued in power after the June 1997 election. There were 9.5 times as many contributors inside the coded categories as outside them.

they do not do much to identify what businesses expected in exchange for their money. The next section addresses this question.

6. PRAGMATIC EXCHANGES

6.1 Illegal transactions

Pragmatic donations are interested. Three alternative interpretations are considered here: illegal transactions, the trading of access as a discrete exchange, and a reciprocal exchange of money for the opportunity to develop networks of mutual obligation. Financial scandals were a regular part of Canadian politics. A Canadian political scientist wrote in 2000:

> The last three premiers of British Columbia have resigned because of illegal fundraising schemes or accepting personal favours. The Saskatchewan Conservative Party disappeared in shame at the way some now-jailed or fined members of the Grant Devine government diverted public funds to private and party uses. It was just ten years ago that Liberal fundraiser Patti Starr's activities contributed to the defeat of the David Peterson Liberal government in Ontario. And Stevie Cameron's *On the Take* detailed the corruption-filled Mulroney years in Ottawa. Political-finance scandals are in our blood too: the Pacific Scandal, the railway bribing party and politician, brought down John A. MacDonald's Government just six years into nationhood. (MacDermid 2000, 32)

During the sample period, there were a number of prosecutions and convictions, at federal and provincial level, for influence peddling. In one case, a Liberal official approached a number of Quebec companies, which were in receipt of government grants, offering to help them secure the continuation of these grants in exchange for donations (McIlroy and Thanh Ha 1997). An initially similar episode of influence peddling by campaign workers eventually reached all the way to the cabinet. It was alleged that ministers, and officials from the prime minister's office, had intervened to ensure that a 'Tory-linked' firm won out over a firm that contributed to the Liberals (Cohn 1987). Senior politicians came out of another Tory influence-peddling scandal slightly better (Janigan 1987). MP Charles Gravel sold tickets to a dinner with Minister Roch La Salle with the promise of government contracts. Later on the businesspeople complained to LaSalle that the contracts had not been forthcoming. Many scandals did not involve party finances. One of the most damaging affairs during the tenure of the Mulroney government involved a massive personal benefit for Minister André Bissonnette. Ministers' assets were placed into blind trusts to protect them from conflicts of interest. However, a firm paid one million dollars to the administrator of Bissonette's trust and much of the money found its way to the minister and his wife (Cohn 1987). During the sample period, illegal exchanges appear to have been exceptional rather than systemic at the federal level (Corcoran 1993). There was definitely no suggestion of anything comparable to the 'tollgating' that had, in the recent past, financed both Conservatives and Liberals in Nova Scotia:

> [B]usinesses kicked back a percentage of Government contracts to the party in power as the price of securing the work. In the case of liquor distillers, they paid as much as fifty cents a case as a fee for getting their products listed with the Nova Scotia Liquor Commission. (Harris 1983)

6.2 Access and discrete exchanges

When asked what businesses received in return for their money, most politicians and businesspeople would probably have replied, 'nothing' and then launched into a speech about supporting the democratic system and the free enterprise economy. In response to the same question, Canadian journalists would probably have responded, 'access'. They understood business financing of parties as a discrete exchange: businesses provide money and politicians provide access. Articles titled along the lines of 'access for sale', or arguing a thesis summarized by those words, almost became a genre in the Canadian press. These articles were essentially reports on a range of fundraising events, both secret and public, that were vital to the Liberals and the Tories during the sample period.

Events with ministers or MPs could be relatively small. Annual dinners with party leaders often attracted thousands. While individual tickets were available, businesses dominated these events, usually buying up whole tables, which amounted to a cost of several thousand dollars (Clark and Mackie 2003). Usually, the large dinners were preceded or succeeded by smaller receptions for larger or more regular contributors (Matas 1995; Ovenden 2000). Smaller events could provide much more intimate access and were priced accordingly. A foursome on a golf outing with the Liberal Finance Minister Paul Martin cost $10,000. Dinner with Prime Minister Chrétien was sold at the same price, even though on at least one occasion the special guest star failed to appear (Yaffe 2002). Dinners and other events were often secret, even if, of course, associated donations were disclosed (Mittelstaedt 1993; Alberts 1994). Throughout the 1980s both the Liberals and Conservatives held special events for the members of the Laurier Club and the 500 Club respectively. Membership of these clubs was available to those contributing over a set, relatively low, amount. In 2003, $1,000 was needed to qualify for both clubs.

'Access', in the meaning of receiving an opportunity to influence a politician, requires a minimum amount of time, a maximum number of participants, and a minimum level of secrecy. Any degree of publicity increases the politicians' costs so much that lobbying opportunity is likely to be granted. Since Canadian political power is tightly centralized, direct access to a decision-maker must have been difficult. Ministers were in far too much demand to give any time, never mind a proper hearing, to any other than the most significant businesses. Moreover, on many social occasions, there were too many people, and too little time, to even mention an important and sensitive issue. The co-chairman of the supposedly exclusive Laurier club of Liberal supporters said that at their events there was 'too big a crowd to be a significant occasion of exclusive access to the PM' (Howard 1997b). Nonetheless, sometimes, parties did appear to directly sell political access. A Liberal letter before the 1993 election 'promised those in attendance private meetings with the "future prime minister" when he passed through their community and privileged access to party documents' (Mittelstaedt 1993). The Conservatives also promised one-to-one access to members of the 500 Club for large regular contributors (Naumetz 1986a). On other occasions, 'fundraising' letters were targeted not so much at potential supporters, but at those most in need of political access, such as an invitation to media firms to attend a political fundraiser with the communications minister (Globe and Mail 1985; McLaren 1988). Some of these events seem to have been small enough, secret enough, expensive enough, and of sufficient duration to have provided real access opportunities. However, many such direct access packages surely made unrealistic promises. The Tories' chief fundraiser, David Angus, in response to a question about a letter that offered direct access, said, 'Anybody who can write a cheque for $1,000 is smart enough to know that, of all ways, this is the least way they are going to lobby or do anything. These are supporters of the party and there is a little bit of togetherness' (Winsor 1987). Frequently, the access 'purchased' by the firm was already available for free. Another PC fundraiser admitted that the '500 Hotline' probably did not offer much that was not available by contacting a MP or trade association (Winsor 1987). For the largest firms, contributions were unnecessary to gain direct access. As Liberal Terry Mercer said, 'If senior executives wanted to talk to a cabinet minister, a simple phone call will do it. They're already recognized' (Howard 1997a).

6.3 Reciprocal exchange

Conceptualizing access as a direct purchase leaves us with a set of contradictory logic, evidence, and rhetoric. Logically, it seems practically impossible and politically foolhardy for politicians to provide real access to actual decision-makers for the huge number of Canadian businesses that contributed financially to parties. However, there is a range of evidence that the parties, at a senior level, did, sometimes, 'sell' access, even if it often was not delivered. This does not fit easily with the rhetoric surrounding fundraising from business, which emphasized ideological and social motivations for making contributions and attending functions. Liberal Immigration Minister Sergio Marchi denied selling access:

> He points out he is also available for events at no cost—where he says the same things he says at fund-raisers. Many people want to support a politician, but don't have the time or inclination to show up at the campaign office. Through fund-raisers, they not only can give money but also feel they have participated in the political process. (Alberts 1994)

A Tory fundraiser emphasized the social function of such events: 'We need a chance to chew the fat and tell each other how good we are' (Winsor 1987).

One way of reconciling all these statements might be to hypothesize that a naïve and cynical minority was being exploited by a larger group of politicians and businesspeople who understood that access was not for sale and that supporting a political party was not a knowing euphemism and meant just what it said. However, a better way of thinking about the connection between money and influence in the Canadian system would be to stop thinking of money and access as a discrete exchange. Instead, it was a reciprocal exchange. Money and access were both parts of a symbiotic system of lobbying and political finance, in which businesses and politicians developed mutually beneficial relationships over a period of time. So, for example, the annual leaders' dinners, and other large fundraising dinners starring cabinet ministers, are likely to have provided little or no access to businesses that invested in tickets. Nevertheless, sometimes attendees could be lucky: a representative of a pharmaceutical company reported enthusiastically that 'I was chatting and for fifteen minutes I had the ear of two cabinet ministers and a senator. It was well worth the money' (Curtis 1999). Instead, such events served to build and maintain relationships that might, on a later occasion, increase the chances of real access and the chances that such access achieves its aim of influencing a decision. Real access consists of an often brief, but secret, one-to-one meeting or communication with a decision-maker, as well as some real expectation that the 'pitch' will be considered favourably. This sort of access is more likely to be provided through a broker such as a member of a minister's staff office, one of the party's 'bagmen', an MP, or a provincial politician, who not only realizes that the firm is a regular and substantial political contributor, but may well remember a name and a face and have some understanding of the needs and problems of the firm. In other words, the decision-maker would need to be convinced, often through his trust of the broker, that he and his party are obliged to the firm. The centralization of the system meant that substantial fundraising was much easier if a cabinet minister was produced. The parties' money men knew this and put a lot of energy into insisting that ministers attend fundraising events when on official business outside of the capital (Matas 1995). The really large firms, 'Bay Street', expected that the solicitation of funds would be accompanied by a visit from one of a handful of senior fundraisers, who were directly answerable to the party leader or prime minister, and could set up meetings with ministers (Stanbury 1993, 315). Thus, businesses calculated that their money could be useful, when, and if, the need arose. Even so, money did not guarantee anything. In a sense, Liberal fundraiser senator Leo Kolber was absolutely correct when he said that he 'did not promise a bloody thing' when fundraising from business (Stanbury 1993, 315). On occasion, politicians found it expedient to boast that businesses had nothing to gain from making financial contributions:

> [Jean Chrétien] said he told Mr. Bronfman that the controversial privatisation of Toronto's Pearson Airport shouldn't take place just before an election. 'I told (Mr. Bronfman) that in his face,' he said. 'I guess you can say he paid $1,000 to receive that message.' (Mittelstaedt 1993)

Chrétien also pointed out the most reliable big contributors had been the banks, but their merger request was flatly refused (Chrétien 2007, 398). Political contributions help develop a relatively diffuse obligation to help out firms. Often the relationship and the money may have achieved nothing other than 'the answer to a phone call—or a quicker answer to a phone call' (Allen 1989a; Curtis 1999). They are not sufficient to establish an obligation in relation to a specific issue of the firm's choosing. In order to prevent the perception or reality of such a definite obligation arising, until at least 1980, the Liberals imposed on themselves a relatively low limit for corporate donations of $25,000 and $50,000 in election years (Sheppard 1980). There does seem to have been a relatively firm, if unarticulated, consensus between parties and businesses that no really large donations would be proffered or accepted.

Once understood in the wider context of reciprocal exchange, many of the supposed anomalies regarding political donations become less puzzling. Large firms, that already have access, make payments to develop a sense of obligation amongst the political elite, beyond the objective social and economic importance of the enterprise. Many of the best attended and expensive fundraising events provide little or no access to the decision-maker, but they demonstrate that other political actors present may have direct access to the 'star' politician giving the keynote speech. Firms that are aware of the utility of developing a relationship with a party, and especially with well-connected individuals within it, see a clear rationale in attending such an event. Thus, the donations constitute an investment in a small but real increase in the probability of successful lobbying.

Pragmatism was an important motivation for the business payments to parties. This pragmatism took several forms. One rare form was illegal transactions. Right throughout the period access was bought and sold in discrete exchanges. However, the dominant form of pragmatism was a reciprocal exchange, aimed at building a relationship with politicians and parties through financial contributions and face-to-face meetings that could result in a small but significant increase in the chances of beneficial decision, should the need arise. These reciprocal exchanges depended on networks of businesspeople and politicians. The next section aims to extricate two different interpretations of business–political networks in Canada.

6.4 Networks of interest, networks of loyalty, and the unification of the right

It was frequently difficult to tell whether the system of political finance and high-powered socializing reflected networks of interest or networks of loyalty. The previous section argued for networks of interest: the network is used to foster reciprocity that can further business interests. An alternative interpretation is that of networks of loyalty: business cash is used to maintain loyalties to a personal network. In practice, the two were difficult to separate and complemented each other. Nonetheless, the networks of interest interpretation is more convincing. Crucially, there is the simple fact that business money was being used. As in many other countries, businesspeople could and did use their own substantial wealth to make payments that reflected loyalty to a personal network. Indeed, by mid-century, participation in fundraising had been established as a tradition in some wealthy families (Paltiel 1970, 35; Whitatker 1977, 199).

The story of the unification of the Progressive Conservative and Reform parties provides an excellent opportunity to disentangle networks of interest from networks of loyalty. This section explains the persistent reluctance of businesses to fund Reform, instead of, or even merely as well as, the humiliated Tory party and the timing and circumstances under which the unification was brought about. Thinking of the Canadian system of business political finance as the maintenance of networks of mutual obligation makes a major contribution to explaining these two puzzles. Moreover, the story of the unification of the right has the advantage of the weakness of alternative explanations based on ideology and the sale of access.

The reluctance to fund Reform was hardly ideological. Reform's pro-market zeal should have made it more attractive than the flexible, centrist Tories. As noted earlier on, businesses probably did prefer Reform's policies to those of the Liberals and the Progressive Conservatives. Reform's outlook did clash with that of the business elite on some other issues. It did not prioritize doing a deal with Quebec, never mind making whatever concessions were necessary to preserve the federation, as did the Tories and Liberals. Most businesses clearly preferred the continuation of the federation (McQueen 1995; Toulin 1997). Reform initially suffered from an image as a 'dead-end regional party' and then perhaps managed a partial upgrade to an 'upstart regional party' (Curtis 1999). One Reform MP admitted that their reputation on Bay Street was of a western-oriented party 'riding into town on our horse with a six shooter' (Baxter 2000). A threat to the federation was a threat to Canadian business. After all, its two great centres were Toronto and Montreal. Also, business leaders must have been uncomfortable with the social conservatism of the prairies, with its concern for 'family values' and gun rights (Galloway 2000). Nonetheless, neither of these issues was as central to business as tax and regulation, which reflected Reform's ideologically unambiguous pro-business commitment. Furthermore, as argued above, ideology just was not a primary motivation for most businesses. Reform won many more seats than the Progressive Conservatives in the elections of 1993 and 1997. If political donations were purchases of access they should have favoured the relatively influential Reform party over the Progressive Conservatives, with only two MPs from 1993 to 1997 and twenty MPs from 1997 to 2000.

The seeming irrationality of the preference for the Progressive Conservatives might be construed as a reflection of the strength of the networks of loyalty that bound together the traditional business and political elites. During the sample period, the Canadian business elite largely remained an 'old boys network', centred on private clubs, interlocking directorates, the big five banks and the cities of Toronto and Montreal (Carroll 2007, 269, 275). Nevertheless, by the 1990s, the business elite was becoming less tightly knit as capital moved to the oil-rich west; women and ethnic minorities rose up corporate ladders; businesses formed smaller more meritocratic boards; private clubs shut down and were to some extent replaced by neo-liberal think tanks and interest groups (Carroll 2007, 273, 275). The Liberals, Conservatives, and business elite were members of a wider Canadian elite—the 'Establishment' (Jenkinson 2001). The parties solicited their largest donations from the biggest firms, by following up a letter with a visit from a former business executive (Howard 1997b). Longstanding interpersonal links seem to have played an important role in maintaining funding for the Tory party. The insurgent Reform party came up against these strong connections when trying to get businesses to abandon the Conservatives for a newer and apparently stronger right-wing alternative. One fundraiser said, 'Unlike the Tories, Reform does not have an old boys fund-raising network full of movers and shakers who have cultivated relationships with Bay Street and other corporate pockets.' Another recounted a meeting with a senior banker who admitted, 'My head says you're right, but I've been a Tory for 65 years and I can't emotionally stand the fact that the Tories are defunct' (Curtis 1999).

This can also be interpreted in terms of a network of interest. A sense of reciprocity could not be developed instantly or even quickly. A Tory party that regained power would have links to business as strong as those of the Liberals. Firms would have established relationships with a range of intermediaries as well as some of the senior decision-makers themselves. Moreover, the structure and culture of the Reform party may have been less functional from a business point of view. Reform was a proudly populist party. This must have worried the big businesses, which were used to being able to deal with a handful of trustworthy ministers, without having to worry unduly about the grassroots of parties. Populism was also anti-elitism and the fat cats of Toronto were the elite (Pedersen 2001). Connections to the Tories were likely to be more helpful in the event of a Tory victory than were connections to Reform in the event of a Reform victory.

The rationale for such a network, from a business point of view, was that it could be brought to bear in matters of importance, and might sometimes influence a political decision. The rationale for such a network, from a political point of view, was that it provided a regular source of funds. Politicians were less likely to feel an obligation to firms that only provided money when it was least needed. Moreover, the implicit deal, on which these obligations were based, assumed two parties. The Tories accepted that businesses would fund their competitors for the centre of the Canadian political space. If business were to fund their competitors for the centre and for the right this might be seen as a violation of the relatively well-established pact between politicians and business donors. It would mean that a dollar received by the Progressive Conservatives was less effective than a dollar received by the Liberals. Thus, a positive reason to prefer the Tories was that Tory networks would be more functional for business interests than any new Reform network could be. A negative reason was that abandoning the Tories, or hedging between the two right-wing parties, could jeopardize the sense of obligation, which made the networks valuable in the first place.

The unification of the right took place in two stages. The first was the formation of the Canadian Conservative Reform Alliance, usually known simply as the Alliance. The Reform party failed to make a breakthrough in 1997 and seemed destined to remain a regional party. In order to compete for power with the Liberals, the Reformers needed to match their national presence and match or exceed their fundraising power. Both of these objectives seemed to be in the gift of the Tories, who had continued to receive business funding out of proportion with their electoral and parliamentary importance, and who had effectively been reduced to an Ontario-based party. 1997 was even more depressing for the Tories, who remained electorally marginalized, and could no longer explain away 1993 as a freak election result. Although the Tories received more business funding than Reform, the trend was for greater support for the Reformers and less for the Tories. After not just two mere defeats, but two parliamentary terms as a minor party, the functionality of Tory networks had become highly questionable from the business point of view. However, this did not mean that Reform was going to replace the Tories. Reform did not have the networking strength, or given its western populism, even the networking potential of the old Progressive Conservative party. Also, it did not have the electoral strength, and given Ontarians' aversion to the Reformers, the electoral potential of the Tory party of old.

The 'United Alternative' was the project of leading Reform politicians, including leader, Preston Manning, and some less senior Tories and former Tories. The federal Progressive Conservative party itself remained steadfastly hostile. From its inception, the movement was strongly oriented towards raising business money, and gained the support of senior fundraisers from the two parties. Initially, donors were approached and asked for half of what they were giving the parties, but the hope was that once a unified party emerged it would be very attractive to businesses seeking to support the right (Walters 1998). The new proto-party was more of a threat to the finances of the Progressive Conservatives than those of Reform. 'The Tories are starting to lose donations from major corporations because they are telling [PC Leader Joe] Clark to smarten up. Maybe the money's just not there, but we can hold our own fine. If the United Alternative brought everyone together, we'd do extremely well', said a former Tory MP, who supported the Alternative (O'Malley 1999). After all, a key aim of the movement was to co-opt Tory donors, thereby demonstrating to the Reform grassroots and the Tory leadership that a merger made sense. The defection of established players in Canadian political finance offered a way for businesses to harness their old Tory networks to Reform's electoral power. Although business clearly favoured a united right, the United Alliance idea added further to the confusion for business donors and a substantial number decided to abstain, or continue with traditional policies, until the situation became clearer (Curtis 1999).

The United Alliance idea had to battle its way through the democratic procedures of the Reform party. First, 60 per cent of members voted to study the idea. Then, a two-thirds majority was required to transform the party into the United Alliance (UA). The idea was backed by founding leader Preston Manning and most senior Reformers, but was resisted by many MPs and grassroots members. Committed Reformers admitted that the Alliance's access to business funding was crucial in persuading them to support the new formation: 'One of the things that tipped the balance for me in favour of supporting the United Alternative was when we started seeing the corporate board room doors swing open to UA proponents that were never open to Reform' (Baxter 2000). Stockwell Day, who won the contest to be the UA's first leader, had been a provincial minister for the Progressive Conservatives in Alberta (Cunningham et al. 1999). Businesses reacted enthusiastically to Day's election and contributed with unprecedented generosity (Naumetz 2000). The Alliance quickly demonstrated a capacity for corporate fundraising, which was much more like that of the Tories than the Reform party. It rapidly became clear that much of this money was instead of, not in addition to, traditional donations to the Progressive Conservatives (Cadegan 2000). The UA aimed at and, to a large extent, achieved a different image from Reform: 'We have certainly learned to be more measured in what we say and people have come to know us as responsible people who can now have a real possibility to dethrone the Liberals' (Baxter 2000). However, in the election of 2000, the new formation suffered a rout at the hands of the Liberals, who managed to identify the Alliance with the most unpopular elements of the Reform image.

After the 2000 election fiasco, many corporate donors spoke bluntly to the Tories: 'The strong view of many of our financiers is they don't care whether we merge (with the Alliance) or negotiate—they don't care what the answer is. But they sure as hell know what the question is, and their message to us was they intend to fund the first guy who comes up with the answer' (Jenkinson 2001). The pressure was so strong that Joe Clark, the Progressive Conservative leader, openly pleaded with business not to use donations to force a merger (Winsor 2001). Around the time of the formation of the Canadian Alliance business funding was a carrot to unity. After the 2000 election and the disintegration of the Alliance under Stockwell Day, business money became a stick: 'You have to put the parties together before anyone will pay attention to the Alliance. No one in the business community cares about anything else', said Stanley Hartt, chairman of Bay Street investment bank Salomon Smith Barney Canada Inc. (McNish and Laghi 2002). This would end the splitting of the right-wing vote, weaken Liberal attacks centring on regionalism and extremism, and dilute the democratic consensualism of the Reform heritage, which had made it difficult for the party to react to, and control, the agenda in the manner of contemporary nationwide campaigns. It would also, of course, facilitate effective business networking. The eventual formation of the united Conservative party did attract considerable funding as promised (Greenaway 2003; Willis 2003).

Both the network of loyalty and network of interest interpretations are consistent with the reluctance to fund Reform. However, the defection to the Alliance in 1999 and 2000, and the virtual killing off of the Progressive Conservatives thereafter, is obviously not indicative of a network of loyalty. It is still consistent with a network of interest interpretation. Admittedly, of course, there were some elements of ideology, and maybe even of genuine concern for the democratic process, in the vital role business played in the unification of the right. In general, the most plausible story is that businesses were working for the re-establishment of a party that was both competitive and effectively networked to Canadian businesses. The Tories and big business were already bound together by a tight network, from which the populist Reformers were almost entirely absent. The formation of the Canadian Alliance connected the Reformers to the network through well-established players, who had defected from the Tories or Liberals. The insistence on the unification of the right demonstrated the precedence of the network of interest over the network of loyalty.

7. CONCLUSIONS

In spite of their protestations to the contrary, the evidence that Canadian businesses contributed money 'to support the democratic process' is weak. Ideology also played a relatively marginal role. The Liberals and Progressive Conservatives were treated as government and opposition, rather than centre-left and centre-right. Even during the ideologically polarized election of 1988 the vast majority of Canadian businesses did not use political contributions to signal their ideological preference. The strong relationship between business strategies and incumbency demonstrates that pragmatism was the dominant motivation for business donations to Canadian parties. Businesses pursued increased profits by rewarding the government. Although businesses did express misgivings about contributing to politically or financially weak opposition parties there is, at best, a weak relationship between donations and popular support, as indicated by opinion polls. Illegal transactions, although ever-present, were a relatively marginal phenomenon in this period. Businesses could not buy policy benefits. The Canadian press tended to argue that there were discrete exchanges of cash for access. Businesses could buy access and, indeed, the parties actively marketed their fundraising events as 'access for sale'. The sale of access was a part of the political finance system, but is not a convincing account of most of the payments. The amounts of money were usually too small. The quality and quantity of access on sale was usually insufficient. Larger firms had access to policy-makers, irrespective of whether they made political contributions or not.

Instead of buying access, the money, and the related social events, or visits from the parties' bagmen, served to develop a relationship of mutual obligation between firms and parties and, more concretely, between key individuals in the firms and the parties. This created an expectation of a more favourable hearing from decision-makers if and when a firm decided to lobby for a policy benefit, which could represent a massive windfall for even the biggest firms in the country. Reciprocal, rather than discrete, exchange is the best way of understanding business financing of parties in Canada. Political contributions were akin to venture capital. The probability of success was quite small but the rewards could be massive. The low probability that contributions would make a difference and the lack of simultaneity between a specific contribution and a favourable outcome maintained political legitimacy for the parties and firms. The size of the benefits ensured that the time and money spent in developing and maintaining relationships was rational for a profit-seeking business. The long-term reciprocal nature of exchanges provides much of the explanation for the continuing preference for the two-MP Progressive Conservatives over the Reform Party after 1993. The role business cash played in the formation of the Canadian Alliance and, a couple of years later, of the united Conservative party showed that executives were not merely staying faithful to an old boys network. The network was no good unless it was connected to power, thereby justifying donations as business expenditure.

That most large businesses should seek to further their specific interests through the political system is consistent with the individualist, competitive, and short-term focus of a liberal market economy. The power of the Canadian executive prevented it from credibly committing to policies that could support a co-ordinated economy. The centralization of Canadian politics in the cabinet and prime minister also provided an incentive for a very high proportion of firms to establish a relationship of reciprocity with the principal political parties. Many did this by hedging against the massive and unpredictable swings of power produced by the electoral system. Others followed the distribution of power, awarding huge financial bonuses to governments. The absence of an ideological motivation in Canada makes sense in the context of the largely non-ideological competition between the only two parties ever to have governed. Canadian business money spoke only one language—pragmatism.

The permissive Canadian system ended after our sample period. Bans and limits on corporate donations, and their replacement with public funding, had been spreading across the provinces since Quebec's legislation in the 1970s. Nonetheless, the transfer of such a regime to the national level was unexpected when it came in 2003. Outgoing Liberal leader and prime minister, Jean Chrétien, sprung the reform on a surprised and reluctant party. The Liberals, historically relatively reliant on corporate fundraising, and the National Democratic Party, dependent on unions, were to be the big losers. The Liberals' party president denounced the legislation as 'dumber than a bag of hammers' (Chrétien 2007, 399). The Conservatives and the Bloc Québécois, with their large numbers of individual donations, appeared to be the greatest beneficiaries. Throughout his ten years as prime minister, Chrétien had been dogged by various fundraising controversies. He claimed his aim was to restore the legitimacy of politics because there was an entrenched, albeit misplaced, perception that corporate money bought influence (Byfield 2003; McCarthy 2003; Martin 2003; Winsor 2003). Chrétien later wrote that,

> Perception is everything in politics ... so I decided that it was essential to reform the system in order to clear away the myths and restore the public's trust in their representatives, in the same way that we had established the office of the ethics counsellor and strengthened the regulations involving lobbyists and ministerial conduct. (Chrétien 2007, 398)

While this account sounded dubiously altruistic to many observers, no alternative theory is much more convincing. The ban on corporate contributions was to be accompanied by contribution limits. Parties were compensated with substantial public subsidies (Boatright 2012). In 2011, the Conservative government announced its intention to phase out public subsidies.

In the same year as Chrétien banned corporate contributions, the leaders of the Reform and Progressive Conservative parties agreed to a merger, which was ratified by a referendum of Reform party members and conventions of PC members. The new party called itself simply, the Conservative Party. The merger was controversial, with many Progressive Conservatives worrying that the new party would be too right-wing. Several national politicians refused to join the new party and a handful actually defected to the Liberals. Reformer Stephen Harper was the easy winner of the new party's first leadership election. In the early election of 2004, called by Chrétien's successor, Paul Martin, the Conservative party received fewer votes than its predecessors had in the disappointing election of 2000. Nonetheless, the logic of merger proved itself, as the Liberals were denied a majority and Martin formed a minority government, which lasted only until 2005. The Conservatives, still under Harper, formed minority governments after the elections of 2005 and 2008, finally winning a majority in the 2011 election. The Liberals now find themselves in a situation like that faced by the Progressive Conservatives in the 1990s. They have lost their status as official opposition and a merger with the New Democrats has become a topic of discussion.

4

Australia: Pragmatism and Ideological Bias

1. INTRODUCTION

In Australian political finance, money speaks both the language of pragmatism and the language of ideology. Each year, an average of 13 per cent of the large firms studied here gave money to at least one of the principal political parties at the federal level. As in Canada, the distribution of money clearly tracks changes in government. With the left in power, the parties attract relatively equal amounts of money, but if the right controls government, it receives a much larger share of business funding than the left. Ideology plays an important part in Australian political finance, because, in contrast to Canada, the economy is the dominant dimension of competition in the Australian party system. Given the largely majoritarian configuration of institutions within jurisdictions this creates a policy risk for firms in Australia's liberal political economy. Australia's variety of capitalism has much in common with Canada's and also generates incentives for pragmatic financing of political parties. Reciprocal exchanges of money for relationship-building opportunities form the dominant pragmatic mechanism in Australia. Nonetheless, there is substantial quantitative and qualitative evidence that discrete exchanges may be more important than in Canada. The smaller scale of the Australian jurisdictions should give businesses greater bargaining power with politicians and therefore the capacity to demand discrete exchanges.

This chapter has a similar structure to its Canadian counterpart. So, it begins with an account of Australian political economy and then reviews the regulation of political finance and the overall finances of the principal political parties. The next section is a quantitative analysis of the motivations of business contributors to Australian parties, as well as a case study of the turnover of government in South Australia in 2002. The subsequent sections assess interpretations of the Australian system of party–firm relations. These begin with 'supporting the democratic process' and continue with ideology, which is so much more important than in Canada. Pragmatism is assessed in terms of illegal transactions, as well as discrete and reciprocal exchanges. The conclusion summarizes the chapter, noting similarities and differences with Canada as well as analysing the likely effect of recent legal changes.

2. THE AUSTRALIAN POLITICAL ECONOMY

Australia is a liberal market economy (Kitschelt et al. 1999, 435–6; Estevez-Abe, Iversen, and Soskice 2001, 165; Hall and Soskice 2001, 19–20, 59; Hall and Gingerich 2009, 138). It exhibits each of the institutional complementarities that support the comparative advantage of liberal market economies. Firstly, the stock exchange dominates the market for corporate governance. The value of domestic publicly listed firms is over 100 per cent of GDP, one of the largest in the world. Fifty-five per cent of the population owns stocks. Forty-four per cent hold stocks directly, which is twice the US and UK figures (Lau, Sinnadurai, and Wright 2009, 162). Although Australia is a relatively small economy, its stock market is well diversified (Henker and Henker 2010, 286). Considerations of shareholder wealth dominate board behaviour in Australia (Lau, Sinnadurai, and Wright 2009, 161). The merger of the state stock exchanges and then the demutualization of the Australian Stock Exchange drove the increasing importance of the stock market in the 1980s and early 1990s.

Secondly, in industrial relations, companies rely on the market to govern relations with their employees. Australian levels of employment protection are relatively low, and similar to Canada's (Estevez-Abe, Iversen, and Soskice 2001, 165). This means firms are sufficiently adaptable to chase the short-term results that the stock market requires. Firms also have a lot of flexibility in setting wages. However, this is a big change from the recent past. In 1907, Australia set up an industrial relations system based on compulsory arbitration. This unique system survived most of the twentieth century. The Labour government began reforming this system in 1983 by giving an important role to national negotiations between the government and the Australian Council of Trade Unions (Kidd and Shannon 1996, 730–1). In 1993, it passed an act reducing the authority of the Industrial Relations Commission (Wailes, Ramia, and Lansbury 2003, 625). The Liberal–National Coalition ended formal agreements with the trade unions' peak body. More importantly, it legislated to reduce the arbitration system's role to the setting of minima; constrained union involvement in wage setting; and introduced individual contracts, known as Australian Workplace Agreements (Chester 2011). In 2005, the government pushed the logic of deregulation much further in the Work Choices Act, which overrode state industrial relations systems. Kevin Rudd's Labor government repealed some of this legislation in 2010, but Australia now has a clearly liberal system of industrial relations. Awards covered 80 per cent of employees in 1990 (Kidd and Shannon 1996, 730–1), but only 16 per cent in 2008. In 2007, trade unions organized 20 per cent of workers, down from 57 per cent in 1982 (Chester 2011). Australia's unions have also been closely linked to the Australian Labor Party, politically, organizationally, and financially.

Thirdly, Australia emphasizes generalist training and education, instead of the industry-specific apprenticeships that are so important to co-ordinated economies

(Culpepper 2007, 618–21). Higher education institutions account for three times as high a proportion of GDP as vocational education and training institutions. Moreover, enrolment in higher education has been growing more quickly (Lee and Coelli 2010, 390). The returns to vocational education are small compared to university education, and, in some circumstances, do not improve labour market outcomes (Lee and Coelli 2010, 405). The relative returns to university education have been increasing over recent decades (Borland 1996, 379). Indeed, vocational programmes tend to attract underachieving students and those from underprivileged backgrounds (Dalley-Trim, Alloway, and Walker 2008, 56). Until very recently, lower-income students in vocational institutions have not had the same level of financial support as university students (Chapman, Rodrigues, and Ryan 2008, 1). This system of general education enables and encourages workers to adapt to changing firm strategies and to change employer. Fourthly, contracts and competition and characterize inter-firm relations. Globalization and privatization have had a particularly noticeable effect on competition within Australia's previously oligopolistic economy (Chester 2011). Significantly, business associations play little or no role in the basic economic strategy of Australian businesses. Instead, associations offer lobbying functions or sell marketing and public relations services that could be, and often are, also offered by other firms. Yet again, this fits into the short time horizon of the firm in a liberal economy. Business associations have tended to be weak, divided, and only intermittently effective in politics. Attempts to give them a substantial institutionalized role in policy-making and implementation have failed at both national and, to a lesser extent, at sectoral levels (Bell 1995, 2006). By contrast, lobbying by individual firms has played an important part in Australian politics since the Second World War (Schneider 2006, 115). Senior executives, as well as in-house and external specialists, lobby on behalf of Australian firms (Warhurst 1998, 539–43).

Fifthly, Australia, like Canada, is a federation of majoritarian political systems. Australia is one of the few countries with compulsory voting. It is usually regarded as having reduced the parties operating costs, notably by relieving them of voter mobilization and allowing them to concentrate on voter conversion (McAllister 2002, 387). Electioneering has become very focused on the media and political advertising. Most elections are held under the Alternative Vote according to which voters can rank the candidates in single-member districts in order of their choice. Like first-past-the-post, this is an essentially majoritarian system. It generally produces single party governments of the centre-left or centre-right, or coalitions of two closely allied centre-right parties. Minority governments represent a small but significant proportion of administrations at state and Commonwealth (federal) levels (Sharman and Moon 2003, 255). The current prime minister of Australia, Julia Gillard of the Australian Labor Party, has a minority in the House of Representatives and is reliant on independent members.

The Commonwealth gets much of its power from its control of taxation. It has a monopoly on the collection of income tax and the Goods and Sales Tax of 2000 was another milestone in its fiscal dominance (Weller and Fleming 2003, 18). The states retain responsibility for delivering citizens' most cherished services, such as health, education, and the police. The mutual dependence of the federal and state governments is reflected in the meetings of the Council of Australian Governments. The prime minister dominates the cabinet (O'Malley 2007, 17, 19–20). In turn, the government dominates the House of Representatives, the politics of which is a classic example of Westminster adversarial theatre. However, the use of Proportional Representation by Single Transferrable Vote for elections to the Australian Senate adds a measure of consensualism to Australian politics. Government majorities have been very rare in the Senate, but since party discipline is also strong, the chamber has acted as a significant check on the government, especially in legislation (Thomas 2009, 376–7). The states also have Westminster governments with popularly elected upper houses, excepting Queensland, which has no upper house.

Sixthly, Australia's party system is typical of a liberal market economy. It is based on a simple left–right divide (Kitschelt et al. 1999, 431, 434; McAllister 2002, 384; Iversen 2005). Australia's centre-right is defined by a permanent coalition of the Liberal Party and the smaller National Party, which consistently wins rural seats in some areas. These two parties are often known as 'the Coalition'. In spite of the long-term relationship between the parties there has been very little pressure to merge. The party system has been described pithily as 'a trio in form and a duet in function' (Lipson 1959, quoted in McAllister 2002, 382).

The Liberals can trace their origins back to 1909. They re-branded and re-formed twice during and between the two world wars, but had been unashamedly a classic cadre party, providing almost direct representation for the business elite. They were re-formed again in 1944 under Robert Menzies, as a mass membership party with some autonomy from funders and parliamentarians. The party's organization is still very much dependent on its relatively autonomous state branches. The National Party, previously the Country Party, grew out of rural discontent around 1920. It has played an important role in Commonwealth politics every since. The party is also a significant competitor in the states, except for South Australia and Tasmania. Exceptionally, the National Party ruled as a single party government in Queensland from 1983 to 1990. The two parties have small memberships, ideological flexibility, and strong leaderships. However, the Liberals suffered a decline in membership in the 1980s and 1990s, but the Nationals claim their membership has increased (McAllister 2002, 389). The Coalition faces the Australian Labor Party (ALP), which was founded in 1891. This party has strong links to trade unions. Its membership is larger than its competitors and is relatively stable (McAllister 2002, 389). Unlike the right-wing parties, its organization is relatively strong at the federal level. The ALP has an enduring conflict between highly institutionalized more and less ideological factions, but in recent decades it has managed to avoid splits and has enjoyed greater electoral success. Under Bob Hawke and Paul Keating in the 1980s and 1990s the party embraced the market and economic reform (McMullin 1991, 418–32, 442–3). Since 1973, the party has also gradually reduced union influence within its structures.

The party system has been relatively stable for over a hundred years and parties have maintained a stronger position in politics than in other established democracies (McAllister 2002, 379–80, 382). This contrasts with the dramatic rise and fall of parties that is characteristic of Canadian politics. As in similar political economies, the centre-right has been notably more successful at the federal level (Moon and Sharman 2003, 268–9). The majoritarian electoral system tends to give the right an advantage. The median voter should not support long-term social insurance and means-tested benefits for the poor (Iversen 2005, 124–6, 142). Australia's more flexible centre-right also has an advantage in targeting its electoral campaign at the shifting concerns of the median voter. The Australian liberal political economy incentivizes pragmatism, as firms pursue individual strategies for profit and seek advantages over each other. Its powerful executive has the power to deliver benefits to firms. The left–right structure of the party system, and its majoritarian electoral system, constitute a policy risk for pro-market Australian businesses, which they might choose to try to reduce by making ideological payments to the right. Before investigating the motivations for business financing of Australian parties, the chapter introduces the overall system of political finance in Australia.

3. AUSTRALIAN POLITICAL FINANCE

3.1 Regulation

The contemporary era of the regulation of Australian political finance began with the advent of Hawke's Labor government in 1983. However, disclosure was easily evaded until 1992. Previously, only campaign contributions had to be disclosed, with the predictable consequence that parties classified most payments as contributions to their day-to-day administration. The Political Broadcasts and Political Disclosures Act of 1991 brought all payments to parties within the disclosure regime (Chaples 1994, 31). Both parties reported that this regulation, at least initially, drastically reduced corporate contributions (Cumming 1992; Hartcher 1992a, 1992b). The act also provided for a severe restriction on political advertising, banning it during campaigns, and requiring broadcasters to provide free time instead. Use of this broadcasting time was confined to a figure talking to camera, without any dramatic effects (Chaples 1994, 34). Like Canada's attempted ban on third-party advertising, the broadcasting provisions of the act were struck down as unconstitutional (O'Keefe 1992; Orr, Mercurio, and Williams 2003, 384–5).

Disclosure applies not only to parties, but also to 'associated entities', defined, until 2006, as entities that are 'either controlled by one or more political parties or operate wholly or to a significant extent for the benefit of one or more political parties' (Young and Tham 2006, 10). The revenue of the associated entities rivals that of parties. Income from associated entities ranged from 43 per cent of party income in 2001–2 and 2004–5 to 116 per cent in 1999–2000. However, it seems that the associated entities are more than fundraising vehicles. The ALP received on average only 13 per cent of its income from Associated Entities between 1999 and 2005, while the Liberals received almost 19 per cent. All payments, or in-kind contributions, must be reported and identified as either a 'donation' or 'another payment'. In law, donations are gifts, for which no, or inadequate, consideration has been received (Orr 2006, 107). This distinction does not separate political contributions from payments received in the course of running the party as a business. An employee of the Australian Electoral Commission explained, 'So if you think you got $2000 worth of networking opportunities as well as your meal and the glossy brochure, you don't have to declare it' as a donation (Sexton 2006). Moreover, the Australian Electoral Commission does not have the resources to contest the parties' classification of payments.

The $1,500 limit for disclosure was introduced in 1984 and remained un-changed until 2006, when the limit was raised to $10,000, to be indexed annually (Coorey 2008). This meant that one thousand fewer donations were reported than in the previous federal election year. Also, the percentage of receipts that had to be itemized dropped from 75 to 64 per cent (Young and Tham 2006, 20; Birnbauer 2007; Schubert and Rood 2008). The drop in the percentage of revenue disclosed by associated entities was even greater (Grattan 2008). The limits are per donor, per jurisdiction. Therefore, a firm could have secretly but legally contributed almost $12,500 by splitting contributions of less than $1,500 amongst the nine jurisdictions. Since 2006, donations below $1,500 have been tax deductible.

Public funding has varied across the jurisdictions during our sample period. In New South Wales, the federal level, and Queensland, public subsidies for election campaigns were in place at the beginning of the period. Victoria introduced them in 2002. Western Australia brought in publicly funded elections in 2006, after the sample period. South Australia and Tasmania have not done so. In every case, the funds are limited by a threshold of 4 per cent of the vote and distribute an amount of one to two dollars per first preference vote (Orr, Mercurio, and Williams 2003, 396; Young and Tham 2006, 39). Public funding provided on average 25 per cent of the income of the federal Coalition and ALP from 1998 to 2005. The parties' research foundations also receive small amounts of money (Ramsey 1998), as do their international bodies, which assist in democracy promotion. New South Wales is the only jurisdiction to provide financial support for general party activities between elections (Young and Tham 2006, 42) amounting to between 4 and 5 per cent of the income of the major parties in 2004–5.

Australia does not have the large quasi-independent party foundations found in other countries. However, both parties have important organizations, which exist only to raise funds. The Greenfields foundation collected contributions from businesses and passed them on to the Liberal Party, thereby avoiding the necessity to disclose the identity of the donors. Similarly, auctions or dinners organized outside the party could collect money without identifying the ultimate donors (Duffy 2000; Hannan and Carney 2005). A prominent example was the work of public relations company Markson Sparks on behalf of the ALP (Crabb and Rollins 2001). Both parties actively manage assets through companies, which their opponents suspect might also be conduits for undisclosed donations (The Age 2001; Gordon 2004). A common way for a specific interest to avoid transparency is to make multiple donations in the name of various companies and individuals (Sexton 2005). Sometimes donations have been made on behalf of shelf companies, the ultimate ownership of which remains unknown (Sexton 2006a, 2006b).

3.2 The finances of the Australian parties

The jurisdictions vary in the amounts of money spent and received. Surpluses and deficits reached multiples of a million dollars at the federal level and in the states of New South Wales and Victoria. In the smaller states of South Australia, Western Australia, and Tasmania, there was only one surplus or deficit over a million dollars. Queensland was in between these two groups. There is no strong party-specific pattern across the seven jurisdictions. Even within jurisdictions, the two parties do not usually exhibit markedly different financial situations (see Figure 4.1). However, it can be noted that, at the federal level, the Coalition managed two large surpluses, which the ALP did not and, in Victoria, the ALP never ran a deficit, while the Coalition twice endured substantial deficits. In contrast to Canada, control of government does not seem to have determined whether a party can balance its books.

More money is contributed to the parties in the states of Victoria and New South Wales than at the federal level. Victoria contains the traditional business capital of Melbourne. In recent decades, many firms have transferred their headquarters to Sydney in New South Wales. The small federal capital of Canberra is not a substantial centre of private business and is dominated by government and universities. Perhaps more importantly, the states are responsible for two highly politicized issues: property development and gambling (Horan 1997). Developers have been prominent political contributors in both states (Dubeki and Baker 2004; Tham 2006; Clennell, Smith, and Robins 2008; Millar 2008b, 2009; Skelton 2008; Smith 2008). One fundraiser said, 'You get a lot of funding being in government at state level. If you're a property developer, what can the feds do for you? Getting development approvals or a planning policy change is not something the feds can do. Much of the relevant regulation is conducted at state level' (Elliott 2003). Sydney and New South Wales have become notorious for poker machines, on

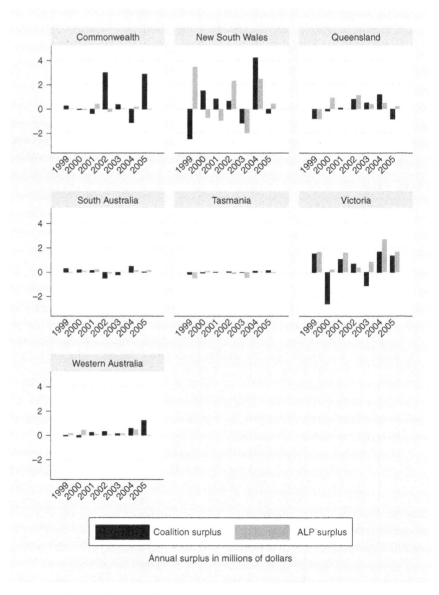

FIGURE 4.1 Finances of the Australian parties by jurisdiction

which clubs, pubs, and hotels often depend to survive (Verrender 2001; Skelsey 2003). This dependence has been reflected in political finance (Wainwright 2003).

Official data show that business is an important source of funding for Australian political parties. There were about 25,000 itemized payments to the Coalition, the ALP, and their associated entities from 1998 to 2005, of which 17,000 were made by 5,400 businesses. The dependence of the parties on business ranges from 23 per cent in 2001–2 to 58 per cent in 2002–3, with an average of 37 per cent. Although not as high as Canada, in comparative terms this is a very high level of dependence on business. The next section uses a large data set to systematically test for different motivations for business contribution to Australian parties.

4. MOTIVATIONS FOR CONTRIBUTIONS TO PARTIES

This section studies annual disclosed payments (not just officially classed 'donations') to the major parties and their associated entities for 450 firms in seven jurisdictions over seven years. Payments were registered in almost 10 per cent of the 22,050 observations. Figure 4.2 shows the distribution of *Bias* in Australia, defined as payments to the ALP as a proportion of payments to both parties. Firms

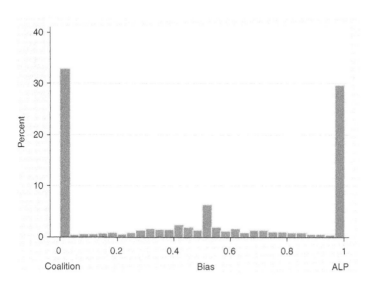

FIGURE 4.2 Distribution of bias in Australia

Note: 2,162 observations; 239 firms. Bias is the proportion of reported contributions to the Liberal–National coalition and the Australian Labor Party paid to Labor in a given jurisdiction in a given year.
Source: Iain McMenamin (2012), "If Money Talks, What Does it Say? Varieties of Capitalism and Business Financing of Parties", *World Politics*, volume 64(1), pp1–38, Cambridge University Press.

clearly cluster around four strategies: non-contribution, a clear preference for one party, or hedging. The big difference with the Canadian sample is the much smaller proportion of hedging payments. The variable the models seek to explain consists of four categories: no contribution; *Left* (ALP proportion of annual business payments to the major parties $> = 0.67$); *Hedge* (ALP proportion between 0.34 and 0.66); and *Right* (ALP proportion $< = 0.33$).

The multinomial logit equations in Table 4.1 predict the logged odds of each of the contribution categories by reference to non-contribution. The following variables are used to explain variation in the firms' contribution strategies. First, there is a dummy variable for *Left* government. John Howard's coalition government of Liberals and Nationals ruled the Commonwealth for all seven years of the sample period. The Australian Labor Party (ALP) dominated politics in the six states, controlling government in all years and all states, except for South Australia from 1999 to 2002. Next is *Years*, which counts the number of years until the next constitutionally mandated election. *Poll* uses monthly opinion polls to compute the probability of the left-wing party winning more votes than its right-wing competitor in the event of an immediate election. The source is the Roy Morgan poll of two-party preferred voting intentions, except for Tasmania's Single-Transferable Vote system (Farrell and McAllister 2006) which necessitates the use of first preferences. Although not the best predictor of election results (Jackman 2005), this poll has the best coverage across the seven jurisdictions. The ALP's dominance of the opinion polls is even more striking than its dominance of government. As Figure 4.3 illustrates, the ALP was more popular than the Coalition in all years in all polities, except for 1999 in Victoria. In Tasmania and Queensland, the opposition's support never came close to that of the Labor governments. The models also include interactions of Left and Poll with the number of years to the next election. The first economic variable is *Income* (logged to reduce the impact of outliers).[1] Large firms are more likely to hedge because of the lower costs of payments relative to their income. Finally, the firms have been classified into seven sectors, based on amalgamations of the United Nations ISIC classification. This was necessary because of collinearity problems in more disaggregated versions. All models have clustered standard errors to account for heteroskedasticity and equations two to six have year dummies to compensate for time dependence.[2] Likelihood-ratio tests also suggested the inclusion of interactions of Left and Poll with the electoral timetable in models two and three. The resulting equations are highly complex: there are three seventeen-variable equations in models four and five. Moreover, the year dummies, Year variable, Left variable, Poll variable, and their interactions are all potentially collinear as they track changes in political context from year to year.

[1] Incomes interpolated for 2000, 2001, 2003, 2004.

[2] Beck, Katz, and Tucker (1998) prefer using cubic splines rather than year dummies, but there was insufficient variation in the data set to compute the cubic splines.

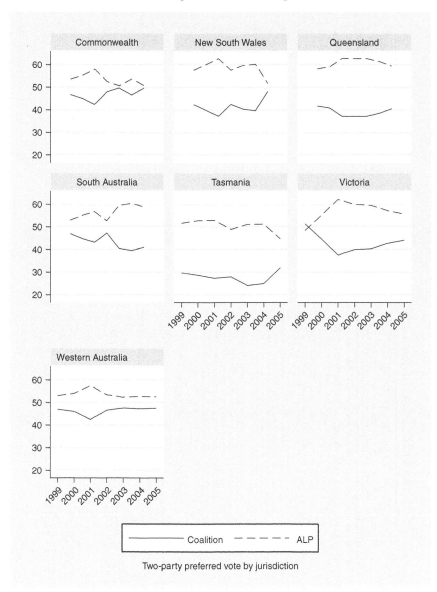

FIGURE 4.3 Popularity of the parties

Notes: First preferences in Tasmania. Liberals only in South Australia and Tasmania.

TABLE 4.1 Multinomial logit estimates of firm strategy in Australia

	Model 1	Model 2	Model 3	Model 4	Model 5	Model 6
	HEDGE	HEDGE	HEDGE	HEDGE	HEDGE	HEDGE
LEFT	0.15	-1.045	-1.187	3.22	0.72	-0.87
	[0.118]	[0.27]***	[0.36]***	[0.83]***	[0.42]*	[0.39]**
YEARS	-0.36	-0.9	-0.13	-.526	-0.945	-1.05
	[0.061]***	[0.15]***	[0.69]	[0.56]	[0.59]	[0.79]
LEFT*YEARS	—	0.62	0.739	0.093	0.16	0.48
		[0.14]***	[0.2]***	[0.24]	[0.2]	[0.21]**
POLL	—	—	1.163	-1.33	-1.36	-1.16
			[1.54]	[1.48]	[1.37]	[1.67]
POLL*YEARS	—	—	-0.9	0.127	0.45	0.27
			[0.82]	[0.76]	[0.72]	[0.9]
Constant	-2.784	-2.14	-3.19	-4.93	-2.95	-1.01
	[0.681]***	[0.64]***	[1.68]*	[1.8]***	[1.3]**	[1.75]
	RIGHT	RIGHT	RIGHT	RIGHT	RIGHT	RIGHT
LEFT	-0.473	-0.973	-0.6	2.99	1.43	-0.81
	[0.08]***	[0.155]***	[0.248]**	[0.43]***	[0.27]***	[0.32]**
YEARS	-0.09	-0.25	0.445	-0.51	-0.65	0.52
	[0.03]***	[0.058]***	[0.315]	[0.31]*	[0.29]**	[0.4]
LEFT*YEARS	—	0.2	0.256	2.99	-0.37	0.22
		[0.063]***	[0.116]**	[0.43]***	[0.11]***	[0.15]
POLL	—	—	-0.657	-5.2	-4.08	-0.3
			[0.77]	[0.86]***	[0.76]***	[0.95]

	(1)	(2)	(3)	(4)	(5)	(6)
POLL*YEARS	—	—	-0.776 [0.396]*	0.9 [0.41]**	0.91 [0.38]**	-0.87 [0.5]*
Constant	-2.52 [0.275]***	-2.11 [0.31]***	-2.06 [0.685]***	-0.21 [0.67]	-0.54 [0.64]	-2.19 [0.8]***
LEFT	LEFT	LEFT	LEFT	LEFT	LEFT	LEFT
LEFT	0.146 [0.113]	-0.82 [0.223]***	-1.53 [0.282]***	2.3 [0.47]***	0.06 [0.3]*	-2.01 [0.34]***
YEARS	-0.163	-0.6	1.43	0.6	0.38	1.63
LEFT*YEARS	[0.029]***	[0.09]***	[0.52]***	[0.45]	[0.45]	[0.63]***
	—	0.458	0.725	0.11	0.24	0.92
POLL	—	[0.1]***	[0.127]***	[0.15]	[0.13]*	[0.16]***
			6.22	3.97	3.74	6.55
POLL*YEARS	—	—	[1.52]***	[1.6]**	[1.43]***	[1.75]***
			-2.32 [0.58]***	-0.88 [0.54]	-0.81 [0.52]	-2.7 [0.69]***
Constant	-3.056 [0.241]***	-2.555 [0.325]***	-8.05 [1.4]***	-9.14 [1.7]***	-7.06 [1.4]***	-7.88 [1.62]***
Year Dummies	No	Yes	Yes	Yes	Yes	Yes
Observations	22050	22050	22050	22050	22050	17110

Notes: Robust standard errors, clustered by firm, in brackets. *** = significant at 1%; ** = significant at 5% * = significant at 10%. Income and sectoral controls included in all equations.

Unfortunately, this also makes for presentational problems, which I confront by presenting several models. The first relatively straightforward model in Table 4.1, without year dummies, ensures maximum comparability across all country cases. Model two, which includes year dummies, combines statistical accuracy and comparability of Canada and Australia, while the subsequent models investigate sources of error that are particular to the Australian sample. Models three and four take account of the fact the sample pools data from seven different jurisdictions. These jurisdictions have economies of very different sizes. Model four includes Gross State Product for the states and Gross Domestic Product for the Commonwealth, all from the Australian Bureau of Statistics, thereby providing a good estimate of how important the different jurisdictions were to the firms. GDP overestimates the relative importance of the federal level. It has a lower contribution rate than the two big states of Victoria and New South Wales. Therefore, model five restricts the Commonwealth to the maximum Gross State Product figure (from New South Wales in 2005). The sixth and final model takes into account the problems generated by the unsatisfactory distinction between donations and other payments under Australian law. Remember that the identification of 'donations' with a pure gift excludes many payments that in ordinary language, and political intent, are donations to the parties. Payments for membership of party-political business clubs and attendance at functions are usually listed as other payments. However, these other payments also include non-political transactions that are part of the running of a political party as an organization. To minimize the effect of these types of payments, the third model excludes the 22 per cent of firms that are the most likely business partners of parties. The nature of multinomial logit coefficients makes their substantive implications difficult to discern and this is, of course, a greater problem with lots of variables and interactions. However, the models can be used to produce predictions in the form of the usual table of strategies.

Left, and/or its interaction with Years, is significantly in the right direction for contribution to the left and the right in all models, except for model one where it predicts contributions to the right but not to the left. Also, it is a weak predictor of contributions to the left in model five. Poll also performs very well. It, and/or its interaction with Years, is significantly in the right direction for contribution to the left and the right in all relevant models, but it is a weak predictor of right-wing contributions in model three. In the context of highly complex equations and potential collinearity, the power and consistency of the basic political variables is very impressive. Table 4.2 uses the coefficients from model three to predict the probabilities of different strategies as government turns over from right to left. Variables are set at sample values, except for Poll, which is held at 0.5, and Left and its interaction, which are manipulated. 0.5 denotes a dead heat between the

TABLE 4.2 *Predicted turnover strategies: Australia*

Right in power	*Left in power*			
	NON-CONTRIBUTOR	HEDGE	LEFT	RIGHT
NON-CONTRIBUTOR	0.086		0.097	
HEDGE		0.0015	0.0021	
LEFT			0.024	
RIGHT	0.281	0.009	0.012	0.036

Note: Contribution rate is to any one of the seven jurisdictions.

Coalition and the ALP. The rank-order of predicted strategies is almost identical for the basic and complex models.[3]

The Australian simulation illustrates a combination of pragmatic and ideological motivations. As in Canada, the contribution rate suggests that financing political parties is a normal part of business in Australia.[4] However, the ranking of strategies is very different. The most likely reaction to a turnover from right to left is to pay to the right when in government, but refuse to fund either party under the left. This is almost three times as likely as its left-leaning equivalent. The same goes for plumping for the right while in government and hedging when the left comes to power. Its probability is four times larger than the opposite pro-left strategy. Ideological purity is not the rarest strategy as in Canada. Cleaving to the right, whether in government, or opposition, is the third most likely strategy and is fifteen times more probable than sticking with the left. These strategies result in more subtle financial ramifications for governing and opposition parties than in Canada. The simulation predicts almost no change in the number of coalition-only donors after a governmental turnover. It should stay stable at about 10 per cent. However, when the ALP controls the executive, the percentage of ALP-only contributors increases by 75 per cent from 2.1 per cent to 3.6 per cent. The inclusion of poll figures allows an even more vivid portrayal of how ideological bias and pragmatism interact in Australian political finance. In an election year, if the Coalition is in opposition with only a 10 per cent chance of winning the election, almost 4.5 per cent of firms will continue to give only to the Coalition. If the Coalition's prospects reverse, and polls give them a 90 per cent chance of victory, the number of Coalition contributors is predicted to rise to 12.6 per cent. If the Australian Labor Party finds itself in opposition, with a one in ten chance of government in an election year, only a miserable one quarter of 1 per cent of firms will give to them alone. However, if the ALP seems almost certain to

---

[3] In model one, the ALP-ALP strategy is fifth instead of sixth and the Coalition-Hedge strategy is sixth instead of fifth.

[4] The predicted Australian contribution rate is to any of the seven jurisdictions, while the Canadian equivalent is to the federal level only. Thus, the Canadian contribution rate is higher than Australia's.

win, with a 90 per cent probability, the number of ALP-only contributors increases by a factor of twenty-four to 6.3 per cent. This example suggests that Coalition-only contributors combine pragmatic and ideological motivations, but ALP-only contributors are almost entirely pragmatic. Australian businesses react to changes in government and likely changes in government, but they are clearly biased towards the coalition of the Liberal and National parties. Nonetheless, if the Australian Labor Party is in power, Australian businesses will be prepared to fund it, or at least desist from funding its competitor. In Australia business money is bilingual: it speaks the languages of both pragmatism and ideology.

In addition to changes in the (expected) distribution of political power, the electoral schedule also has an implication for pragmatic firms. As in Canada, the closeness of an election has a much larger effect on the hedging category than on the other two contribution patterns. In other words, firms react rationally to increasing political uncertainty. Hedging increases much more dramatically as an election approaches than do contributions to the left or the right. Hedging is more likely as elections approach in all equations, but in only half of the coefficients for contributions to the left and the right. Larger firms are more likely to adopt each of the contribution strategies in all equations. Moreover, as predicted, size is most strongly associated with hedging. Economic sector also makes a difference. All sectors impact on the choice of left or right in Australia and manufacturing firms are more likely to hedge.

The conclusion that business financing of parties in Australia is motivated by an interaction of ideology and pragmatism is consistent with the results of other authors using quite different methods (Gilding 2004, 140–1; Harrigan 2007). The analysis contradicts the idea that supporting the democratic process is anything more than a marginal motivation for contributing to Australian parties, since payments seem to be driven by control of government or the identity of the parties, rather than their number of votes or legislative seats. In the following sections, I build upon this basic understanding of the role of business in Australian political finance, by exploring, both quantitatively and qualitatively, support for the democratic process, ideology, and pragmatism.

5. INTERPRETING BUSINESS FINANCING OF PARTIES IN AUSTRALIA

5.1 Supporting the democratic process

Once again echoing their Canadian counterparts, many Australian firms assert that their political donations are aimed at supporting 'democratic processes' (Douez 2001). A variation on this theme is the claim that donations are 'paid to both in parties in recognition of the stable political system Australia operates, like a big thank you' (Elliott 2003). In the more colloquial words of a major property developer, 'It's a genuine belief that if we don't have good governance in this country, then we're stuffed' (Millar 2008d). Coca-Cola's corporate affairs manager, Alec Wagstaff, said it was important that donations were 'predictable' and even-handed to avoid perceived links between political decisions and donations. In contrast to Canada, the democratic motivation does not combine with a desire to support the free-market system, for the obvious reason that one of the principal competitors in Australia has a socialist and labour unionist background. The overall pattern of payments does not support the idea of support for the democratic process. A reward for governing parties and a bias towards the Liberal–National coalition are difficult to construe as support for democracy. If the democratic motivation were a good general explanation for business payments, the distribution of money would be linked to votes or legislative seats, resulting in a fairly stable spread of money between the major parties.

5.2 *Ideology*

The multivariate analysis predicts that, in Australia, the probability of a given firm contributing to a right-wing government is twice that of a left-wing government. Australian discourse tends to underestimate this substantial advantage for a number of technical and methodological reasons, such as a reliance on self-classified donations, the exclusion of associated entities, and recent ALP dominance of government in most jurisdictions. Another reason for the perception of even-handedness is that the right's advantage was so much greater in the past. Traditionally, the Liberals, as the political defenders of the free-market system, found it easy to raise funds from business. Liberal Party treasurer, Malcolm Turnbull, said, 'There used to be a time when the federal treasurer of the Liberal Party could make money by simply strolling up [Sydney's] O'Connell Street or [Melbourne's] Collins Street' (Hewett 2003). The contemporary Liberals hanker after this halcyon age and have consistently reported an increasing reluctance of the traditional business base to support the party (Wainwright 2003; Gordon 2005; Grattan 2005). For example, in 1992, the Liberals' national party president, Ashley Goldsworthy, expressed disappointment that firms raised objections to specific policy commitments as a reason not to contribute. Instead, he thought they should take a broader view and support the Liberals as a 'free enterprise party' (Hartcher 1992b). In the 1980s, the Liberals expressed dismay that business had begun to fund the ALP 'enemy' (Jaensch 1994, 194). Similarly, in 2007, a senior Liberal castigated businesses for treating the Liberals and the ALP equally (AAP 2007). There is little doubt that the Liberals' historic advantage has been reduced. Moreover, it is probable that this reduction has taken place more or less gradually over the last quarter of a century. Nonetheless, it is important to note that a very substantial advantage still exists. In the past, the bias towards the Liberals was probably both ideological and sociological. The sociological element consisted of the close connection between traditional business elites, especially those educated in public schools and members of the traditional and exclusive Melbourne and Adelaide clubs and the Liberal Party. This connection, along with the overall integration of the Australian elite, was never as strong as in some other countries (Gilding 2004, 128–32), notably Britain. However, in the 1980s, the relationship began to break down due to the rise of new business elites from other religious and ethnic backgrounds and the change in economic structure caused by the decline of manufacturing and the rise of globalization (Gilding 1999, 180; 2004, 133). Not only did the business elite distance itself from the Liberal Party, the Liberal Party tentatively distanced itself from the traditional elite. The Liberal Party's inter-war predecessor, the United Australia Party was very much dependent on 'self constituted committees of wealthy supporters' (Overacker quoted in Jaensch 1994, 192). The Liberal Party was designed as a mass membership party that could overcome this dependence. However, while the dependence on funding from business, and resulting influence, reduced, they remained crucial to understanding the party (Jaensch 1994, 192–3). Nonetheless, an excessively close relationship with business came to be seen as problem by those within, as well outside, the party. In 1994, the incumbent Liberal leader, John Hewson, tried to rally support against a challenger by claiming that if his opponent won 'the Liberal Party would be run by the Melbourne Club' (Carney 1994). Harrigan (2007) provides some strong evidence that the remaining Liberal bias was ideological, not sociological. In a study of the 2006 donations, he showed that coalition-only donors were less integrated into the overall business elite than hedging corporations. The only institution that brought Coalition supporters together was the right-wing think tank, the Centre for Independent Studies.

There are several related reasons for the erosion of the Liberal Party's ideological advantage, perhaps the most fundamental of which is the ALP's transformation in the 1980s. Labor's shift towards the centre made it more difficult for the Liberals to make an ideological claim to business support. Many Labor policies received backing from business (Carney 1994). Vital as the change in the ideological platform of Labor has been, there are still clear differences between the parties. For example, a classic left–right disagreement on labour market regulation was one of the central issues of the 2007 federal election. Nonetheless, the new Labor government eschewed a fundamental unravelling of the Coalition's 'Work Choices' reforms (Hall 2008).

The reduction in the Liberals' traditional advantage was probably also due to a specific fundraising drive by the ALP. In speeches to meetings of businesspeople and in targeted letters, the ALP called for an 'even handed approach' to political contributions. In a letter sent in 1995, ALP national secretary Gary Gray wrote, 'Of course it is your right to decline our request, and for you to continue your past policy of supporting only one side of the political process and we respect that. That is your choice. However, most people I speak with regard moderate contributions to both sides of politics as the most reasonable way to underwrite the strength and integrity of our democracy' (Gordon and Ceresa 1995). The intensification of fundraising and the institutionalization of a system of paid access have made it more difficult for firms to indulge in ideological funding of the Liberals. Malcolm Turnbull suspected that motivations were becoming more pragmatic: 'The corporate dollars are moving to those corporates which have a vested interest in making donations; people like developers, the liquor industry, the gaming industry, people whose agenda is very transparent' (quoted in Koutsoukis and Schubert 2004).

Nevertheless, the ideological bias of business contributors makes a difference to Australian politics. Using simulated contribution strategies,[5] the Coalition should receive $3.5 million from sample firms while in government and the ALP $2.1m, while in opposition. In government the ALP does a little better getting $2.6m to the Coalition's $2.9m. If all business contributors were to behave in the same way, the implications are quite striking. In government the Coalition would receive 46 per cent of its income from business, with the opposition ALP getting only 28 per cent. Obviously with the ALP in government this big difference would shrink: the ALP would rely on business for 34 per cent of its income, not much less than the Coalition's 38 per cent. Indeed, in an important respect, this is a very conservative estimate. In Australia (Harrigan 2007), as in many other countries, the smaller the business the more it tends to identify with right-wing politics. Of course, there are other reasons why it would be foolhardy to use these simulations to predict money flows in a specific Australian jurisdiction, but there is no doubt that ideological business financing of parties in Australia is substantively important. The next sub-section looks at the pragmatic motivation for funding politics.

5.3 Pragmatism

Many large Australian firms appear to have formal policies on political finance. Most disclosed policies refer to consistent hedging or 'no donations' policies. These latter policies indicate that negative publicity can be a significant cost for donor firms. Prime Minister John Howard thought some businesses had stopped contributing because of concerns about appearances (Metherell 2005). Others thought that neutrality was best maintained by refraining from any donations, as opposed to hedging between the big parties: 'It's driven by the fact that we made a decision to be politically impartial, we have to work with all governments, especially in the industry we are in', said a spokesman for healthcare giant Mayne Nickless (Elliott 2003). Some very large companies publish 'No Donations' policies in their annual reports. The Australian Shareholders Association wants public companies to stop donations,

---

[5] Taking the mean value of all hedged contributions, the mean value of contributions coded as Coalition, the mean value of contributions coded as ALP and using simulated contribution strategies from a simple model without poll values and interactions and excluding finance because of the large skew from large payments from banks.

which it considers a form of bribery (Baker 2006). In at least one case, shareholder activism caused a large firm's virtual withdrawal from political funding (Coultan and Sexton 2004). In 2003 alone, the Liberals reportedly lost $750,000 from recurrent donors because of changes in board policy (Koutsoukis and Schubert 2004). It has become increasingly common to pay to attend, or sponsor, events without making a direct cash donation. A Telstra spokesman said the telecommunications company did not make direct donations, but did attend functions, and had 'a demonstrable business case for doing so' (Hayes 2004). Other large firms like Lend Lease and NRMA have a similar policy of not making donations but attending 'ticketed political fund-raising events from both sides of politics' (Gilmore and Benns 2008; Millar 2008d). It is not entirely clear what the basis of this distinction is. Party fundraisers claimed it was easier to get an executive to attend a function, where he or she might mix with ministers or future ministers, rather than to get the board to approve a direct donation to a political party (Korporaal 1995). Thus, the executive could avoid the company politics around donations and develop a potentially useful political network.

According to the previously reported models, changes of government are predicted to produce substantial increases in the probability of a contribution to the newly governing party in Australia. There seems to be no equivalent of the common Canadian policy of regularly donating twice as much to the government as to the opposition. Instead the incumbency bonus results from Australian firms' calculations in particular contexts. Tony Abbott, the Liberal Health Minister, said there were 'very few altruistic donors'. He 'suddenly became popular for fund-raisers when Pharmaceutical Benefits Scheme drugs were being discussed' (Grattan 2005). WMC, a large mining firm, candidly admitted that it makes decisions on funding 'having regard to policies that impact our company and shareholders'. Its chief executive, Hugh Morgan, sat on the boards of several Liberal fundraising companies and WMC donated almost exclusively to the Coalition. After Morgan's retirement the firm refrained from political donations (Coultan and Sexton 2004). Many businesses exhibit a clear bias towards the Coalition, by giving only, or predominantly, to the Liberals and Nationals. Some, however, do give equally to the ALP and the Coalition (Tingle and Cookes 1997; AAP 1998; Colebatch 2000). Although it is not written in official policies, it is widely acknowledged that changes of government and the stage of the election cycle strongly affect the level of donations (Tingle 1996; Daily Telegraph 1997; Hewett 2003). While a governing party can raise funds right throughout its term, the opposition often has very little success until the election approaches (Wainwright 2003). Some commentators think that that poor poll results influence corporate receipts (Bildstein 2006) and this is also borne out by the quantitative analysis. Concerns about leadership may also affect donations. It is frequently claimed that Alexander Downer would not have been deposed as Liberal leader had not party treasurer, Ron Walker, complained that corporate donations were falling (Brown 1999). Attractiveness to business donors has also influenced the rise and fall of leaders of the New South Wales Liberals and has been an attribute of all recent successful leaders of both parties (Elliott 2003).

5.4 South Australian case study

The South Australian election of 2002 is the only turnover in the data set. This state has a population of 1.6 million. Its government depends on support in the 47-seat assembly. In South Australia, the Australian Labor Party reflected quite closely the political transformation undergone at federal level in the 1980s and 1990s (McMullin 1991, 439). The National party has been so marginal as to not feature in government (Parkin 2003, 120). The Liberals had been in power since 1993, but since the 1997 election they had oscillated between bare majority and minority government, as a number of members moved in and out of the Liberal Party. The Liberals surprised their opponents by replacing media-savvy John Olsen with avuncular Rob Kerin only six months before the election (Manning 2002, 577). Business associations were vocal in emphasizing government spending on infrastructure rather than services, which seemed to be the main concern of the electorate as a whole (Stock 2002, 541). The Liberals' record of privatization was a liability with most voters, and the performance of private monopoly utilities was also the target of criticism from businesses. The ALP's last period in government had ended with the disastrous collapse of a state bank. Therefore, the Labor campaign was very concerned to project an image of economic confidence, with leader, Mike Wrann, constantly referring to Ernst and Young's imprimatur for his party's budgetary plans (Manning 2002, 578). In spite of this, as the election approached, after second preferences, the polls were predicting almost no difference between the Labor and the Liberals. In the end, Labor lost the popular vote, but had more seats, and was able to form a minority government with the help of an ex-Liberal independent.

Table 4.3 presents data on firm strategies in reaction to the South Australian turnover. The interpretation of these figures is complicated by a large increase in the contribution rate after the election. The largest category consists of new contributors to the recently elected ALP government. Next come those firms that have maintained an ideological commitment to the right, in spite of the Liberals losing power. The third largest group contains those that have

TABLE 4.3 *Turnover strategies in South Australia, 2002*

Right in power	Left in power			
	NON-CONTRIBUTOR	HEDGE	LEFT	RIGHT
NON-CONTRIBUTOR	0.885		0.024	
HEDGE		0.007	0.002	
LEFT			0.007	
RIGHT	0.009	0.006	0.01	0.014

Notes: The election was in February and the accounting year for the Australian Electoral Commission begins in July. The figures are the mean of three different measurement strategies: leaving out 2002, counting 2002 as a year of Liberal government, and counting 2002 as a year of Labor government. The mean number of contributors was fifty-two. There were 3.3 times as many contributors inside the colour-coded categories as outside them.

pragmatically shifted from the right to the left. None of the other categories reach 1 per cent. In contrast, the model of overall Australian behaviour suggests that a larger number of Liberal contributors should greet a government of the left by abstaining from political finance. Similar to the other Australian jurisdictions, there are very small numbers of hedging firms. The case study provides a concrete example of the power of both ideological and pragmatic motivations for business payments to Australian political parties. The next section investigates the nature of pragmatic exchanges in Australia.

6. PRAGMATIC EXCHANGES

6.1 Party fundraising

Corporate policies are as much a reaction to parties seeking funds, as they are a way for the firm to promote its interests in the political system. The parties feel great and increasing pressure to raise money. As late as 2003, it was reported that MPs usually distance themselves from fundraising, leaving it to campaign committees or their party's central apparatus (Peake 2003). However, a couple of years later, the situation had changed. One senior Liberal Victorian MP said, 'We've caught the American disease we've got a fund-raise or perish mentality. MPs are directed by party headquarters to attend coffees with key business supporters just because it might lock in our next $15,000 cheque' (Baker 2006). During the sample period, fundraising initiatives did not tend to be tightly controlled by the party's centre, with major discrepancies in the prices of events, confusion about the ultimate destination of funds, and enormous pressure on the time of ministers. The fundraising system can be very intense. In one six-month period, Prime Minister John Howard's New South Wales Liberal Party branch organized 'fourteen lunches, one golf day and two receptions for major party donors to meet either him, his ministers or his parliamentary secretaries' (Clark and Glendinning 2001). As in Canada, party bagmen call on large firms that have been regular supporters (Colebatch 2000). In Victoria, the donations of the largest firms are acknowledged to be 'few in number, large in sum, and well disclosed' (Bachelard, Baker, and Millar 2007). Sometimes these approaches can be blunt. A Victorian property figure remembers taking a call from a senior Liberal fundraiser: 'He called and said, "I've put you down for $100,000, OK"' (Millar 2008a). An aggressive proactive approach has spread across the parties (Baker 2006), with fundraisers targeting contributors to their political competitors and firms in politicized sectors. In Victoria, 'an ALP insider' claimed that the party deliberately targets companies in 'regulation high' and 'issues rich' industries: 'development, infrastructure, gaming, alcohol, and, in the past, tobacco' (Millar 2008a). A relatively systematic newspaper investigation concluded that donors to the ALP were heavily concentrated in these sectors. In an interesting twist, one source says that Victorian Labor has encouraged their donors to also contribute to the Liberals, thereby reducing Labor's political vulnerability if something 'uncomfortable occurs' (Millar 2008d). Economic, as well as political, competition has been cited as a justification for some types of fundraising. NSW Premier Bob Carr of the ALP linked his party's activities to competition for investment: 'We're concerned that without access to a minister or public servants they'll take that investment to another state (or nation)' (Hanna 2003). Parties and politicians accept money from virtually any legal source and are frequently exposed as having received money from embarrassingly disreputable donors. On the other hand, Labor decided to refuse donations from tobacco companies in 2004 (Newcastle Herald 2004; Schubert 2006) and in New South Wales some individual politicians turn down contributions from property developers.

The other side also feels the intensity of fundraising. Many lobbyists and businesspeople find themselves struggling against a constant avalanche of events. 'If you went to all of them you'd never get any work done, and you'd have a serious health problem', said one lobbyist (Bachelard, Baker, and Millar 2007). 'We have been inundated with invitations', said Mr David Charles, the chief executive of the NSW branch of the Australian Hotels Association. 'We could spend $1000 a day going to these things. There are only so many lunches and dinners you can go to' (Korporaal 1995, 1). His organization's solution was to hold its own dinners to allow members hear each party outline its policy for the hotel industry (Clennell 2007a). Ian Smith, chief executive of consultancy group Gavin Anderson, which advises corporations on political donations, sees political finance as a core expense, not an optional luxury: 'Any company should recognise that, as they have a marketing budget and an operations budget, there should be an allocation of political donations as part of that process. It's not about the purchase of someone's vote, it's about making sure your opinion and your issues are in the domain' (Gettler 2004).

Some allege that this pragmatism is a collective delusion. 'Big companies are remarkably naive, and they still think ministers make decisions, and not many of them actually do—it's all up to the public servants', said one senior Victorian lobbyist. 'Ministers in this government are very cautious. There is never anything untoward in these functions . . . I can't see what the businesses get out of it. They do it because others are doing it, and it's the way business is being done' (Bachelard, Baker, and Millar 2007). Victorian Labor lobbyist David White goes further. He denies companies can expect any outcome from spending money on donations: 'The culture in Victoria (has been) exactly the same since 1955 . . . [I]f there was any undue influence in the ALP it preceded 1955. Since then it doesn't exist' (Bachelard, Baker, and Millar 2007). Businesspeople often find their efforts disappointing. Fundraising events are not worth it according to one guest at a federal Liberal dinner: 'It was a $50 meal. We had one of the Prime Minister's advisers at our table, but there is no reason to suspect we would be recognized, let alone warmly welcomed, if we took a problem to Canberra, simply because we had supported the party by taking three seats at the dinner' (Day 1995). Moreover, these events are often anything but entertaining, as businesspeople have to endure boring, and sometimes ill-informed, speeches by politicians (Davies 2006). In spite of these statements, there is a strong consensus in the available participant testimony that businesses do gain something from their financial contributions to parties. The lobbyists' comments may be disingenuous and the businessperson's comment probably rests on a misunderstanding on the nature of the system. The next three sub-sections analyse the three principal types of benefits made available to business contributors: illegal transactions, reciprocal exchanges, and discrete exchanges, notably the trading of access. These are the same three types that were discussed in the Canadian chapter. Indeed, one of the most striking aspects of the Australian interface of parties and firms is its similarity to Canada.

6.2 Illegal transactions

Illegal exchanges between politics and business are rare in Australia, partly because reaction to past problems has been quite robust. New South Wales, Queensland, and Western Australia have anti-corruption commissions, with sweeping powers (Colebatch 2007). Nonetheless, the decade before the sample period saw the eruption of massive scandals in Queensland and Western Australia. The Western Australian scandal was perhaps one of the most spectacular and damaging ever to take place in a rich country. Brian Burke was the flamboyant Labor premier from 1983 to 1988. His commitment to a close and ambitious partnership between business and the state earned his style of government the title of 'WA Inc.' His period in power lead to a rapid and widespread corruption of the political, administrative, and economic systems of the state. He used political donations to fund his stamp collection and anonymous gold trading through a state enterprise. Attempts to rescue his cronies' enterprises ended up costing the state hundreds of millions of dollars. His political associates took bribes and he and other Labor politicians colluded to hide the true relationship between the state and a range of companies and businesspeople (Wainwright 1992). Burke was convicted twice (although the second conviction was overturned on appeal) and served over a year in prison. Amazingly, Burke was not only later allowed to work as a lobbyist, but was very successful in working with the Labor Party to which he had done so much damage. Less surprisingly, his activities resulted in a further round of scandals and ministerial resignations (Cohen 2007).

The Queensland scandals reflected corruption that was more deep-seated but not so grand in scale. The problem was clearly related to National Party's constant presence in government between 1957 and 1990. Until 1983, it governed with the Liberals, and thereafter alone. Sir Joh Bjelke-Petersen managed a record nineteen years as premier. Like Burke, he was a champion of developmentalism (Wanna 2003, 101), but at a less frenetic pace. Five of his ministers were jailed on various corruption charges, while another died awaiting trial. The former police commissioner, who had been extraordinarily close to the premier, was convicted of receiving regular payments in return for tolerating prostitution and gambling. Bjelke-Petersen's perjury trial ended with a hung jury (AAP 1991; Jones 1994). In the twenty-first century, there have been many minor controversies, but major scandals have been restricted to the local level. These scandals tend to reveal the very abnormality of the behaviour in question. In the New South Wales town of Wollongong a scandal, variously described as a 'soap opera' (Frew and Besser 2008) or the 'plot of a bad detective novel' (Ferguson 2008), reached up into state politics. Frank Vellar, the developer at the centre of this 'sex-for-development' scandal reported to his wife, 'For the first time in my life I've been put into a position of yes or no in terms of a bribe . . . Normally it's done really discreetly' (Ferguson 2008).

In spite of these episodes, it is virtually universally accepted that only in very rare circumstances can a financial contribution directly buy a decision. Mr Riordan, corporate affairs manager for WD and HO Wills, said it would be 'pretty dumb' to make demands of a political leader because of a donation (Day 1995). Liberal Senator Gary Humphries said parties would have to be 'pretty desperate' to be influenced by donations of a few thousand dollars (Canberra Times 2007). Instead of bribery, pragmatic donations are mostly interpreted as discrete exchanges of cash for access or as one half of a reciprocal exchange that could eventually deliver a valuable decision.

6.3 Reciprocal exchanges

Australian participants outline the same subtle process of network development as do their Canadian counterparts. Financial contributions do not buy a direct, clear, and simultaneous benefit. Instead, by building a record with the party and relationships with politicians and their advisers, financial contributions establish a basis for possible reciprocal benefits in the future. Ministers have a clear incentive to maintain a distance from contributors. Senior politicians often claim that they separate themselves from fundraising, other than attendance at functions. They assert that an absence of knowledge of the source of donations protects them from conflicts of interest. Steve Bracks, a Victorian ALP premier, said, 'I divorce myself, and am completely separate, from any donations that are given to the party.' Therefore, any allegation that a donation had influenced his government was 'personally insulting, outrageous and totally without foundation' (Rollins 2001a). His successor said he made a point of not knowing who contributed to Labor: 'I don't ask, nor would I ask. Nor would I want to know who it is who has donated. I see the list at the end of the year when it's published' (Millar 2008c). In a similar vein, Liberal prime minister, John Howard, said:

> You never ever have any bank accounts over which you have control. You don't have leader's accounts, you don't control money, you don't ask people to give you cheques, or accept cheques, even to pass on to other people. While obviously you go to functions which involve people who are current or prospective party supporters, you must be careful not to be in any way directly involved in the raising of money. (Brown 1999)

Martin Riordan, a former press secretary to John Howard, agreed that political leaders try to keep their distance from party donors. However, it is not possible to maintain a strict separation. 'They would prefer not to know. But in reality they spend half their lives at fundraisers so they get to know who's who and who wants what' (Day 1995). Indeed, senior politicians sometimes admit to knowing who their donors are. Prime Minster Howard accepted that he and his ministers listen to business donors but was 'very confident' that decisions were never influenced by political donations (Clark and Glendinning 2001). Similarly, NSW Premier Bob Carr said, 'They'll be listened to by government but they'll know they get as many knock backs on policy requests as they get tick-offs' (Hanna 2003). As assertions that policy cannot be bought, these statements are undoubtedly correct. However, it is almost equally undoubtedly true that regular payments can help develop a relationship, which, in turn, provides a small, but real, increase in the probability of successful lobbying. The denials are literally true but are only true because they insist on a framework of discrete exchange: blunt simultaneity and certainty connecting payment and benefit. Instead, payments are aimed at reciprocal exchange. They hope, over a period of years, to develop a relationship, which may or may not deliver a policy benefit that was not otherwise available. However, the payments do increase the probability of successful lobbying. Remember that the value of one lobbying success almost undoubtedly dwarfs the value of a long period of substantial financial contributions. A variety of well-informed sources reveal this logic.

A former Victorian ALP minister frankly admitted:

> As a minister, are you not going to give a company or a businessman who has just personally donated $1000 to your local campaign a little more time than you really should? Are you going to take an extra special interest in the progress of their particular proposal or issue? Of course you probably are. It's human nature, you can't just accept someone's money and not feel that you owe them something. (Bachelard, Baker, and Millar 2007)

The deputy leader of the Victorian Liberals, Louise Asher, said, 'It doesn't mean I would vote on a bill the way they wanted me to, but it certainly means they would get access or a return phone call or whatever it is they may want' (Birnbauer 2007). Peter Botsman, political historian and ALP member, says, 'There's a relationship established around a donation to a political party which brings also a personal phone relationship and a conversation at a critical time maybe all that is needed' (Ferguson 2008).

Actually the system can and does work in this way, even if the actual decision-makers do not have a relationship with donors. Instead, an effective relationship can be developed with their assistants or with other brokers. Of course, brokers issue the same strenuous denials that they facilitate the purchase of policy. Graham Richardson was once the Labor Party's leading bagman and the political fixer of choice for a swathe of big businesses. It was widely believed that only the prime minister was more powerful. He candidly admitted, 'I've always, when getting a large donation off someone, said to them that I'd make sure if they had a problem with Government, they'd be able to at least talk to the person with whom they had the problem.' However, he also maintained, 'You won't find one person who gave me money and then got a government decision. You can't find that. I know you can't because I've been very careful for a long time' (Wilkinson 1996). Richardson is still a broker, but now works on behalf of property developers rather than the ALP (Frew 2008).

John Mant, the acting commissioner of the NSW Independent Commission Against Corruption from 1993 to 1994, explained, 'If you're going to do a big development in New South Wales you have to make a decision as to whether you're going to go down that path of making a contribution, turning up at the dinners, employing the appropriate lobby group to work on your behalf... [Using a fixer who knows the system] give[s] the developer, particularly the nature of the ex-minister, they do give the developer a real inside run' (Ferguson 2008). A former Howard staff member made it clear that those outside the ministerial ranks were encouraged to take political finance into account: 'Staff and MPs are encouraged to engage with donors. Not a week would go by without hearing the phrase, "They're a good supporter"' (Baker 2006). A Victorian 'property industry source' gives the following rationale for political contributions:

> Yes, people do donate because they think it curries favour; it's part of business practice. But it's all about the relationships. That relationship will matter in due course when the Government has something that requires some decision. An adviser may turn to a decisionmaker and say 'you remember you met such and such at that function'. And he will say: 'They've got the capacity to deliver this haven't they?' And the adviser will say 'yes'. (Millar 2008d)

Apparently, some Australian corporations describe the system of political finance as 'Aussie guanxi: political donations are entrenched as another cost of doing business' (Elliott 2003). Guanxi is a Chinese term for 'a web of personal relationships based on kinship, shared educational background, and past favours given and received' (Moise 2008, 25). As a term that suggests something subtle, complex, long-term, and very useful, guanxi is appropriate for understanding the rationale of business financing of political parties in Australia. Thinking about reciprocal exchange reveals a system that is much less mysterious, and much more rational, than the usual framework of discrete exchange.

6.4 Access and discrete exchanges

Yet again like Canada, the political debate on political finance is not dominated by discussion of the nuances of relationships and probabilities but rather by the seemingly straightforward sale of access. In the previous chapter, I argued that, in Canada, the number of payments forming part of a reciprocal exchange probably vastly outnumbered those that were one side of a discrete exchange. There are several reasons to believe that access is substantially more important in Australia than in Canada. The simulations do not directly measure exchange processes, but they can provide some hints. Hedging, and especially consistent hedging, should be associated with a long-term expectation of reciprocity. The model predicts that on average just less than one-third of Canadian contributors should hedge, but only 14 per cent of Australian contributors. The figures suggest that 13 per cent of Canadian contributors should hedge consistently, but the Australian probability is less than one hundredth of 1 per cent.

There is a huge difference in scale between Canada's population of thirty-three million and the Australian states ranging from half a million in Tasmania to seven million in New South Wales. The Australian Commonwealth has a population of twenty-one million. Especially outside of the big two states, with their powerful quality daily newspapers, there is a much lower visibility for politicians than there is for the Canadian national government. Indeed, some of the states are so small that politicians cannot avoid access at ticketed events by virtue of the sheer number of attendees. It is not possible to get thousands of paying Tasmanian businesspeople into a ballroom. For the same reason, parties depend on a much smaller number of businesses and, therefore, are under pressure to provide more than an opportunity for mere relationship building.

The size of contributions also provides some evidence on the relative importance of discrete and reciprocal exchanges. As Figure 4.4 shows, the total average annual payments to the major parties represent a much larger proportion of the sample firms' average income than in Canada. This suggests that Australian businesses place a higher value on the returns for contribution than do Canadian firms.

In addition, the average business payment is worth more to the Australian parties than it is to the Canadian parties. The proportion of average party annual income represented by the average annual payments of a firm is larger than the Canadian proportion for all Australian jurisdictions and measures (see Figure 4.5). However, the New South Wales proportions are quite close to Canada's, especially after excluding sectors that are relatively likely to have a business relationship with the parties. Payments are two to four times more important than in Canada for

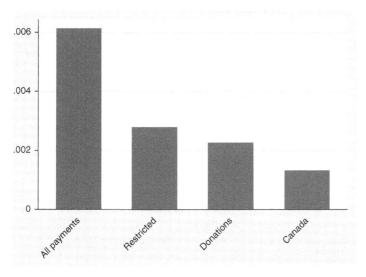

FIGURE 4.4 Comparison of the size of Canadian and Australian firms' payments

Notes: Compares sample mean total contributions over zero as a proportion of mean income per annum per jurisdiction. The restricted Australian sample excludes finance, insurance, and business services. The different reporting thresholds do not affect the comparison. The Australian threshold is 0.0000993 per cent of mean income. The same percentage of the Canadian mean is $137, which is less than the threshold.

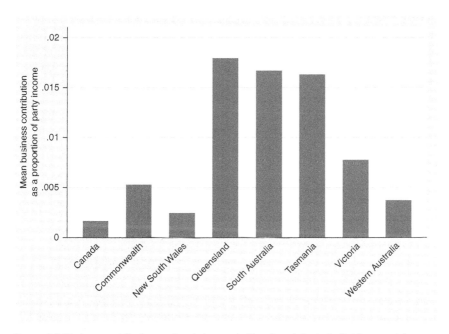

FIGURE 4.5 Business contributions and party income in Canada and Australia (total payments)

the Australian national government and in Western Australia and Victoria. In Queensland and South Australia there are big differences between total payments and the restricted measure (not shown), ranging from double to ten times the Canadian figure. In Tasmania, both measures are approximately ten times as large as for Canada. At almost 2 per cent, the loss of an average firm's payments would represent a noticeable reduction in the annual income of a Tasmanian party.

The comparative rarity of hedging and consistent hedging, along with the smaller scale of Australian jurisdictions compared to Canada, and the larger value of payments in relation to firm and party incomes all imply that firms tend to receive a greater benefit from parties for their political contributions. Newspaper reports suggest that this is indeed the case. Moreover, they give the impression that the difference is of kind, as well as of degree. In other words, real access to decision-makers, as opposed to networking opportunities, is more available in Australia than it was in Canada. Access is sold more explicitly and is often of a higher quality. Payments are more likely to form part of discrete exchanges in Australia.

A document from Marketplace Communications, which was engaged to attract corporate sponsorship for a cabinet visit to Brisbane in 1995, claimed that for $20,000 a sponsor could have 'one-on-one' access to the prime minister and other ministers during a cocktail party. Senator Robert Ray of the ALP said the firm had been 'overzealous' and had been admonished. He admitted the party had made a mistake in not making clear the line between political donations and access to ministers. He said, 'I have made it very clear that I do not believe access can be a thing that is auctioned, and that access to ministers must be available to everyone without charge' (Chamberlin 1995). The Liberals charged €11,000 a seat at the prime minister's table, as part of a fundraiser that included ten-minute private briefings with ministers (Koutsoukis and Schubert 2004; Baker and Bachelard 2007). At least one other event with the prime minister reached a similar price (Colebatch and Austin 2007). The New South Wales ALP offered an 'intimate dinner' with Premier Bob Carr and Treasurer Andrew Refshauge (Sydney Morning Herald 2005). Another popular approach has been to package a year's access:

> A glossy ALP brochure is offering five levels of 'business dialogue', starting at $100,000 for a foundation partner and working down to $10,000 for an executive partner. For a $100,000 donation to ALP coffers, a partner would receive a private boardroom lunch with senior Iemma government ministers, five places at a federal MPs' dinner, 10 invitations to the Premier's Christmas drinks, a VIP table at the budget dinner and favoured treatment at ALP functions. (Mitchell 2006; Clennell 2007c)

In the attached material, the New South Wales ALP general secretary Mark Arbib said the commitment 'would provide a unique opportunity for your business to develop a working relationship with NSW Labor' (Mitchell 2006). In 2008, the new Rudd government introduced a similar scheme at the federal level. This offered several forms of very high-quality access, in terms of small numbers and extended duration. Moreover, the repeated use of the word 'specific' seemed like an invitation for relatively straightforward lobbying. The access on offer included a 'three-day retreat' to 'liaise with the entire ministry, discuss specific issues with ministers in smaller settings, and hear an address from the Prime Minister'. Another more exclusive variant was the 'leadership event' involving the prime minister and three other senior ALP politicians. Apparently, the prime minister's office's insistence in approving every public fundraiser had made such events too difficult to organize. The membership strategy was the only remaining feasible approach (Milne 2008).

Access is not only traded at a fixed price; it is openly auctioned. Dinner with a state premier has been offered for auction on more than one occasion (Verrender 2001). One winning bid amounted to $48,000, but the Hong Kong billionaire and casino owner in question never availed of his opportunity (Clennell 2007b). On the other hand, auctions can also result in relatively cheap access, such as a $5,100 winning bid at a 'Golden Luncheon Auction' securing access to the NSW Planning Minister (Gibson and McClymont 2008). The NSW premier has asked not be involved in any more raffles of this kind (Gibson and McClymont 2008).

The Australian Hotels' Association has often hosted very small events, which were likely to provide a high level of access. In 2003, their dinner with the National Party state leader was to be attended by forty-five and their Liberal dinner only thirty-five. The parties themselves provide once-off access on an even cosier scale, such as a lunch for sixteen with the South Australian Police and Urban Planning Minister (Castello 2008), or a dinner for seventeen with the NSW Planning Minister (Jopson 2008). An apparent opportunity for relatively direct lobbying, rather than mere networking, was a NSW Liberal invitation for only fifteen donors to spend 'an intimate three hours with [the leader of the opposition] and the Opposition planning spokesman' (Davies and Norrie 2006). There are also larger events with politicians distributed around tables in a ballroom (Gordon and Carty 2008), but these seem to be less common than in Canada.

The strength of the effect of payments on access depends on the importance of the firm. An executive from a medium-sized property development company said, 'If you've got a big project you're going to need to talk to the Government, so you go along to a meet-and-greet. A company of our size wouldn't be speaking to the minister, you'd speak to the chief of staff or adviser so at least you've got something on their desk. It just smoothes the path to get something heard' (Bachelard, Baker, and Millar 2007). The head of a public relations firm that has done a lot of fundraising for the ALP says that if you are rich enough to pay for membership of party's business membership scheme you almost certainly do not need to pay in order to obtain access: 'If you are worth hundreds of millions of dollars you have access to any of the politicians, whenever you want to. The Prime Minister would happily take the phone calls of the leading members of the business community' (Coultan and Sexton 2004). Ashley Mason of construction company Leighton Holdings makes the same point, 'It's part of the system. I don't think you get very much at all. Certainly, a company like ours, you get a meeting whenever you like. It's seen as part of the process, and we do it in a bipartisan way. The biggest problem we have is to get people to go along from the company—it's just another bloody dinner ... Our people generally regard it as a bit of a chore' (Bachelard, Baker, and Millar 2007). This is another assertion that is literally true, but a distraction from the real nature of the process. It is probably correct that the big businesses find these meetings boring and that they are not strictly necessary for the firm to make direct contact with a policy-maker. However, as argued earlier, they are almost undoubtedly part of a strategy of relationship development and maintenance. This relationship involves an obligation on the part of the politician and political party that increases the chances of successful lobbying.

It is not clear to what extent these access events actually do allow opportunities for lobbying. One oft-neglected aspect of the fundraising system is that it provides access to decision-makers outside of the constraints of a government context:

> For it is at these fund-raising events, away from bureaucrats, office staff and, importantly, freedom-of-information laws that may record official meetings, that a politician can talk in private with a banker, unionist or real estate agent who has paid for the pleasure of their company. (Baker and Bachelard 2007)

According to this persuasive logic, small fundraising events provide the best possible opportunity for effective lobbying. However, the same authors write in another newspaper article that, 'It's an unwritten rule that there will be no overt lobbying: businesses are there to be seen, to put a face to the name, to establish a profile in the minister's mind' (Bachelard, Baker, and Millar 2007). While these events may be small and all proceedings are off-the-record, the fact that it is widely known that places in the room have been sold must raise the costs for politicians. Ironically, the clear incentives and opportunities to deliver real access may make it less likely that access, in the sense of an actual opportunity to lobby, is actually granted. In 2003, Queensland ALP premier Peter Beattie scrapped a scheme called 'Queensland First', which sold access to senior ministers (Courier Mail 2004). This demonstrates that the sale of access does constitute a substantial cost for politicians. While this counter-pressure is important, the logic of scale in Australian polities, and the relative size of many payments, along with the widespread 'intimacy' of events, suggests that, in most cases, access is for sale. Sometimes, what is billed as access is merely an opportunity to develop a relationship. Indeed, often the parties' promotional pitch emphasizes this very aspect. A relationship is a real benefit because it brings with it a small but real increase in the probability of successful lobbying.

7. CONCLUSIONS

The pragmatic motivation of Australian firms is obvious in their reaction to changes of government. Australian firms obtained similar benefits to their Canadian counterparts. There were some illegal transactions, discrete exchange of cash for access, and reciprocal exchanges of cash for the opportunity to form a relationship of mutual obligation. Indeed, the similarity of the ways in which access was traded and networks developed in the two countries is remarkable. However, it appears that the frequencies of these two types were very different. Discrete exchange was more important, and correspondingly, reciprocal exchange, much less important in Australia than in Canada. Also, there are differences in the forms of access and the way they were traded. In Australia, access was often traded in a very explicit manner. Ethanol giant allegedly demanded guaranteed access to the ALP's Simon Crean, then leader of the opposition, in return for a $50,000 donation. The ALP decided to return the donation. Conversely there have been reports that politicians demanded money before granting access to businesses (Gettler 2004). Canadian parties did not use access so aggressively, but neither was it so often sold on such a transparent basis. Frequently, Canadian firms seeking good quality access had little option other than to get involved in the subtle process of networking. Related to this difference is the popularity of business membership programmes in Australia, which gave firms rights to regular access. In Canada, access tended to be sold on an ad hoc basis. Firms could not purchase regular access. This could only be achieved through assiduous networking. These conclusions do not necessarily imply that Australian politics is more penetrated by business interests. The aim of networking is to develop a sense of mutual obligation between firm and party. Once this is achieved, firms can expect not just access but a relatively favourable hearing. Firms that have purchased access often receive a relatively perfunctory hearing. Indeed, if the opportunity to lobby is widely known to have been sold, politicians will be very wary indeed of making a beneficial decision. In this respect, it is also worth remembering that the Canadian businesses were much more likely to contribute to parties than were Australian firms.

The other, and much greater, difference between Canada and Australia is the persistence of ideological donations in Australia, as opposed to the virtual absence of an ideological preference between Liberals and Conservatives amongst Canadian businesses. Australian firms tend to give twice as much to Coalition governments than they do to ALP governments. The ideological motivation interacts with pragmatism. On average, Australian businesses' strategy towards Labor governments is to desist from supporting the Liberals, rather than switching to the ALP, or hedging between the two major parties. So, while the system of political fundraising in Australia shares its techniques, and perhaps even much of its culture with Canada, the overall relationship between parties and business is fundamentally different.

There have been important changes in the regulation of Australian political finance, but so far these seem unlikely to have brought about an out-of-type change in behaviour. At the end of 2005, the Coalition government raised the threshold for disclosure to $10,000 and indexed this to the consumer price index. From July 2011 to June 2012 the amount was set at $11,900. In 2010, New South Wales introduced new limits on donations (Costar 2011, 4), followed by Queensland in 2011 (Queensland 2011). The same legislation also introduced a much wider definition of an associated entity. Predictably, these changes lead to sharp drop in itemized income and a sharp rise in the income of associated entities relative to political parties. New South Wales has recently gone further and banned donations from all legal persons. There is a risk of constitutional challenge, but legal opinion seems quite confident that the law will stand. In 2008, the new ALP Commonwealth government, lead by Kevin Rudd, published a very wide-ranging paper on political finance regulation. It put the issues of banning or capping business contributions on the agenda (Australian Government 2008). Therefore, the uniformly transparent and permissive system, which facilitated this study, no longer exists. Of course, the behaviour analysed here still exists, but it is not clear how it has been affected by the decrease in transparency and it is difficult to predict how it will be affected by reductions in permissiveness. A decrease in transparency reduces the political cost of accepting contributions and especially reduces the cost of a discrete transaction relative to a reciprocal exchange. If payments can be kept secret, there is less need to keep business at a distance by refusing discrete exchanges and only offering vague, but real, hopes of reciprocity. Limits on business financing of parties should have the opposite effect: by reducing the amounts parties can receive, they should reduced the temptation for discrete exchanges. Such limits might have a bigger effect on the smaller scale politics of Queensland than on New South Wales, which has attracted so many business payments that parties should have been comfortable offering merely reciprocal exchanges. An observable implication of this argument is that hedging should become relatively more popular. The next chapter studies Germany, which has a very different political economy and business–political relationship than liberal Australia and Canada.

5

Germany: Symbolic Expenditure

1. INTRODUCTION

In Germany, money tends to speak ideologically. A small number of companies grant a certain but small benefit to right-wing parties as an expression of a political preference. Nonetheless, a handful firms did contribute to the Social Democrats after they returned to government in 1998. The German case study has a similar structure to its Canadian and Australian predecessors. It starts with an account of German political economy and then reviews the regulation of political finance and the overall finances of the principal political parties. The next section is a quantitative analysis of the motivations of business contributors to German parties. The penultimate section uses qualitative evidence to assess interpretations of business financing of parties in Germany. The conclusion summarizes the chapter, comparing Germany to Australia and Canada.

2. THE GERMAN POLITICAL ECONOMY

Germany is the archetypical co-ordinated market economy (Hall and Soskice 2001, 21–7; Casper, Lehrer, and Soskice 2009) and provides a contrast to liberal Australia and Canada in all six spheres. Firstly, in the market for corporate governance, networks of firms and banks provide opportunities for finance that complement the stock exchange. Germany's domestically owned, publicly listed firms are half as valuable as a percentage of GDP as their equivalents in Australia and Canada. German firms have a two-board system. The supervisory board has equal shareholder and employee representation, although the shareholder-nominated chair can cast a tie-break vote (Vitols 2001, 343). Workers are also represented through works councils. The management board needs the authority of the supervisory board for major decisions and tends to operate by consensus. Its members usually have significant autonomy in managing their sections or functions within the firm. In the middle of our sample period, 90 per cent of listed companies in Germany had a shareholder with at least a 10 per cent stake in the company (Vitols 2001, 342). This 'stakeholder' model of corporate governance (Vitols 2001, 337) means that German firms tend to pursue multiple goals such as profitability, market share, and employment security. It also allows, and incentivizes, long-term strategies while reducing incentives for, while erecting obstacles to, the pursuit of short-term share price and profitability.

Secondly, employment security is very high and the institutionalized equalization of wages within sectors reduces incentives for workers to move from employer to employer. This encourages firms to commit to long-term specializations and incremental innovation. Employers invest in training in order to increase productivity to match the externally imposed high costs of labour. To 'compensate for such external rigidities, firms have to increase their internal flexibility' (Streeck 1992, 32). Moreover, having no option but to invest in expensive skills, firms are forced into competition for high value-added products. However, given that they cannot change their labour force, or incentivize radically new thinking through wages, they concentrate on incremental innovation. The 'pattern of innovation is one that is more likely to generate improvements of existing products of existing firms and sectors than to give rise to new sectors' (Streeck 1997, 41).

Thirdly, training and education is often highly specific to a particular company or industry. Germany operates a 'dual system of vocational education in which companies pay the bulk of the costs of in-firm training while public funds support the provision of complementary education in schools' (Culpepper 2001, 277). This education is highly specialized and, at the beginning of our sample period, there were about four hundred nationally standardized occupational profiles (Streeck 1992, 30). This system matches employees' qualifications and incentives to the relatively long-term and niche strategies of firms.

Fourthly, inter-company relations exhibit institutionalized and informal cooperation, as well the market relationships of competition and contract. Firms are 'social institutions, not just networks of private contracts or the property of their shareholders' (Streeck 1997, 37). Indeed, the German conception of contract law is 'regulatory' in contrast to the 'classical' approach of common law systems. This approach to contracting goes well beyond the written contract to embrace a wider concern with fairness, which is based on private norms and the balance of power between contracting parties. In doing so, the courts tend to grant legal status to standards that have evolved within trade associations (Casper 2001, 391). Thus, not only are German business associations deeply embedded in history (Shonfield 1969, 240; Crouch 1994, 21) and the economy, they are also embedded in German law (Edinger 1994, 177–8). Indeed, they are mentioned in the Basic Law and were also present in the Weimar Constitution (Shonfield 1969, 243). 'Associations . . . are typically granted some form or obligatory or quasi-obligatory membership, helping them overcome the free-rider problems associated with collective goods production' (Streeck 1997, 39). Business associations often play a vital role by facilitating the diffusion of technology across firms, and ensuring that the state plays an effective role in supporting and subsidizing research and training, sector by sector (Streeck 1992). Associations are powerful organizations, which tend to speak authoritatively for the interest they represent (Streeck 1983). Their import-ance depends on, and reflects, their indispensability to the basic strategies of member firms. Associations continue to dominate lobbying in Germany (Ronit and Schneider 1998; Schneider 2006, 115–19). Indeed, as late as 2002, a practi-tioner reported that there was virtually no market for public affairs expertise in Germany (Behrens 2002, 175).

Fifthly, Germany's highly constrained consensual politics guarantee the stabil-ity of this environment and thereby the rationality of the long-term investments and strategies of German firms (Streeck 1992, 36; Wood 2001). The 'immobility and predictability of government policies preclude[s] rapid political innovation and allows economic agents to develop stable expectations [and] pursue long-term objectives (Streeck 1997, 38). Germany's political system was designed in the aftermath of the Second World War to avoid the catastrophe of its recent past. After the First World War, Germany was ruled by an unstable and incoherent democratic system, one that was relatively easily transformed into a totalitarian state by Hitler and the Nazi party. Therefore, the Allies and the German democratic parties put in place institutions that would be both stable and limited in their power (Pulzer 1995, 46–7).

The constructive vote of no confidence stipulated that a Chancellor (prime minister) could only be forced to resign if there were a parliamentary majority for a successor. The electoral system avoided extreme fragmentation by evenly dividing the seats in the Bundestag (or lower house of parliament) between those elected by first-past-the-post and party list proportional representation (PR) and imposing a threshold of 5 per cent of the national vote for PR seats. The strong federal system was the most obvious limitation on power. Power and taxes were divided between the federal government and the *Länder* (states) (Pulzer 1995, 48). All of the twenty-one states have an executive responsible to the legislature, in every case except Bavaria unicameral (Conradt 1996, 259). The western states are generally larger and richer. Some, such as Bavaria and the city-state of Hamburg, have a clear historical continuity, while the borders of others have been set by Germany's twentieth-century history. The states have primary responsibility for education, law enforcement, the environment, broadcast media, and public admin-istration. The Bundesrat (the upper house of parliament) is composed of represen-tatives of the governments of the states. It has a veto over about 60 per cent of federal legislation (Conradt 1996, 193). It is especially significant when the parties comprising the federal government do not control the Bundesrat, as occurred during most of the 1990s. However, it is not primarily a party political chamber, and sometimes Bundesrat representatives do not vote in accordance with their co-partisans in the Bundestag.

Germany is famous for its legalistic culture. It is a Roman law system, based on systematic legal codes, in contrast to the tradition of incremental judge-made law in common law systems. Most regular court cases are held at the state level, with only a small number proceeding to the national high courts of appeal (Conradt 1996, 241). After the Second World War, a powerful constitutional court was introduced. It has blocked the Bundestag and federal government on many occasions with decisions on abortion, international treaties, and the electoral system. Moreover, it has frequently been involved in party finance. Germany has had a highly independent central bank, the Bundesbank, since the Second World War. The chief sources of its independence were the government's inability to remove its members, along with its clear inflation target in setting interest rates. Since 1999 that power has transferred to the European Central Bank. As part of the negotiations leading to the abandonment of the successful Deutschmark for the euro, Germany insisted on transferring the organizational form of the Bundesbank to the European level. Germany is constrained in many other ways by its membership of the European Union (EU). For example, the German government does not decide on trade or industrial regulation policy, but can only pursue its interests in these areas through the complex mix of European institutions. Other areas where the EU is very important include competition law, agriculture, fishing, energy, transport, and environmental policy. Indeed, the EU has some effect on virtually every activity of the German state. German policy-makers are not just constrained by other public authorities, but also by private institutions. This is partly because strict divisions between public and private often do not exist. Germany's welfare state is largely administered by almost two thousand health and social security funds, on which business, labour, and professional interests are represented. Such corporatism, the attribution of public functions to private organizations, is common throughout the German political, economic, and social systems.

Sixthly, and finally, Germany's political parties have less ideological flexibility and a weaker right-wing bias than their counterparts in liberal market economies. The parties are 'semi-constitutional organs' (Scarrow 2002, 78). The Basic Law privileges them with public finance and the right to bring cases to the constitutional court, but holds them to standards of intra-party democracy and insists that they raise over half of their funds from private sources. The party system has been dominated by struggles between left and right (Scarrow 2002, 78). The left's main representative has been the Social Democratic Party (SPD), the organizational roots of which go back to 1863. The SPD's ideological history under the Federal Republic has seen several shifts in to the centre and out to the left, as well as considerable internal debate. In the aftermath of the Second World War, the party had reasons to be optimistic. It had a proud record of resistance to the defeated fascist regime and the emerging communist regime in the east. It had quickly resurrected its organizational structure and many viewed the inter-war period as a failure of capitalism. Nonetheless, they lost election after election to Konrad Adenauer's Christian Democrats. The Social Democrats sought to escape from the constraints of their official loyalty to Marxism and their inability to reach out beyond their working-class base. They did so in their congress at Bad Godesberg in 1959, which set out a new programme (Smith 1982, 98–101; Pulzer 1995, 70). The new approach sought to replicate the Christian Democrats' success in establishing a 'People's Party', which represented the interests of all Germans, not just one sector of society. The new formula, 'As much freedom as possible, as much planning as necessary' (Smith 1982, 197–8), could be interpreted as differing only in emphasis from the SPD's right-wing competitors. In 1965 the SPD joined a grand coalition with the Christian Democrats and ruled with the Free Democrats from 1969 to 1982. During this period, a new generation of activists tried to reconvert the party to Marxism (Pulzer 1995, 125), just as the techno-cratic Helmut Schmidt led the party and government through economic difficul-ties (Pulzer 1995, 137). The foundation and success of the Green party meant the SPD had to defend its left wing in the 1980s and 1990s. However, Gerhard Schroëder successfully sought to define a 'New Middle' for the SPD in the late 1990s (Padgett 2003), leading to a breakaway under finance minister, and former chancellor candidate, Oskar Lafontaine.

The Christian Democratic Union (CDU) was founded after the Second World War:

> A succinct formulation of the [their] new approach is the idea of a 'double compromise': the one between Catholicism and Protestantism, the other between capital and labour. Together the two compromises gave the CDU its claim to be a party of the whole people. (Smith 1982, 89–90)

The CDU has dominated government in the Federal Republic, and was in govern-ment from the state's pre-history under the Allies until 1969. Thus, the party has been strongly identified with the state and the status quo. In spite of its self-conscious identification as a people's party and its dedication to the social market economy, the CDU has always defined itself against the left (Pridham 1977, 305; Smith 1982, 198, 202; Pulzer 1995, 137; Wood 2001, 266). In contrast to the organized mass party of the SPD, the CDU initially had an anti-organizational culture (Pridham 1977, 133, 246, 259). However, a membership drive and bur-eaucratization in the 1960s has resulted in two principal parties with much more similar organizational structures. In 1950s and early 1960s the CDU mopped up a variety of small right-wing, centrist, and regionalist parties. It is in a permanent parliamentary and electoral alliance with the Bavarian Christian Social Union (Pridham 1977, 303). Nonetheless, the CSU has a separate organization with its own leadership, congresses, and headquarters.

For almost three decades, the Free Democrats were the third party in Ger-many's 'two-and-a-half' party system. It is a liberal party that has calibrated the balance of its emphasis on economic and social freedoms over time, partly in response to coalition opportunities with the CDU/CSU or the SPD. In the 1990s, the German party system became more complex with the arrival of two small left-wing parties. The Green party travelled from its anti-political roots to federal government with the SPD in 1998. The former rulers of the German Democratic Republic rebranded themselves the Party of Democratic Socialism (PDS) and have consistently won seats in the east. In 2007, the PDS merged with Lafontaine's defectors from the SPD to form the Left Party. These two parties have constrained the SPD's ability to compete for the centre with the Christian Democrats (Kitschelt 1999, 329). It is important to remember that Germany has a dual party system, with the same parties operating with slightly different priorities, and often completely different coalition strategies, at the federal and state levels.

Not since Adenauer's dominance of post-war Germany have Christian Democratic leaders had authority and flexibility comparable to their equivalents in the Australian and Canadian centre-right. The CDU finds it difficult to pursue right-wing policies as it genuinely straddles the centre and has important links to Christian labour unions (Wood 2001, 254, 271). The ideological distance between the SPD and the Christian Democrats was at its greatest in the 1950s (Smith 1982, 98–101; Pulzer 1995, 50). German parties have relatively weak capacities and incentives to manoeuvre ideologically in pursuit of the median voter. However, leaders' dependence on left-wing or broadly consensual party structures means their parties can credibly commit to policies that support individuals' and firms' investment in highly specialized skills and markets.

Thus, the German variety of capitalism finds it difficult to engage in either price competition or radical innovation (Vitols 2001, 358–9). Its comparative institutional advantage is in diversified quality production. Economic change and economic globalization seem to have accelerated Germany's concentration in this area of comparative advantage. Craft industries have expanded into diversified quality production, while large enterprises that formerly competed on cost have moved upmarket into more expensive and varied products (Streeck 1992, 6). Even in high technology areas, Germany finds it easier to compete in 'segments characterized by less risky, cumulative technologies' (Casper, Lehrer, and Soskice 2009, 218–19). Moreover, German firms have moved out of sectors characterized by radical innovation, or moved the radically innovatory parts of their firms to Anglo-Saxon countries with better environments for this sort of business (Vitols 2001, 357). Germany's co-ordinated economy reduces incentives for pragmatic contributions to parties, as firms' political interests, in regulation and training, are channelled through business associations. Germany's political system guarantees the stability of the rich array of institutions that underpin incremental innovation. Consensual political institutions constitute only a minimal risk of major policy shifts, thereby also reducing incentives for ideological financing of political parties. The next section provides an overview of the German system of political finance.

3. GERMAN POLITICAL FINANCE

3.1 Regulation

German parties have a very different legal status to their counterparts in Australia and Canada. The Basic Law stated that, 'They shall publicly account for the sources of their funds and for their assets' (Basic Law, Art. 21 (1)). It also required parliament to concretize its provisions in legislation, but this did not happen until 1967 (Nassmacher 2001, 105). There have been several twists and turns since the late 1950s, instigated by either the parties themselves (Koss 2011, 109–20) or the Constitutional Court (Poguntke 1994, 191). Essentially, the right-wing parties, which dominated the early decades of post-war German democracy, resisted disclosing large donations from businesses and wealthy individuals. They did, however, introduce a substantial tax credit in 1954, which the Constitutional Court declared unconstitutional in 1958, on the grounds of 'equality of opportunity', since the law primarily benefited those on higher incomes (von Armin 1993, 206). In the same judgement, the Court suggested that public subsidy would be acceptable, a proposal to which the parties reacted immediately (Koss 2011, 107). In 1966, it restricted public finance to the 'necessary costs of a reasonable election campaign', banning general party financing, and limiting state funding to below half of a party's income. However, these statements of principle had little effect on the size and distribution of state subsidies (Koss 2011, 107). Nonetheless, this decision finally prompted the politicians to pass a Party Law. The Party Law of 1967 distributed funds on the proportional results of elections for all parties winning over 0.5 per cent of the vote (von Armin 1993, 209). The state also provided matching funding of 50 per cent on membership fees or donations up to a ceiling (General-Anzeiger 2002a).

There has also been a series of more detailed changes. In 1984 disclosure was introduced for assets and expenditure. The size of tax benefits was increased hugely in 1988, after a surprise court decision of 1986. There is also the matter of the complicated equality provisions, which are supposed to compensate for the unequal effects of tax benefits, and the 'base payments' that are intended to compensate for the unintended effects of the equality provisions (Landfried 1994, 135). These latter funds were small in comparison to the original public subsidy, calculated on vote share. The Constitutional Court eventually decided that its original insistence on election expenses was impractical and switched to continuous 'partial government funding' (Fischer 2000). These changes did not modify three basic characteristics of the 1967 law: disclosure of income, permissiveness in relation to business contributions, and substantial public financing.

Disclosure is, by its nature, problematic to assess. Disclosure issues in German political finance arise from state funding and private donations. The level of state funding is difficult to estimate because German law insists on artificial distinctions between various party bodies, which are difficult to police. Parliamentary groups and party foundations receive substantial amounts in an opaque process that lacks the constitutional and legal framework of disclosure, to which the parties themselves are subject (Rademacher 1994). The parliamentary caucuses receive far less than the parties, but the foundations receive much more. Parliamentary groups, as institutions of state, must have full public funding. However, parties, as coalitions of citizens, must generate at least half of their income themselves. As in other countries, there are numerous allegations about the misuse of parliamentary funds for party purposes (Bollmann 2001). However, even the largest figures only represent a small proportion of a party's annual income. There is no suggestion that the party foundations are mere front organizations, as may be the case with some of their Australian equivalents: they clearly are involved in a massive aid, research, consultancy, and educational activities. It is widely agreed that the separation from political activities is quite strict (Scarrow 2002, 99; Nassmacher 2010, 57). Nonetheless, it is possible that some of their funding is in fact channelled towards party activities in the narrow sense. Most notoriously, Germany's party foundations have been accused of transferring to their mother parties large amounts of state money that they were supposed to pass on to democratic parties in Spain and Portugal in the 1970s (von Nowak 2000). There is also potential for money to come to the parties from the EU parliament, which has lighter regulation than Germany (Tillack 2004). Another possible, but probably not very lucrative, such channel is to divert money donated to a local referendum campaign (Der Tagesspiegel 2008). Taking into account these channels, as well as public relations benefits from government, political scientist Karl-Heinz Wetting estimates that the state funding rate is closer to 70 per cent in reality than the 50 per cent legal maximum (Funk 2007). Moreover, there is little doubt that the proportion of income accounted for by the state has been increasing gradually since the 1970s (Landfried 2000).

There have also been controversies in relation to the disclosure of business donations, and this is much more pertinent to this book. Parties had to disclose all donors of over 20,000 Deutschmarks per year, which is very close to the euro limit of 10,000 in operation since 2002. The limit was raised to 40,000 in 1986, but was struck down by the Constitutional Court in 1992 (Saalfeld 2000, 100; Nassmacher 2001, 106). The 1967 legislation also compelled parties to report their income by major categories. Donations in-kind must be reported, although, since they do not go through a bank account, they pose a greater temptation to evade disclosure. An example is the printing and distribution of a paper for the Baden-Württemberg CDU, which was unreported even though it was valued at hundreds of thousands of euros (Schöll 2005). BMW leases cars at a low rate to parties and claims to report all sponsorships and donations (Hengst, Kazim, and Volkery 2007).

Secret funding has been an almost constant, and sometimes substantial, source of party finance in Germany since the Second World War. The largest and oldest such fund was the 'Civic Association', which was set up in 1954, by Christian Democratic chancellor, Konrad Adenauer, a banker, and the head of the Federation of German Industries. From 1969 until 1980, it channelled about 214 million marks, mostly to the CDU, CSU, and FDP, but also, in far smaller amounts, to the SPD (Lersch and Palmer 1999). Sending funds through this intermediary charity allowed full tax deductibility of donations, but also, and perhaps much more importantly, made it very difficult to trace a donation from a business to a party. Indeed, the Civic Association itself did not maintain a direct relationship with the parties, favouring a plethora of foundations and bank accounts in Liechtenstein, Switzerland, and elsewhere. It seems that the Association's funds were not successfully used to influence particular decisions, even though there were some determined attempts (Koss 2011, 80). In the 1970s, the public became aware of the widespread fraud by parties and firms in relation to political donations. In 1975, tax investigations and prosecutions relating to political finance began. Approximately 1,860 cases commenced (Lersch and Palmer 1999). Public protest twice prevented the parties from passing an amnesty for these offences (von Armin 1993, 206). The Flick group was particularly active: it distributed about 26 million marks to all major parties during the 1970s. Its manager, Eberhard von Brauchitsch, called this 'maintenance of the political landscape' (Lersch and Palmer 1999). A parliamentary inquiry began into the Flick scandal, but in 1985 the parties agreed to discontinue it (Walther 2004).

It seems likely that the Civic Association has not raised or transferred new funds to the federal CDU since 1979. Nonetheless, it is still unclear whether large amounts of money collected by the Civic Association continue to be held in bank accounts and are available to German parties (Agence France Presse 2000a; Boenisch et al. 2000; Scherer 2004). The Hesse CDU admitted to falsifying its accounts (Associated Press 2000a; Focus 2000a) and many thought the source of its funds might date back decades to the heyday of the Civic Association and the Flick affair. Since the early 1980s, the Hesse CDU has been drawing on over twenty million marks that had often been transported to banks in Switzerland and Liechtenstein in black briefcases (von Bartsch 2004). This money entered the accounts of the party, disguised as loans or bequests (Agence France Presse 2000a).

The most famous disclosure scandal in German political finance centred on the CDU's Helmut Kohl. He was chancellor from 1982 to 1998 and was credited, inside and outside Germany, with a historic role in German unification. Kohl collected 2.1 million dollars in donations for the CDU between 1993 and 1998. This was less than half of 1 per cent of the annual income of the party (Nassmacher 2001). He did not declare these donations and when they were discovered he stubbornly refused to name their source (Jacobi 2000). Kohl then began a campaign of 'restitution' to raise funds from individual and corporate donors on a personal basis. Some mentioned their appreciation of Kohl's political career, while others expressed concern for the financial health of the CDU itself (Focus 2000b). Kohl's faithful lieutenant, Wolfgang Schäuble, also fell victim to the affair, confessing to taking cash from an arms dealer (AFX 2000). His mishandling of the issue led to his resignation as CDU leader (BM 2000) and his replacement by the current CDU leader and chancellor, Angela Merkel.

The CDU's financial punishment for the 'Donations affair' has been something of a saga. The Bundestag President, Wolfgang Thierse of the SPD, imposed a 41 million mark fine on the CDU for their false financial statement of 1998, equal to the amount of state money they had received (Meyer 2000). He went on to impose a further 7.7 million of sanctions to the value of double undisclosed donations (Associated Press 2000b). This was overruled by the Administrative Court, which held that compliance was merely formal and administrative, since the Political Parties Act says nothing definite about what should happen if a report is inaccurate (von Irion 2001). The CDU and SPD then appeared to do a deal whereby the CDU only had to pay back a figure linked to the value of the undeclared donations (Berliner Morgenpost 2001). Nonetheless, the CDU also appealed this figure (Die Welt 2002). In 2002, the main parties agreed to reform the law to introduce prison terms and fines for party officials who submit inaccurate financial reports (Froehlich 2002). The law also banned donations by companies with greater than 25 per cent public ownership and required the parties to disclose media ownership stakes of greater than 20 per cent, as well as corporate investments (Hamburger Abendblatt 2002). In spite of these recent scandals, it is generally agreed that corruption in contemporary German party politics is a marginal activity (Koss 2011, 86).

3.2 The finances of the German parties

The major parties are under constant financial pressure because of declining votes and membership numbers. Therefore, they support greater state subsidies (von Jungholt and Marx 2007). The CSU is reported to have suffered a serious financial crisis (Focus 2000c). Nonetheless, in contrast to Canadian parties, their financial problems never seem to have been so serious as to threaten the day-to-day operations of a party. German parties indulge in large deficits in election years, but are able to compensate by running surpluses in other years. Incumbency does not seem to bring a financial benefit and neither does the left or the right appear to have a financial advantage. Figure 5.1 shows the annual surplus of the CDU, CSU, and SPD for the sample period of 1992–2005.

In contrast to Canada and Australia, the German press does not report systematic fundraising by parties from business. The FDP seems to compete with the CDU for the donations of medium-sized companies. In 2002, it integrated fundraising into the general election campaign itself. For instance, it asked doctors to pay for FDP posters highlighting the failures of the SPD–Green government in health policy (Henning 2001). Since the 1970s, the major parties have had fairly

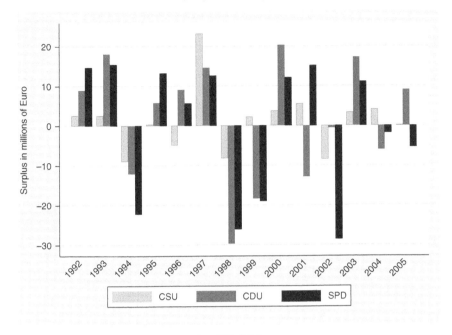

F<small>IGURE</small> 5.1 Annual surplus of German parties, 1992–2005

similar financial models, with most money coming from the state and from their membership. This reflected the CDU's move towards a mass membership model in the 1960s, prior to which it had been reluctant to demand money from members and may have been heavily dependent on business funding (Pridham 1977, 133, 256, 258–66). The disclosure records do not make it clear to which level of a party money was given. The party headquarters are more dependent on state funding than other sections of the parties (Landfried 2000). There are legal provisions for sharing money between richer and poorer states and the federal level (Rademacher 1994). Moreover, district associations have to transfer much of their income from membership dues to the federal level (Fahrun 2005). Candidates are usually expected to make substantial financial contributions to their own electoral campaign (General-Anzeiger 2002b). This is also the practice for lower tier elections (Stuttgarter Zeitung 2002; Schunder 2004; Scheinpflug 2010). Notwithstanding these complexities of party finance, it is widely assumed that larger donations are aimed at the federal level (Clemens 2000, 28).

Figure 5.2 shows the parties' income from legal persons. This includes major donations from business associations and labour unions, as well as from firms. Income from legal persons is of substantial importance to the CSU, amounting to about 10 per cent of income from 1994 to 2005, and over 30 per cent in 1992 and

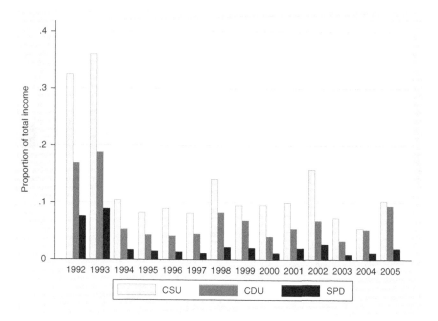

Figure 5.2 German parties' income from legal persons

1993. It also provides a noticeable share of income to the CDU of around 5 per cent, except, again for 1992 and 1993, when it approached 20 per cent. The drop after 1993 is probably related to the removal of tax deductibility from donations by legal persons (Reitz, Barrey, and Oschwald 1993; Rademacher 1994). Legal persons have made only a relatively trivial contribution to the SPD's finances. To some extent, the SPD compensates with income from its extensive media empire, estimated in 2001 to be worth 385 and 510 million euros (Associated Press 2001). In 2002, it transferred about 5 million euro to the party (Hornig et al. 2004).

Income from the sample contributors only exceeded 1 per cent of annual income for the CSU in 1998 and 2002 and for the CDU in 2005. It only exceeded half a per cent for the SPD in 2002 and 2005. Contributions by big business do not seem to have been affected by the tax-deductibility changes. However, as Table 5.1 shows, the payments of individual big businesses are worth more to German parties than they are to Canadian parties. Nonetheless, these payments still seem too low for German firms to have any serious leverage over the parties. The table also demonstrates that the payments are worth less to the German firms than they are to the Canadian or Australian firms, largely because of the giant size of many of the firms in the German sample. The next section investigates the motivations for business financing of parties in Germany.

TABLE 5.1 *Value of payments to firms and parties*

	Proportion of firm income	Proportion of party income
Australia	0.00008	0.01
Canada	0.00004	0.002
Germany	0.00002	0.007

Notes: Firms: Australian measures based on explicitly identified donations, or excluding those sectors most likely to trade with parties, reduce the Australian score to lower than the Canadian figure, but still higher than Germany. Eliminating Australian and Canadian payments to below the German threshold (using the exchange rate) maintains the same clear ranking of countries. Parties: Changing the Australian measure to include only explicitly identified donations reduces the Australian score to slightly below Germany. Excluding those sectors most likely to trade with parties reduces the Australian score to slightly below Canada. Eliminating Australian and Canadian payments to below the German threshold (using the exchange rate) brings Canada up to Germany's level, while extending Australia's lead.

4. MOTIVATIONS FOR CONTRIBUTIONS TO PARTIES

This section uses a large data set to systematically test for different motivations for business contribution to German parties. The CDU and CSU are treated similarly to the Australian Liberal and National parties. They are a permanent electoral coalition; agree on a chancellor candidate; and share control of government. Indeed, after the CDU found itself with a 21 million euro fine to pay after the donation scandal, it received a 2.3 million euro subsidy from its sister party the CSU (Stuttgarter Nachrichten 2007). Payments were registered in only 4.3 per cent of the 4,410 observations of the 315 firms over fourteen years. Fifty-nine firms, almost 19 per cent of the total, made at least one payment in the sample period. Figure 5.3 shows the distribution of *Bias* in the Germany, defined as payments to the SPD as a proportion of payments to the SPD and CDU/CSU.

The vast majority of payments are exclusively to the right, with only a small number hedging or choosing the SPD. Due to the small number of payments and their skewed distribution it was necessary to reduce the number of categories in the dependent variable. The model seeks to explain variation in three categories: no contribution; left-wing contribution or hedge (SPD proportion of annual business payments to the major parties ≥ 0.34); and right (SPD proportion ≤ 0.33). The multinomial logit model includes a binary variable, *Left*, for SPD government. *Years* is the number of years to the next constitutionally mandated election. There is also a measure for the annual *Income* of each firm, logged as usual, as well as sectoral indicators that are not shown. Likelihood ratio tests suggested that dummies for time dependence, poll values from Politbarometer (weighted by the populations of the former East and West Germanies), and interactions of Left and Years did not need to be included.

Table 5.2 presents the results. Income is statistically significant in both equations, and, in line with theory, the coefficients are bigger for the category that

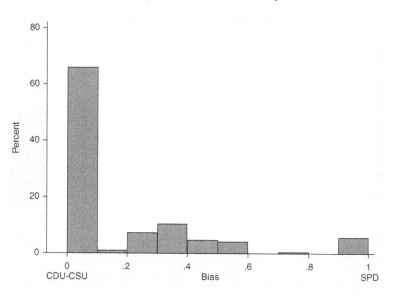

Figure 5.3 Distribution of bias in Germany

Note: 191 Observations; 59 firms. Bias is proportion of reported contributions to the Social Democrats and Christian Democratic Union—Christian Social Union paid to the Social Democrats in a given year.
Source: Iain McMenamin (2012), "If Money Talks, What Does it Say? Varieties of Capitalism and Business Financing of Parties", *World Politics*, volume 64(1), pp1–38, Cambridge University Press.

Table 5.2 *Multinomial logit estimates of firm strategy in Germany*

	RIGHT
LEFT	−0.21
	[0.175]
YEARS	−0.108
	[0.066]
Constant	−4.939
	[0.604]***
	HEDGE/LEFT
LEFT	0.684
	[0.33]**
YEARS	−0.215
	[0.128]*
Constant	−8.14
	[1.272]***
Observations	4410

Robust standard errors, clustered by firm, in brackets. *** = significant at 1%; ** = significant at 5% * = significant at 10%. German incomes imputed from data for 1997, 1998, 1999, 2002, 2005, excluding banks and insurers for which no income figures were available.

TABLE 5.3 *Predicted turnover strategies: Germany*

Right in power	Left in power		
	NON-CONTRIBUTOR	HEDGE/LEFT	RIGHT
NON-CONTRIBUTOR	0.915	0.0114	
HEDGE/LEFT		0.00007	
RIGHT	0.0363	0.0005	0.0012

includes hedging. In Germany financial firms are more likely to contribute to the right and the primary sector is more likely to hedge or give to the left. Years is significant for Left/Hedging, but insignificant for Right. This suggests that ideological payments to the right are not affected by the electoral timetable, but the more pragmatic approach of firms that do not support the left is influenced by the proximity of an election. The Left government coefficient is small and statistically insignificant for contribution to the Right. This can be construed as evidence of the weakness of pragmatic motivations for contributing to the German right. The absence of an incumbency effect on right-wing contributions suggests that many German businesses contribute in order to express their support for right-wing policies rather than hoping for benefits targeted at their own firm. Left-wing government is significantly associated with contributions to the left and hedging. The SPD received its small number of contributions after entering government. Thus, there is evidence for a limited amount of pragmatism.

Following the familiar format, the simulation in Table 5.3 predicts firm strategies in the even of a turnover from left to right. It assumes the mean income and years to an election. The simulations were done sector-by-sector and then aggregated with a weighting for each sector's sample frequency.

The largest category is that of contribution to the Right when in government, followed by no contribution under the Left. It numbers more than three times as many as the next biggest category. Firms pursuing this strategy are comfortable expressing their support for a right-wing government, but feel it is wise to refrain from doing so under the left. Nonetheless, they do not pursue their pragmatic interests by making actual payments to the left. The next biggest category is of non-contributors under the right who hedge or pay to the left, when the left takes power.

The contrast between Germany and the other two cases is stark. The vast majority of German companies do not involve themselves in party finance.[1] The

---

[1] Nominally, Germany has a higher disclosure threshold than the other countries and this complicates cross-national comparison. The German firms had larger incomes than their counterparts in Canada and Australia. If the German threshold is calculated as a proportion of the mean income in the sample, it is barely higher than the Australian and Canadian thresholds. Given that pragmatic firms

ideological category of consistent payments to the right is larger than any of the categories that could be interpreted as indicators of neutrality or left-wing bias. The highest probability relates to firms, which paid to the right under a right-wing government and do not contribute at all under the left. This is actually reminiscent of the behaviour of Australian firms, but it is important to remember that it is on a far smaller scale. These ideological contributions reflect the Christian Democrats' enduring 'anti-left' identity and perhaps also a tradition established when ideological competition was much sharper and the risk of a major change in the business environment was imaginable (Lersch and Palmer 1999; Wiegrefe 2001). A small number of German firms speak the language of ideology, but pragmatism can motivate them to refrain from expressing their preference for the right.

These conclusions are highly consistent with a comparable study of the top 100 firms from 1984 to 2005. Goerres and Hoepner (2011) also found a relatively low contribution rate, predominantly right-leaning donations, and limited hedging. Exploiting more detailed economic data, this research showed that interlocking directorates increase the probability of donations. Donors to the right tended to be family-owned and 'personally interwoven with other large firms'. Hedging was particularly likely in the automobile sector. The German party system is more complicated than the two-party framework used here. To the left of the Social Democrats are the Greens. However, they have reported only occasional business donations. Thus, there is no overestimation of ideological bias, because of their exclusion. To the right (on business matters, at least) of the Christian Democrats and Christian Socials are the Free Democrats, who do attract business donations. Thus, the bias to the right may be greater than that reported above. The chapter continues with a qualitative investigation of motivations.

5. INTERPRETING FINANCING OF PARTIES IN GERMANY

Allegations of links between reported contributions and decisions are rare. A recent example is of the FDP ensuring a reduction in VAT for hotels after receiving a 1.1 million euro donation from the company owning the Mövenpick hotel chain (BM 2010; Maron 2010; Poschardt 2010; Tretbar 2010). This is not the only time a large contribution has caused a problem. The SPD mayor of Wuppertal accepted and reported a €255,000 donation to his almost bankrupt local party from

should undertake a cost-benefit analysis of contributions, this seems like a reasonable approach to assessing differences in thresholds. A more obvious, but less theoretically appealing, alternative is to apply the German threshold on the basis of purchasing-power parity. This reduces the contribution rates for Canada and Australia, but they are still three times that of Germany.

a construction company (von Heimeier 2006b). The Wuppertal District Court held that the developer Uwe Clees expected benefits in relation to various construction projects in the city. Politicians and lawyers judged the payment to have been so large that it could not merely represent support for 'general policy' (von Heimeier 2006a). Similarly large, but secret, contributions have been linked to benefits in other German cities too (Beucker 2006; Richter 2007). Firms are well aware of the costs of perceived impropriety. Daimler-Chrysler announced it was stopping donations until the CDU explained the origin of the donations in the Kohl affair (Fischer 2000). Other smaller companies made similar declarations (Impulse 2000).

German parties do not generally sell access. Indeed, there is only one clear example of the sale of access during the sample period. The North Rhine West-phalian Christian Democrats sold access to regional Prime Minister, Dr Jürgen Rüttgers, at the party's annual congress. The episode exhibits a lot of similarity with Australian and Canadian systems of access and may well have been a conscious attempt at importation. As is common in Australia, there were different levels of access with their own brand. For €5,000, a firm could get a mini-stand and a couple of tickets for the evening event. €16,000 bought the 'Partner Package III', which included the placement of a representative of the firm at one of the top VIP tables, and the opportunity to meet the prime minister and conduct a private conversation with him (Appenzeller et al. 2010). A public relations firm organized the scheme, allegedly without the knowledge of the prime minister, who fired the secretary-general of the party. Australian and Canadian politicians have on occasion reacted to an access controversy in almost exactly the same way. The access payments were classed as 'sponsorship', rather than 'donations', and did not have to be reported. In recent years, sponsorship of conferences has become more important for all parties (Schmale 2010; von Ulla 2010). However, it is usually, but not always (Beikler 2008), transparent, with sponsors often prominently displayed on the internet. Moreover, sponsors receive some space at the conference venue rather than access to senior politicians. Reports on the North Rhine Westphalia CDU agreed that the episode was very unusual. '[T]he 'Rent-a-Rütt-gers' system went far beyond what is usual with other parties' (Schmidt and Wyputta 2010). 'Bundestag President Wolfgang Thierse (SPD) [could] not remember having heard before of similar cases' (Appenzeller et al. 2010). The 'Rent-a-Rüttgers' scandal is not the only time that the fundraising efforts of public relations specialists have caused problems for German politicians. Associations with 'relationship-broker' Mark Hunzinger played an important role in the downfall of Rudolf Scharping of the SPD and Walter Döring of the FDP, as well as the temporary retirement of the Green, Cem Özdemir.

The ideological motivation seems to be taken for granted, partly because it is so deeply ingrained in the German party system. In the early post-war period, donations to the CDU were clearly, and often aggressively, ideological. In one instance, a Hessian mining company used its financial influence to force the

CDU to switch coalition partners from the SDP to the FDP. However, the ideological motivation could also work to the advantage of the CDU. In 1958 the Schleswig-Holestein CDU, faced with a reduction of funds, successfully demanded a continuation of the flow of money on threat of a coalition with the SPD. In an episode remarkably similar to the unification of the Canadian right forty years later, business donors used their financial leverage to force a unification of the small arch-conservative German Party (DP) and the CDU in 1960 (Wiegrefe 2001). In contrast to Australia and Canada, it is hard to find statements from firms that they are supporting the democratic system by contributing to political parties. One such example comes from the spokesman for conglomerate RAG who said, 'We support relevant institutions in the democratic system' (Blorne 2006). The firm has important coal-mining interests and donates to all the major parties except the Greens. Overall, the qualitative evidence backs up the conclusions from the quantitative section.

6. CONCLUSIONS

Business does not play an important role in German political finance. While a good democrat must be vigilant, there is little evidence to suggest a serious threat of German parties becoming dependent on German business. Financial contributions are rare. They are small from a party and a business point of view, whether considered individually or collectively. Ideology is the dominant motivation of the small band of contributing businesses. They consistently express a preference for the right over the social democratic left. This ideological approach is tempered, but only marginally, by pragmatism, as seen in the small number of payments to governing Social Democrats and the abstention of right-wing supporters when faced with a left-wing government.

These clear quantitative patterns are reflected in the emphasis of press coverage, which rarely tried to uncover a pragmatic rationale for business contributions to parties. In Canada and Australia, there was regular and sometimes intense reporting of the system of business contributions to party finance. There is no such genre in the German press. Instead, there was ongoing coverage of regulatory developments and violations. Journalists and politicians acknowledged the exceptionality of the Rüttgers controversy. German businesses cannot reasonably expect to buy access or develop a potentially useful relationship with a political party.

The data set covers a period during which the CDU/CSU alternated with a SPD–Green coalition. It ended with the formation of a Grand Coalition of the CDU and SPD, which ruled from 2005 to 2009, with the CDU's Angela Merkel as chancellor. After the 2009 election, the SPD left government and the CDU continued, but this time in partnership with the liberal Free Democrats. The party system is also in some flux with the Greens threatening to displace the SPD as the main party of the left, and the Free Democrats suffering an evaporation of support that threatens their ability to pass thresholds for election to parliament. While German politics in general has been eventful, in contrast to Australia and Canada, there have been no major recent changes to the political finance regime.

6

Widening the Argument

1. INTRODUCTION

Different varieties of capitalism are associated with the different patterns of business financing of political parties in Australia, Germany, and Canada. This chapter widens the argument to include alternative explanations and additional country cases. It draws some inspiration from the wider literature on political finance and the very general literature on political institutions. Also, by relaxing the constraints of full disclosure, full permissiveness for business financing of parties, and a clear turnover of government, it is possible to gain some relevant evidence from three extra liberal economies, the United States of America, the United Kingdom, and New Zealand as well as two additional co-ordinated economies, Denmark and Norway. The next section briefly recapitulates theories of business financing of parties, emphasizing the role of public funding, the degree of consensus demanded by political institutions, and the polarization of the party system. The following section presents and discusses measures of independent and dependent variables for all eight cases, before assessing each hypothesis in turn. The penultimate section considers how the theory might be applied to dependent market economies.

2. ALTERNATIVE THEORIES OF BUSINESS FINANCING OF PARTIES

As mentioned already, the literature on political finance usually considers business funding from a party perspective. Several authors note the rise of public funding of political parties in recent decades (Katz and Mair 1995, 2009; Casas-Zamora 2005, 4; Koss 2011; Nassmacher 2010). This funding may have replaced business funding of political parties (Nassmacher 2010, 265–6). Perhaps public funding has freed political parties from the often time-consuming and politically costly process of raising money from business. This argument is explicitly targeted at the mix of funding for political parties, rather than the motivation for business funding of parties. Nonetheless, it has an implication for the importance of business funding. Political institutions can inspire a separate theory on the pragmatic business financing of parties. Pragmatic contributions should follow the distribution of power, with hedging where parties share power, and all contributions going to the governing party, where power is concentrated. So, there should be more hedging in consensus democracies. The nature of party competition could also drive business motivations. The more polarized a party system, the more ideological contributions should be expected. Finally, the institutional and party system logics should interact. Polarization should be neutralized by consensual institutions. Therefore, the relatively polarized and majoritarian polities should have a greater predominance of ideological motivations than less polarized and majoritarian systems. Institutions should have a greater effect if polarization is held more or less constant. Polarized consensus democracies should have more hedging than polarized majoritarian states. Similarly, less polarized consensual countries should have more hedging than less polarized majoritarian systems.

Theoretically, economic arguments can centre on the importance of the number of firms in a group or the size of potential policy benefits. Empirically, these two explanations converge on sectoral differences. Sectoral variables did not have a large or consistent effect across the three quantitative studies. While most sectors mattered in Australia, only one in Canada, and one in Germany made a difference. Larger firms tended to hedge in all three countries, but the country with the least hedging, Germany, was also that with the largest firms. The difference between German firm behaviour and that in the two liberal countries is so large that a different distribution of firms across sectors would not affect the overall conclusions. Australia and Canada are much more similar. While both enjoy considerable natural resources, in the Canadian sample primary firms are much better represented than in Australia. Redoing the Australian simulation, but with the Canadian sectoral distribution, does not change the strong contrast between pragmatic Canada and Australia's interaction of pragmatism and ideology. Of course, the dominant sectors influence the overall political and economic context in each country, such that firms in the same sector behave differently from country to country. This insight is not economic, but political-economic. The next section tests the political economy and political approaches on the extended sample of eight countries.

3. EXTRA CASES

This chapter adds five new country cases to those that have already been studied intensively (Table 6.1). Each country meets most, but not all of the case selection criteria put forward in Chapter 2. Therefore, while these cases provide useful data,

TABLE 6.1 *Business financing of parties in eight countries*

	Public funding	Consensus	Polarization	Business funding	Dominant motivations
	(% of party HQ's income)	(Lijphart)	(CMP)	(% of party HQ's income)	
UK	13 for opposition; Tiny for government.	−1.39	9.4	13 Conservative; Tiny for Labour.	Ideology and Pragmatism
US	8	−0.52	36.9	20	Pragmatism and Ideology
Australia	17	−0.67	27.5	25	Pragmatism and Ideology
New Zealand	0	1.25	39.2	Low	Pragmatism
Canada	6.4	−1.07	25.3	50	Pragmatism
Germany	56	0.23	32	7 CDU; 16 CSU; <1 SPD.	Ideology
Denmark	26–82	1.45	49.6	<66 Conservative. Tiny for others.	Ideology
Norway	64–83	0.92	48	Labour 0; Progress 5.1; Conservative 5.5; Centre 2.3; Others <1.	Ideology

Notes: Average public funding of party headquarters for 1980s and 1990s for Canada and Germany from Nassmacher 2010, 319. Germany is average of SPD and CDU/CSU. Canada is average of Liberals and Progressive Conservatives. UK average of Conservatives and Labour for 2001–10 from McMenamin 2011, 1027. Average of ALP and Coalition from Young and Tham 2006, 14. US figure from Ansolabehere, Figueiredo, and Snyder 2003, 108. New Zealand public funding from Geddis 2007, 7. Norwegian public and business funding from Statistics Norway 2010a. Business Funding for UK 2001–10 from McMenamin 2011, 1027. Canada this volume, see p. 000. Australia Young and Tham 2006, 29. Germany Nassmacher 2010, 265. USA: Proportion of corporate contributions of soft money to parties in 1996 (Clawson, Neustadtl, and Weller 1998, 136) multiplied by ratio of hard to soft money of parties in 1998 (Ansolabehere and Snyder 2000, 600). New Zealand from Edwards 2007, 2. Contribution rate for Australia from data set for Commonwealth only. Danish information from Folktinget 2010. Norwegian bias from Statistics Norway 2010b. New Zealand's bias from Elections New Zealand 2008. Consensus democracy scores are for Lijphart's first (executive-parties) dimension from 1971–96 (Lijphart 1999, 312). However, New Zealand's score is estimated from data I calculated for the 2005–8 parliament (EPP = 3, Cabinet = 0; Executive dominance = 2.25; Disproportionality = 0.01; Pluralism = 3). Polarization scores are the difference between the scores of the two largest parties from the Comparative Manifesto Project (Budge and Klingemann 2001, 21; Pontusson and Rueda 2008, 328–9), for the period corresponding to the other data for all countries, except for New Zealand, Denmark, and Norway for which the score is for after 2000.

they also offer weaker evidence than is available for Australia, Canada, and Germany.

New Zealand fits the criteria of formal permissiveness and transparency. The Electoral Act of 1993 requires parties to disclose the identity of donors giving NZ $10,000 or more. However, if the donor is not 'known', the contribution can be listed as 'anonymous'. The law also allows donations by conduit organizations and the splitting of donations amongst 'straw donors' (Geddis 2007, 2). These legal deficiencies, along with the parties' cavalier attitude to other regulations, indicate that the data must be treated sceptically. New Zealand's political economy has always had much in common with Australia, but it is poorer and lacks its larger neighbour's bountiful natural resources. In the 1980s and 1990s, New Zealand undertook economic reforms that surpassed those of Australia (Wailes, Ramia, and Lansbury 2003). New Zealand once epitomized majoritarian Westminster democracy (Lijphart 1999, 21–7), but a change of electoral system in 1996 has brought about fundamental change. The new system is highly proportional; has introduced more parties to parliament; and, most importantly, all governments under the new regime have been minority coalitions. Therefore, New Zealand is now a highly consensual democracy. New Zealand's party competition is moderately polarized. The difference between the two traditional parties, the centre-left Labour and centre-right Nationals is larger than that of consensual Germany, as well as liberal Canada, the UK, and Australia. There is no public funding of the parties, but parliamentary support and broadcasting rights are very important. The largest parties in New Zealand report a handful of donations. In 2007, in the middle of a minority Labour government's term, the parties reported four business donations over the threshold for both Labour and the National party. Three businesses gave identical amounts to each party. Labour's identified business donations were 50 per cent of its income from anonymous sources, while the Nationals' itemized donations were 15 per cent of their income from trusts.[1] Thus, reported bias is very low, but if most of the anonymous and trust fund money comes from business, there is a moderate bias towards the National party. Since parties do not report income, it is impossible to quantify the parties' dependence on business, but Edwards (2007) suspects it is low. The loopholes in the disclosure legislation also make it impossible to calculate a contribution rate, but again the data, and Edwards' impressions, suggest that it is small.

The US has an elaborate system of disclosure, but does not meet the permissiveness criterion. The precise rules of American political finance are constantly changing as fundraising practise, legislation, and jurisprudence interact over time. A similar phenomenon has occurred in Germany (Poguntke 1994, 191), but the US situation is more complex and less stable. Corporate donations to

---

[1] These data are consistent with Edwards' (2007) impression of low bias amongst New Zealand donors.

campaigns are banned, but corporations may sponsor a Political Action Committee, which can make donations up to a low maximum. However, until the Bipartisan Campaign Reform Act of 2002, there has also been the option of 'soft money'. Money for general political activities, other than electioneering, was exempted from the corporate ban and PAC limit. The USA is the paradigmatic example of a liberal market economy (Hall and Soskice 2001, 27–33), but is much less reliant on natural resources than Canada or Australia. Lijphart scores the USA as majoritarian on the executives–parties dimension. Most of his measures do not really suit presidential regimes, and he makes a number of ad hoc adjustments for presidentialism. Obviously, the representative of only one party occupies the presidency and completely controls the executive. However, the president often faces 'divided government', when the other party controls Congress. Even when the president's own party controls Congress, the president is not the dominant figure that a prime minister is under parliamentarism. American legislators compete in candidate-centred elections and fellow party members frequently do not vote together. The different and weaker role of parties in presidential systems requires the application of a similar caveat to the score for polarization. The USA's score is similar to New Zealand's. That the difference between the Democrats and Republicans is bigger than the gap between the big parties in Australia, Canada, Germany, and the UK seems very plausible. The figure for public funding relates to matching funds as a proportion of the total income of parties and candidates in the 1999–2000 election cycle (Ansolabehere, Figueiredo, and Snyder 2003, 108). Again this is a far from perfect analogue to the direct subsidization of party headquarters in party-centred parliamentary regimes, but it does indicate that public subsidy is low without being trivial. The figure for party dependence on business is a good estimate and is the figure most comparable to the other parliamentary cases. The contribution rate of the largest firms was up to 40 per cent in 2000.[2] In spite of the usual problems of comparing the USA to elsewhere, it is clear that the level of participation in political finance is higher than any other case, except perhaps Canada. Businesses contribute to both Democrats and Republicans, but there is also a substantial bias towards the Republicans (Clawson, Neustadtl, and Weller 1998, 139–66; Kim 2008, 6; Hacker and Pierson 2010, 177–8). Incumbent politicians and those holding particularly powerful positions attract more and larger contributions. In the USA, there are large numbers of ideological and pragmatic firms, and also very many motivated by an interaction of ideology and pragmatism.

The UK sets no limits to business contributions, and its disclosure requirements are probably the most rigorous of all the cases examined here. However, since a government turnover is so recent under this regime, it is not possible to make

---

[2] Ansolabehere, Figueiredo, and Snyder (2003, 108) say 60 per cent of the Fortune 500 have Political Action Committees (PACs), but overall 33 per cent of PACs are inactive.

inferences as strong as those from Australia, Canada, and Germany, and to a lesser extent, the USA. The UK is very obviously a liberal market economy. Its membership of the European Union and particular reliance on financial services distinguish it from the other liberal economies considered here. The UK is the archetypical majoritarian Westminster democracy (Lijphart 1999, 10–21). It has the least polarized party system of all those examined here. In the 1990s, the Labour Party, under the determined leadership of Tony Blair and other 'modernizers', completed a decisive move towards the centre, acquiescing to, and championing, many of the market-friendly policies of the Conservative Party. Blair even asserted that Labour was the 'natural party of business' (Coen and Grant 2006, 17). Public funding is provided only to the opposition, on the very reasonable grounds that the governing party has the massive advantage in political communication. This funding provided 25 per cent of the income of the main opposition party, the Conservatives. Income from business provided almost an identical proportion of the Conservatives' income, with the Labour Party only receiving a negligible income from business. The failure of New Labour to gain financial backing from businesses is in stark contrast to the importance of business funding to the centre-left parties of Australia and the United States. In spite of the importance of business funding to the Conservatives, the contribution rate amongst the top 1005 has been tiny since disclosure was introduced (McMenamin 2011, 1032). The Conservatives' income comes from smaller firms. The small number of very large contributing firms has been biased towards the Conservatives. Overall, there is a high level of ideological bias in Britain. However, there are some indications of pragmatism amongst business contributors. In contrast to individual donations, business donations to the Conservatives seem to reflect opinion poll values, and thus the electability of the party. Amongst large firms, Conservative opinion poll leads, and the nearness of an election, increase bias towards the Conservatives. There have been occasional scandals relating to the sale of access by individual politicians (Ivens 2009; Watt 2009; Groves 2010; Nassmacher 2010, 283) and recently the treasurer of the Conservative Party tried to sell access to the prime minister (Syal, Wintour, and Meikle, 2012). Previous research, under a less transparent regime, a Conservative government and a Labour Party with a more left-wing image, has shown a high contribution rate amongst the largest firms (Fisher 1994; Bond 2007). If large firms donate once again to the Conservatives under the current coalition government that will show that it was the change of government, rather than regulatory or party system change that reduced the contribution rate (McMenamin 2011).

Denmark is highly permissive and all donors of over 20,000 Danish crowns (€2,684) must be named, but amounts do not have to be specified. Denmark is a co-ordinated economy (Hall and Gingerich 2009, 139), with a particular reputation for high-quality, low-technology products. It is also noteworthy for 'flexicurity', very high levels of unemployment protection, combined with the lowest level of employment protection amongst co-ordinated economies (Estevez-Abe, Iversen, and Soskice 2001, 165, 168). It is a highly consensual democracy, and a record holder for minority government (Damgaard 2003, 282). Currently the biggest parties are the Venstre (liberal) party, the Social Democrats, the right-wing populists of the People's Party, the Socialist People's Party, and the Conservatives. Public funding provides most of the income of the major parties, with the exception of the Conservatives who also had a substantial income from private contributions in 2007, while junior partners in a coalition with Venstre. Both the Social Democrats and Conservatives reported one business donation over the threshold. The Conservatives reported gaining two thirds of their income from private contributions in 2007. Potentially, this indicates a high dependence on small contributions from business. The contribution rate is probably very small, unless the Conservatives' private income comes mostly from the largest businesses. Again the substantial sub-threshold Conservative income makes bias difficult to assess. If the private income includes a substantial business component, bias is high. Moreover, if ideology and pragmatism interact like in Australia, Conservative supporters might stop donating if their party leaves government.

Norway has a permissive and transparent system of political finance regulation. It is a moderately consensual democracy, more consensual than Germany, but less consensual than New Zealand. It is a co-ordinated economy (Hall and Gingerich 2009, 139) that has benefited from the bonanza of North Sea gas and oil in recent decades. The declining dominance of the Labour Party in recent times has moved Norway towards majoritarianism and the highly corporatist system of interest groups has traditionally been its most consensual feature. Historically, Norway's parties competed on a remarkable six dimensions, with the left–right labour market dimension dominating. Since the divisive referendum on joining the European Economic Community in 1973, electoral volatility has been high (Strøm and Narud 2003, 526). The polarization score is probably somewhat exaggerated as a systemic score. While the social democratic Labour Party and right-wing populist Progress Party are indeed far apart, other smaller parties occupy the centre. Public funding is generous and provides the vast majority of the income of all parties. The Conservative and Progress parties get over 5 per cent of their income from business. Other parties receive much smaller amounts. In 2009, the opposition Conservatives, representing 14 per cent of the electorate at the previous election, reported thirty-one businesses contributing over the threshold of 30,000 crowns (€3,812). The largest opposition party, the Progress Party, with 22 per cent of the vote, also reports several business contributions above the threshold. The other major parties report none. The contribution rate must be low, but depending on the size of the contributing businesses may be similar to Britain's. Bias is obviously high with opposition parties receiving all reported donations. The next section combines the country evidence to test the various explanations.

4. ASSESSMENT

Parties in liberal economies are more dependent on business than parties in co-ordinated economies. In four out of five liberal cases, the average major party receives at least 10 per cent of its income from business. New Zealand is probably a negative case. No party system in a co-ordinated economy depends on business, but, if the German CSU is counted separately, at least one substantial party in each country depends noticeably on business funding. In three out of five liberal economies there are more pragmatic donors than in any of the co-ordinated economies. In all liberal economies there are more pragmatic donors than Denmark or Norway. It is difficult to make reliable inferences from the UK because of the lack of a turnover. However, there is good evidence that pragmatism interacts with ideology for a large proportion of Conservative donors, so it probably has more pragmatic donors than Germany, as well as Norway and Denmark. New Zealand's reported donations suggest it has fewer pragmatic donors than Germany, but more than Norway or Denmark, which have none. However, it is possible that the unreported donations would lift the numbers of pragmatic donors to a level more similar to Germany. In four out of five liberal economies, there are more ideological contributors than in any co-ordinated economy. In Australia, the UK, and the USA there are vastly more ideological donations than in any of the co-ordinated economies. Canada's system of business financing of parties was dominated by pragmatism, but the simulations suggest many more ideological donors than in Germany. This makes sense given the massive difference in contribution rates between the two cases. In New Zealand there is little or no evidence of ideology in contemporary political finance, but again disclosure deficiencies should not be forgotten.

It is difficult to find intra-case variation with which to further test the political economy argument. Again and again, the varieties of capitalism literature emphasizes the deep roots of institutional complementarities. However, Australia and New Zealand went through substantial qualitative change in their political economies that approached an out-of-type change (Kitschelt et al. 1999, 431–2). In both countries there seems to have been a shift away from ideological and towards pragmatic payments and this is consistent with the theoretical argument and cross-case conclusions. However, these profound changes in political economy happened more or less simultaneously with improved transparency and a narrowing of ideological differences between the parties. Clearly, disclosure did not cause a change in political economy or party ideology. There is a good argument for the priority of political economy change over party ideology. A breakdown in the complementarity between existing trade and industrial relations institutions and competitiveness was surely important in bringing about fundamental ideological changes in the Labour parties of both countries. Overall, the distinction between liberal and co-ordinated economies explains the motivations behind contributions, or the lack of contributions, very well.

Public funding is a second potential explanation of cross-national differences in business financing of parties. In four out of five cases of public support below 10 per cent of income, the average major party depends on business for at least 10 per cent of its income. In all three case of public support above 10 per cent, business dependence is below 10 per cent. The clear negative case is New Zealand, which has no public funding and very low business dependence. It is obvious that public funding co-varies strongly with varieties of capitalism. Public funding is higher in the three co-ordinated economies, and lower in four of the five liberal economies, the exception again being New Zealand. Time-series of sources of party income within countries ought to be able to separate public funding from varieties of capitalism. This essentially means looking at co-ordinated economies before and after the introduction of substantial public funding. Public funding is low in liberal countries and does not provide sufficient intra-case variation. In Denmark and Norway, the era of public funding seems to have coincided with an increase in dependence on money from firms (Sundberg 2003, 199; Nassmacher 2010, 266). By contrast, in Germany it is assumed that public funding displaced corporate funding. Indeed, Koss argues convincingly that the right-wing parties pushed for state funding to free themselves from reliance on business (Koss 2011, 110–12). Unfortunately, it is difficult to test this argument straightforwardly because the literature and German law have only intermittently treated firms as a separate category from business associations and wealthy individuals (Nassmacher 2010, 265). In a wider evaluation of a similar hypothesis, Casas-Zamora also found inconclusive evidence (Casas-Zamora 2005, 39). Nassmacher provides no general assessment, but mentions cases that do, and do not, seem to fit the theory (2010, 265–9). Of course, any such evaluation is tricky because of other features of regulation that can change the effect of public funding (Casas-Zamora 2005, 36). Fortunately, Australian federalism provides an excellent laboratory in which to test the impact of public funding on business financing of parties.

South Australia and Tasmania are the only Australian jurisdictions without public funding of elections. Western Australia introduced it in 2006, outside the sample period and Victoria introduced it in 2002, in the middle of the sample period. Queensland and New South Wales had public funding in place at the beginning of the study period. The funding schemes are broadly similar, centred on election expenses (Young and Tham 2006, 39). However, New South Wales is more generous than the others, also providing funding to parties between elections. If public funding replaces business funding, then, all other things being equal, South Australia, Tasmania, and Western Australia, should have higher contribution rates, followed in turn by Victoria, Queensland, and New South Wales. Table 6.2 reports the difference between the sample contribution rate and contribution rates as predicted by the composition of government, years to the election, and interaction of government and years to election and Gross State Product. If the states with no or less public funding have a higher contribution rate all other things being equal, their contribution rates should be underpredicted.

TABLE 6.2 *Public and business funding of parties in Australian states*

	Underprediction as proportion of sample contribution rate
New South Wales	0.03
Victoria	0.47
Queensland	0.47
South Australia	0.46
Western Australia	0.4
Tasmania	−0.57

South Australia has almost the most underpredicted contribution rate, but it is virtually indistinguishable from Victoria and Queensland. Western Australia is part of the same group. Tasmania obviously does not fit the hypothesis. Only its score is overpredicted. The official data on public funding received by the parties fluctuate very considerably, presumably because of elections, as well as the timing and deficiencies of the parties' reports. However, the totals per jurisdiction produce the same ordinal ranking as the regulatory approach used here, and therefore also serve to reject the hypothesis that public funding displaces business funding. The Australian evidence suggests public funding does not displace business funding.

In summary, the varieties-of-capitalism approach does better than public funding. An emphasis on public funding matches the cross-national spread of business dependence quite well, once again excepting New Zealand. However, it is contradicted by intra-case evidence from Denmark and Norway, and well-controlled evidence from Australia. Moreover, variations in public funding do not generate any ideas about the motivations of donors. The varieties-of-capitalism theory suffers from a lot less negative evidence and also explains the motivations of contributors. The co-ordinated economies tend to have greater public funding. All were co-ordinated economies before they introduced public funding and public funding matches the logic that explains why ideological contributions are rarer in co-ordinated than in liberal economies. Parties surely hoped that public funding would stabilize party competition, and perhaps in particular benefit smaller parties that were important coalition partners of larger parties (Nassmacher 2010, 327–30). This would be associated with further reduced policy risk, and thus less need to bolster right-wing parties.

The third approach looks at political institutions. In three out of four consensus democracies, hedging is marginal or non-existent compared to plumping for one party or side of politics. In New Zealand, hedging is the dominant strategy amongst the handful of contributors. Of the four majoritarian countries, only in the UK is hedging unimportant. Strategies do not map onto the distribution of power at a given point in time.

The institutional variation across the Australian states and Commonwealth provides a useful test of the relationship between political institutions and business financing of parties. As in the cross-national analysis, hedging should be more popular in consensual than in majoritarian systems. Also, incumbency and opinion poll effects should be stronger in majoritarian polities. The two outliers in the Australian system are relatively consensual Tasmania and relatively majoritarian Queensland. Tasmania's consensualism is related to its electoral system and the small scale of the society. Tasmania's electoral system is very similar to Ireland's Proportional Representation by the Single Transferrable Vote. Voters rank candidates in multi-member constituencies. This system encourages candidates with a personal following, such as those with 'a high local profile because of their sporting achievements or commercial visibility' (Kellow 2003, 145). This, in turn, leads to a need to negotiate compromises within parties between regional or local interests. Moreover, legislation requires the consent of the Legislative Council, which is dominated by independent members within even more pronounced particularistic loyalties. Rather than programmatic competition, Tasmanian politics has been dominated by a 'parade of parochialism and personalities' (Herr 2002, 584). Thus, policy-making consists of brokerage and compromise, in which it is frequently not sufficient, or even always meaningful, to rely on the support of the government of the day. The distribution of business money fits the consensual account of Tasmanian politics. It is the only Australian polity where hedging is important (see Figure 6.1). Also, a period of Australian Labor Party (ALP) control of government and a commanding lead in opinion polls did not lead to a significant shift towards funding the left. However, the consistent bias towards the Coalition does not sit well with the non-programmatic characterization of Tasmanian politics. By contrast, John Wanna writes, 'More than any other Australian jurisdiction, incumbency in Queensland is characterized by majoritarianism and a "winner takes all" philosophy' (Wanna 2003, 96). It is the only unicameral state; it has an underdeveloped committee system (Wanna 2003, 81); and appointments to the senior public service continue to be highly politicized. This majoritarianism seems to feed into the calculations of pragmatic businesses. Queensland has the smallest proportion of hedging businesses (Figure 6.1). It is the only state where ALP dominance of government and public popularity has been reflected in ALP dominance of business donations. The marginality of Coalition donors in Queensland is remarkable in comparison to the bias towards the Coalition under popular multi-term ALP governments in Victoria, New South Wales, and Western Australia.

The Australian evidence suggests that institutions do influence the calculations of pragmatic firms, but the cross-national evidence suggests no relationship between institutions and firm strategy. Institutions do co-vary with varieties of capitalism. Indeed consensus democracy is one of the institutional configurations that underpin a co-ordinated economy. These patterns suggest that the incentives

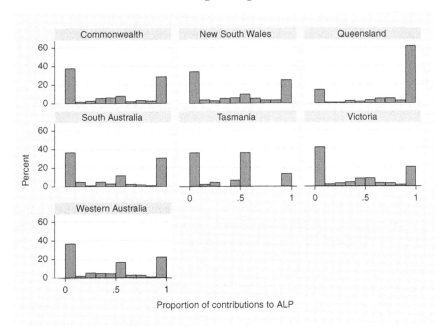

FIGURE 6.1 Bias by Australian jurisdiction

created by co-ordinated political economy are much more powerful than those created by consensual institutions alone.

Finally, the polarization of the party system might explain some of the differences between the cases. Ideological contributions predominate over pragmatism in two out of the four most polarized countries. Pragmatism dominates in two of the four least polarized cases. There are large numbers of ideological donations in the UK, which has the least polarized party system, according to the comparative data. Interactions of institutions and polarization might fare better. Polarization should be neutralized by consensual institutions. Therefore, the relatively polarized and majoritarian USA should have a greater predominance of ideological motivations than less polarized and majoritarian Canada, the UK, and Australia. However, Canada has less ideological behaviour and the UK more than the USA. Institutions might have more effect when controlling for polarization. The relatively polarized consensus democracies of Norway, Denmark, and New Zealand have no greater a tendency towards hedging than polarized majoritarian USA. Similarly, less polarized consensual Germany has no more hedging than less polarized majoritarian Australia, Canada, and the UK.

Explanations based on economic sector, political institutions, or party polarization fare badly in explaining cross-national patterns of business financing of political parties. However, controlling for varieties of capitalism there is evidence

that political institutions can be important. So far this chapter has shown empirically that a political economy approach generalizes well beyond the core cases of
Australia, Canada, and Germany. The next section illustrates theoretically how it
can analyse varieties of capitalism beyond the core Western types of liberal and co-
ordinated economies.

5. DEPENDENT MARKET ECONOMIES IN EAST-CENTRAL EUROPE

This chapter has widened the empirical scope of the research, by including five
other co-ordinated and liberal economies, as well as a number of competing
hypotheses. The varieties-of-capitalism approach fits the new cases and outperforms the competing hypotheses. The new cases did not introduce any radically
different varieties of capitalism. This is an empirical, not a theoretical limit. If
different political economies adapt permissive and transparent regulatory systems,
the variety of capitalism, in particular the nature and extent of competition
amongst firms and the policy risks the political system generates, should also
influence the nature of business involvement in political finance. Leaving aside
hybrids and variants, the literature has so far only proposed one additional variety
of capitalism, the dependent market economies of East-Central Europe.

The distinctive co-ordination mechanism of this political economy is 'dependence on intra-firm hierarchies within transnational enterprises' (Nölke and
Vliegenthart 2009, 680). Capital is provided by foreign direct investment and
foreign-owned banks. Corporate governance consists of control by headquarters in
another country. In industrial relations, transnational enterprises opt for appease-
ment of skilled labour through company-level collective agreements. Investment
in the education and training system is very limited. Innovation is transferred
across borders, but within firms. Countries such as Poland, the Czech Republic,
Slovakia, and Hungary have comparative advantage as assembly platforms for
semi-standardized industrial goods.

A dependent market economy would seem to create limited incentives for
pragmatic or ideological financing of parties. Instead of seeking private goods to
gain an advantage over their competitors within a country, transnational firms can
decide to bring their investment elsewhere. East-Central European economies are
so dependent on foreign capital that they will compete for the investment of
individual firms. If firms perceive a competitive disadvantage, they will opt for
'exit' rather than 'voice'. The dependence on foreign capital also reduces the
policy risk that can motivate ideological payments. Dependency is rooted in the
countries' position in the international economic system, and therefore, regardless
of political rhetoric, general policies that welcome foreign capital are unlikely to

be changed. Receiving business contributions always imposes a political cost. This cost is much higher when a firm is foreign and is likely to be higher still when society is acutely aware of its extreme dependency on foreign capital. Moreover, in Poland, Slovakia, and Hungary moderate nationalist parties have been and are important. Such parties are very quick to capitalize upon any hint that their competitors might be foreigners' lackeys or traitors.

Nölke and Vliegenthart admit that their account of dependent market economies is weak on domestic politics (2009, 673). Given that comparative advantage is concentrated in foreign-owned sectors, domestic firms may have particularly strong incentives to seek private goods from politics by offering to fund political parties. Weak business associations were not in a position to be important representatives of firms (McMenamin 2002), or conduits for their money. Parties' weak membership bases should mean that business financing would be particularly useful. Furthermore, the legacy of communist domination of the economy, and ongoing fundamental reforms, have left many regulations and policies half-formed or inappropriate, thereby creating a potentially large supply of private goods for firms. The strong dependency of the economies on, as well as accession to, and later membership of, the European Union should have minimized policy risk and incentives for ideological contributions. There is some evidence of pragmatic, and beneficial, associations between businesses and politics in East-Central Europe (McMenamin 2004; McMenamin and Schoenman 2007). However, the lack of transparency and/or permissiveness makes it impossible to conduct an empirical study comparable to the others in this book.

6. CONCLUSIONS

This chapter has tested a number of theories that could potentially explain patterns of business financing of political parties. The strongest of these is varieties of capitalism. Theoretically, it explains more dependent variables than any alternative. Empirically, it faces less anomalous evidence. This is not to say that the other approaches have been completely rejected, just that over a number of dependent variables and eight countries they do not perform as well as varieties of capitalism. They may be important in specific times and places. For example, Koss and Nassmacher are probably correct in arguing that public funding has displaced a lot of business funding in Germany. Institutions may not be as powerful as the overall patterns of political economy, but where they vary within one variety of capitalism, they may be important, as appears to be the case in Australia.

It should not be very surprising that varieties of capitalism, a political economy approach, outperforms the alternatives, which are centred on politics or economics alone. Business financing happens at the interface of politics and the economy and it makes sense that it should be impacted by general patterns of how politics and economics interrelate. In the earlier case study chapters, simulations showed that the differences between the countries remained, even if sectoral frequencies were changed to be the same in each country. Firms from the same sector behaved differently in each country. Just as a one-sided political approach is inadequate, so is a one-sided economic approach. Business financing of parties is not best studied with the tools of traditional political finance, or of economics, but is better suited to a political economy approach. The next chapter, the conclusion, explores how this book's analysis can illuminate debates on political corruption and political finance reform.

7

Conclusion: Money is Multi-lingual

1. INTRODUCTION

This book is the first systematic cross-national study of business financing of political parties. The core of its analysis was the three country studies of Australia, Canada, and Germany, based on quantitative and qualitative data spanning several elections. It found that 'money talks' is an unsatisfactory way of thinking about business money in politics. We need to know what money has to say. Money can speak the languages of pragmatism or ideology, and its fluency varies from country to country.

In the liberal market economies, the competitive, short-term focus of firms generated considerable demand for private goods that could help firms develop an advantage over their rivals. Pragmatism was an important motivation for business financing of parties and since pragmatism is embedded in the basic profit-seeking purpose of the firm the contribution rates were impressively high. The preference for less state intervention, and the awareness of the state's power to disrupt the business environment, engendered a widespread awareness of the importance of public policy goods to the overall business sector in Australia. The resulting ideological contributions have made a big difference to the pro-market Liberals in their competition with the centre-left Australian Labor Party. In Canada, the two main parties were pro-business, so there was little policy risk, and relatively few ideological contributions. A more subtle difference between Australia and Canada was the type of pragmatic exchange. The vast majority of business contributions to Canadian parties appear to have been intended as one half of a reciprocal exchange. Better access to policy-makers or a more favourable hearing for lobbyists was expected, but not promised, or guaranteed, at some point in the future. In Australia, perhaps because of the smaller scale of jurisdictions, discrete exchanges of cash for access also seem to be common.

In co-ordinated Germany, the most important policies for firms tend to be the public goods defined, championed, and then partially delivered by business associations. In this context, the pragmatic motivation for contributions to political parties is much weaker. The combination of consensual political institutions and constrained parties means there is a very low risk of major policy change from election to election. So, there is also likely to be low interest in ideological financing of political parties. Since both motivations are undermined by the political economy, the contribution rate is very low.

The difference between co-ordinated and liberal economies also fits the more limited data available for Denmark, Norway, New Zealand, the USA, and the UK. The next best explanation is public funding, but theoretically this explains fewer aspects of behaviour and empirically suffers from more disconfirming evidence. The ideology of political parties, the configuration of political institutions, and the sector of firms fare poorly, unless integrated into a varieties-of-capitalism perspective. This book ends by considering how these conclusions can contribute to the debates on corruption and political reform in established democracies.

2. CORRUPTION AND BUSINESS FINANCING OF PARTIES

This research has several important implications for debates about the potential of business to corrupt the political system. This discussion takes a neo-classical approach to corruption, according to which an understanding of corruption arises from democratic deliberation. A democracy argues about what is the proper use of politics, and what is its abuse, or its corruption. Thus, corruption is a matter of political values, and contested values at that. This is very different to a legal approach to corruption that seeks to adjudicate on which behaviours are, or are not corrupt, but assumes that the definition of corruption is self-evident and politically uncontested. These seemingly abstract concerns about definition capture much of the debate about business financing of parties. Indeed, they also illuminate many of the shortcomings of such debates. Discussion of business financing of parties is dominated by two positions, both of which have been rejected in this book. The first is that business cash in politics is bribery and the second is that it has no influence. Unhelpfully, those who talk of bribery frequently mean influence and those who dismiss worries about business influence mean there is no bribery. Some people think it is an abuse of the political system to allow its penetration by private interests, while others think penetration by private interests is inevitable, or even desirable, unless they can directly buy decisions. So, this is a debate about political values. However, it is also a controversy about political behaviour. One of this book's aims has been to propose a way of structuring such a debate. As such, it does not proclaim what is and is not corrupt. Instead, it shows how democracies might relate their political values to the types of behaviours prevalent in their political systems.

3. POLITICAL AND ECONOMIC IMPLICATIONS

In Germany, business financing of parties does not seem to threaten any sort of systematic corruption. German business money in politics speaks ideologically, but does not amount to remotely enough to bias the political system to the right. This ideological motivation limits incentives for the right-wing parties to deliver concrete benefits to individual businesses. So, corruption as an abuse of power for private, rather than public interest is not caused by business financing of politics. In Canada, business financing of parties could have been construed as a potential source of systematic corruption of the political system. Canadian business money spoke the language of pragmatism. It seems likely business financing of parties was one half of a system of reciprocal exchange. Regular contributors could expect to develop a relationship with a party and key individuals therein. Compared with otherwise identical non-contributors, they could expect a better opportunity to lobby for private goods and also could expect a higher likelihood of success. Given how lucrative political decisions can be, any small, but real, increase in probabilities of access and success made payments and the associated socializing a worthwhile investment. This was not bribery. There was no direct exchange of money for a decision. Moreover, it was, probably intentionally and definitely conveniently, difficult, or impossible, to link a business payment and policy gain. Reciprocity reduced the visibility of the exchange, and the vital political costs, to the extent that accepting small amounts of money made sense for the political parties. Indeed, these exchanges became so widespread that Canadian parties depended on business for half their incomes. Reciprocal exchange can be construed as corruption. The political system is abused because the private interests of contributing firms were considered instead of, or in addition to, the public interest.

In Australia, business cash is bilingual. The languages of pragmatism and ideology are both important. Ideological payments give an important advantage to the Liberal–National Coalition, one that makes a substantial difference to their finances. This could be interpreted as corruption in the wide sense of a small number of people and organizations tilting political competition towards their own view of society, regardless of the preferences of the majority of voters. It might also be viewed as good for democracy, as the advantage the Coalition receives from business can counterbalance the union funding that only the Australian Labor Party receives. This fits in with the generally utilitarian view of political parties in Australia (McAllister 2002). Of course, it can be argued that businesses represent one share, one vote, while unions operate according to one member, one vote and therefore do not violate political equality, which is a basic principle of democracy. Pragmatic money speaks more loudly than ideological money in Australian political finance. Both parties receive pragmatic business donations. As in Canada, reciprocal exchange is an important way of raising money by offering benefits, while minimizing political costs. However, there are good reasons to believe discrete exchanges are much more prevalent in Australia. Pragmatic plumping for one party suggests a short-term aim of discrete exchange, rather than a medium-term aim of reciprocal exchange. The difference in contribution rates is a little harder to interpret. Canada's higher rate might suggest that contributions are more valuable. On the other hand the higher rate might represent the need to build up reciprocity over time, versus the possibility of a discrete exchange in Australia. Business money in Australia facilitates a widespread and quite direct opportunity to pursue private goods. For those who see politics as concerned with public, rather than private goods, this is an abuse of the political system and a type of corruption. Even for those who see politics as a way of distributing private goods, few would see financial contributions to parties as a valid influence on political decisions.

Business financing of parties should also have economic consequences in liberal economies. In a liberal economy, ideological contributions should serve to protect the coherence of the liberal model by increasing the volume of free market voices in the debate on economic policy. However, pragmatic contributions should undermine the liberal model, by incentivizing competition on the basis of political connections rather than business efficiency. Finally, political action, not just political debate, is considered.

4. POLITICAL REFORM

This research is also relevant to would-be political reformers. The nature of a co-ordinated economy means that public goods are comparatively more important to firms than they are in liberal economies. It may be harder for politicians to target private goods at a firm, but it is still possible. Private goods may be less valuable than in a liberal market economy, but they can still boost profits. So, it could be that the introduction of disclosure of business financing increases political costs sufficiently and reduces the value of private goods sufficiently to largely remove pragmatic financing from the political economy. The case for disclosure is straightforward in a co-ordinated economy. If disclosure can minimize both pragmatic and ideological financing, there is little reason to introduce bans or limits on business funding. Indeed, such measures might even reintroduce much more dangerous exchanges hidden from public view. Public funding also tends to be much higher in co-ordinated economies, and while it seems to have reduced dependence on business in some countries, the overall picture is difficult to assess. However, like disclosure, it costs very little in comparison to a state's total budget and might be able to contribute to the alleviation of party dependence on business.

In a liberal economy, disclosure surely increases the political costs of pragmatic donations, thereby reducing the contribution rate, the ratio of pragmatic to ideological contributions, and the ratio of discrete to reciprocal exchanges. However, this book has presented very strong evidence that disclosure is unlikely to end widespread pragmatism. A reduction in relatively easily observable discrete exchanges probably signals a shift towards reciprocal exchange, which reduces visibility, and political costs, under conditions of high transparency. Moreover, discrete exchanges can remain important even when disclosure levels are high. This is perhaps most likely to happen in relatively small-scale polities, in which small numbers of business contributions make up a noticeable proportion of a party's income. Limits on contributions should manage the virtual elimination of discrete exchanges, but the logic of reciprocal exchange can still apply when payments are very small. In liberal economies, too, bans risk moving some activity into the illegal or a-legal zone, where much more dubious exchanges may take place. Nonetheless, in the context of a strong rule of law, like all the countries studied in this book, a ban is likely to immediately remove business financing of parties as an important part of the political system. Pragmatic incentives are higher in liberal than co-ordinated economies and some firms may seek to donate to parties illegally or through roundabout channels that evade the law. Nonetheless, the potential political cost of engaging in such activity will be very high for politicians, as will be the potential reputational cost for larger and better-known companies. Public funding is a less drastic way of reducing the impact of business money on politics. However, it is difficult to know what impact it would have in liberal contexts. It has reduced dependence on business in some co-ordinated economies, but not in others. No liberal economy studied here has really substantial public funding and the evidence from Australia is not encouraging. Of course, public funding has other disadvantages, such as reduced competition amongst parties (Katz and Mair 1995, 2009), but this is also disputed (Nassmacher 2010).

These are attempts to predict what consequences reforms of the political finance regime might have. Of course, whether they are desirable depends not only on the normative question of whether ideological and pragmatic business financing are corrupt phenomena, but also on how prevalent the two motivations are in a given political economy. For example, the Canadian ban of 2004 was aimed at pragmatic financing and was not expected to disadvantage either of the two main parties more than the other. The introduction of low limits in Ireland, which has also traditionally been dominated by two pro-business centrist parties, probably had a similar effect. If, as the limited data suggest, business does treat New Zealand's parties equally, a ban or low limit might also be a straightforward proposition. A ban in Britain would be very different, as it would target ideological payments, and probably give the Labour Party a structural financial advantage. Bans in the US or Australia would also disadvantage one party more than the other, but would hopefully end pragmatic exchanges that pervade both major parties in the two countries.

A wave of disclosure regulations has swept across states that permit unlimited business financing of political parties. This means there will soon be opportunities to conduct research like this in other countries. None of the variables used in the quantitative analysis are idiosyncratic to the case study countries. Moreover, the concepts that dominate the qualitative analysis are often found in the literature on US campaign finance. Controversies will surely arise in these countries and they will probably be conducted at cross-purposes like they have in those systems with long-established transparency. Therefore, it should be possible to carry out research, clarify corruption debates, and analyse political reform proposals using the logic of this book. 'Money talks' is not a truism. It is a normatively important empirical question.

Appendix 1

TABLE A1 *Legal transparency and permissiveness of political finance regimes*

	Disclosure of contributions by parties	Corporate donations	Unlimited donations
Australia	Yes	Yes	Yes
Canada (pre-2004)	Yes	Yes	Yes
Cape Verde	Yes	Yes	Yes
Colombia	Yes	Yes	Yes
Denmark	Yes	Yes	Yes
Ecuador	Yes	Yes	Yes
Georgia	Yes	Yes	Yes
Germany	Yes	Yes	Yes
Ghana	Yes	Yes	Yes
Latvia	Yes	Yes	Yes
Lesotho	Yes	Yes	Yes
Moldova, Republic of	Yes	Yes	Yes
Namibia	Yes	Yes	Yes
Netherlands	Yes	Yes	Yes
New Zealand	Yes	Yes	Yes
Nicaragua	Yes	Yes	Yes
Norway	Yes	Yes	Yes
Papua New Guinea	Yes	Yes	Yes
Peru	Yes	Yes	Yes
Seychelles	Yes	Yes	Yes
Singapore	Yes	Yes	Yes
Thailand	Yes	Yes	Yes
United Kingdom	Yes	Yes	Yes
Venezuela	Yes	Yes	Yes
Argentina	Yes	Yes	No
Armenia	Yes	Yes	No
Belgium	Yes	Yes	No
Bolivia	Yes	Yes	No
Brazil	Yes	Yes	No
Costa Rica	Yes	Yes	No
Ireland	Yes	Yes	No
Italy	Yes	Yes	No
Japan	Yes	Yes	No
Lithuania	Yes	Yes	No
Niger	Yes	Yes	No
Russian Federation	Yes	Yes	No

(*Continued*)

TABLE A1 Contined

	Disclosure of contributions by parties	Corporate donations	Unlimited donations
Spain	Yes	Yes	No
Ukraine	Yes	Yes	No
Albania	Yes	No	
Andorra	Yes	No	
Antigua and Barbuda	Yes	No	
Benin	Yes	No	
Bosnia and Herzegovina	Yes	No	
Bulgaria	Yes	No	
Canada (2004 onwards)	Yes	No	
Chile	Yes	No	
Czech Republic	Yes	No	
Estonia	Yes	No	
France	Yes	No	
Hungary	Yes	No	
Israel	Yes	No	
Mali	Yes	No	
Mexico	Yes	No	
Paraguay	Yes	No	
Poland	Yes	No	
Portugal	Yes	No	
Romania	Yes	No	
São Tomé and Principe	Yes	No	
United States	Yes	No	
Belarus	Yes		
Austria	No		
Azerbaijan	No		
Bahamas	No		
Bangladesh	No		
Barbados	No		
Belize	No		
Botswana	No		
Burkina Faso	No		
Central African Republic	No		
Cyprus	No		
Dominica	No		
Dominican Republic	No		
El Salvador	No		
Fiji	No		
Finland	No		
Grenada	No		
Guatemala	No		
Guyana	No		
Honduras	No		
Iceland	No		
India	No		
Jamaica	No		

Table A1 Contined

	Disclosure of contributions by parties	Corporate donations	Unlimited donations
Kiribati	No		
Madagascar	No		
Malawi	No		
Malaysia	No		
Malta	No		
Marshall Islands	No		
Mauritius	No		
Micronesia, Federated States of	No		
Morocco	No		
Mozambique	No		
Palau	No		
Panama	No		
Saint Kitts and Nevis	No		
Saint Lucia	No		
St Vincent and the Grenadines	No		
Samoa	No		
San Marino	No		
Senegal	No		
Sierra Leone	No		
Slovakia	No		
Solomon Islands	No		
South Africa	No		
Sweden	No		
Switzerland	No		
Tanzania, United Republic of	No		
Trinidad and Tobago	No		
Tuvalu	No		
Uganda	No		
Uruguay	No		
Vanuatu	No		
Zambia	No		

Appendix 2: Descriptive Statistics

TABLE A2 *Income: Australia*

Mean	S.D.	Minimum	Maximum
1.51	3.7	0.147	40.85

Metric is billions of Australian dollars.

TABLE A3 *Categorical variables: Australia (per cent)*

Australian Labor Party government	78
Non-contributors	90
Hedge	2
Coalition contributions	4
Labor contributions	4
Construction and infrastructure	8
Financial intermediation	12
Manufacturing	33
Primary	4
Real estate, renting, and business activities	15
Wholesale and retail	28

Sectors are amalgamations of the UN ISIC classification.

TABLE A4 *Income: Canada*

Mean	S.D.	Minimum	Maximum
1 472 989	3 402 493	−286	4.49e + 07

Metric is thousands of C$

TABLE A5 *Categorical variables: Canada (per cent)*

Liberal government	53
Non-contributors	49
Hedge	19
Progressive Conservative contributors	15
Liberal contributors	17
Construction and infrastructure	15
Financial intermediation	12
Manufacturing	29
Primary	27
Real estate, renting, and business activities	9
Wholesale and retail	10

Sectors do not total to 100 due to rounding. Sectors are amalgamations of the UN ISIC classification.

TABLE A6 *Income: Germany*

Mean	S.D.	Minimum	Maximum
0.6324397	1.037568	−1.101168	14.47132

Metric is standardized according to income of non-banking observations.

TABLE A7 *Categorical variables: Germany (per cent)*

Social Democratic Government	50
Non-contributors	96
Hedge/SDP	1
CDU–CSU contributors	3
Construction and infrastructure	10
Financial intermediation	18
Manufacturing	38
Primary	3
Real estate, renting, and business activities	10
Wholesale and retail	21

Sectors are amalgamations of the UN ISIC classification.

References

AAP (1991), 'The ultimate disgrace for a top cop', *The Advertiser*, 6 August.

AAP (1998), 'Liberal Party tops the fund raising stakes', *AAP Newsfeed*, Nationwide General News, 2 February.

AAP (2007), 'Top Lib slates businesses for equal party donations', *The Canberra Times*, 25 June, p. 7.

AFX (2000), 'CDU-Krise Schauble-Entschuldigung—Ausschuss will alles prufen', *AFX-TD News*, 20 January.

Age, The (2001), 'A guide to the subtle art of giving but not revealing', *The Age*, Late Edition, 14 February, p. 13.

Agence France Presse (2000a), 'Kiep: Hessen-CDU-Gelder eventuell aus Staatsbuerger-licher Vereinigung—Ex-Schatzmeister sagt vor Wiesbadener U-Ausschuss aus (mit Vernehmung Staatsanwaltschaft)', *Agence France Presse—German*, 29 November.

Agence France Presse (2000b), 'Die Koepfe des Jahres', *Agence France Presse—German*, 18 December.

Alberts, Sheldon (1994), 'Chrétien's private fund-raiser evokes memories of Mulroney', *Calgary Herald*, 5 November, p. A7.

Allen, Gene (1989a), 'Questions of influence: politicians, developers and land', *The Globe and Mail*, 16 September.

Allen, Gene (1989b), 'Charity used as channel for donations, inquiry told', *The Globe and Mail*, 3 October.

Ansolabehere, Stephen and Snyder, Jr., James M. (2000), 'Soft Money, Hard Money, Strong Parties', *Columbia Law Review* 100(3): 598–619.

Ansolabehere, Stephen, de Figueiredo, John M., and Snyder, James M. (2003), 'Why is There so Little Money in U.S. Politics?', *Journal of Economic Perspectives* 17(1): 105–30.

Appenzeller, G., Funk, A., Sirleschtov, A., and Zurheide, J. (2010), 'Wie gesehen, so gekauft; NRW-Ministerpräsident Jürgen Rüttgers (CDU) wird Käuflichkeit vorgeworfen. Was ist passiert?', *Der Tagesspiegel*, 23 February, p. 2.

Appollonio, Dorie and La Raja, Raymond (2004), 'Who Gave Soft Money? The Effect of Interest Group Resources on Political Contributions', *Journal of Politics* 66(4): 1134–54.

Associated Press (2000a), 'Neuer Hoehepunkt in CDU-Parteispendenaffaere; Zusammen-fassung Darstellung der hessischen CDU zu Vermaechtnissen falsch- Schaeuble beruft Kommission ein; SPD legt Zeugenliste fuer Untersuchungsausschuss vor', *Associated Press World Stream—German*, 14 January.

Associated Press (2000b), 'Thierse streicht der CDU 7,7 Millionen Mark Staatsgelder-Erste Zusammenfassung Strafe auch fuer Schreiber-Million', *Associated Press World Stream—German*, 1 December.

Associated Press (2001), 'CDU/CSU will der SPD Medienbeteiligungen gesetzlich verbie-ten Unionsfraktion legt Entwurf eines neuen Parteiengesetzes vor; Barspenden ueber 1.000 Euro sollen verboten warden', *Associated Press World Stream—German*, 16 July.

Atkinson, Michael M. and Thomas, Paul G. (1993), 'Studying the Canadian Parliament', *Legislative Studies Quarterly* 18(3): 423–51.

Australian Government (2008), *Electoral Reform Green Paper: Donations, Funding and Expenditure*, December.

Bachelard, Michael, Baker, Richard, and Millar, Royce (2007), 'Taking their toll', *The Age*, First Edition, News, 14 May, p. 9.

Baker, Richard (2006), 'Are our politicians for sale? Focus—political donations', *The Age*, First Edition, News, 24 May, p. 15.

Baker, Richard and Bachelard, Michael (2007), 'Show me the money: campaign funding', *The Age*, First Edition, Insight, 3 February, p. 5.

Baxter, James (2000), 'Alliance broadening appeal: new party to appeal to Bay Street', *Windsor Star*, 31 January, p. B2.

Beck, Nathaniel, Katz, Jonathan, and Tucker, Richard (1998), 'Taking Time Seriously: Time-Series-Cross-Section Analysis with a Binary Dependent Variable', *American Journal of Political Science* 42(4): 1260–88.

Behrens, Peter-Alberto (2002), 'Germany: Public Affairs Reinvented', *Journal of Public Affairs* 2(3): 173–6.

Beikler, Sabine (2008), 'Bürgermeisterin Wanjura wird Fall für den Staatsanwalt; Berlins Korruptionsbeauftragter Fätkinhäuer will Umgang mit Spenden prüfen CDU-Politikerin weist die Vorwürfe von SPD, FDP und Grünen zurück', *Der Tagesspiegel*, 31 January, p. 12.

Bélanger, Éric (2003), 'Issue Ownership by Canadian Political Parties, 1953–2001', *Canadian Journal of Political Science* 36(3): 539–58.

Bell, Stephen (1995), 'Between the Market and the State: The Role of Australian Business Associations in Public Policy', *Comparative Politics* 28(1): 25–53.

Bell, Stephen (2006), 'A Victim of its Own Success: Internationalization, Neoliberalism, and Organizational Involution at the Business Council of Australia', *Politics and Society* 34(4): 543–70.

Ben-Amar, Walid and André, Paul (2006), 'Separation of Ownership from Control and Acquiring Firm Performance: The Case of Family Ownership in Canada', *Journal of Business Finance and Accounting* 33(3–4): 517–43.

Bennett, Robert J. (1999), 'Business Routes of Influence in Brussels: Exploring the Choice of Direct Representation', *Political Studies* 47(2): 240–57.

Berliner Morgenpost (2001), 'Meldungen', *Berliner Morgenpost*, 3 March.

Bernard, Prosper H. (2008), 'Varieties of Capitalism and Inequality: Canada from a Comparative Perspective', *Journal of Humanities and Social Sciences* 2(2): 1–17.

Beucker, Pascal (2006), 'Genosse vor Gericht; Der Kölner SPD-Spendenskandal geht in eine weitere Runde: Jetzt ist Ex-Oberstadtdirektor Heugel dran', *Die Tageszeitung*, 3 May, p. 1.

Bildstein, Craig (2006), 'Libs want MPs to help pay for next election', *The Advertiser*, State Edition, News, 8 April, p. 7.

Bird, Heather (1988a), 'Why Liberal debt problems persist', *The Toronto Star*, 23 January, p. D3.

Bird, Heather (1988b), 'Federal parties hope money can help buy voters' love', *The Toronto Star*, p. D6.

Birnbauer, Bill (1996), 'Liberal cash overwhelms ALP message', *The Age*, Late Edition, News, 28 March, p. 8.

Birnbauer, William (2007), 'How business muscles in on parties: political donations—democracy at work', *Sunday Age*, First Edition, News, 11 February, p. 5.

Blome, Nikolaus (2006), 'RAG kassiert Subventionen und spendet an Parteien; 170000 Euro an SPD und CDU—Grüne wollen Rechnungshof befassen—Anzeigenkampagne gerügt—Milliarden-Beihilfen für Steinkohle', *Die Welt*, 4 April.

BM (2000), 'Schäuble will nicht aufgeben; Merkel und Wulff kündigen personelle Konsequenzen an', *Berliner Morgenpost*, 17 January.

BM (2010), 'HotelierSpende; Westerwelle bestreitet Vorwurf der Käuflichkeit', *Berliner Morgenpost*, 19 January.

Boatright, Robert J. (2012), 'The End of the Reform Era? Campaign Finance Retrenchment in the United States and Canada', *The Forum: A Journal of Applied Research in Contemporary Politics*, forthcoming.

Boenisch, Georg, Dettmer, Markus, Hildebrandt, Tina, Krach, Wolfgang, Mascolo, Georg, Palmer, Hartmut, Schimmoeller, Heiner, Schmidt-Klingenberg, Michael, Schreiber, Sylvia, and Schumacher, Hajo (2000), 'Die verlogene Ehre', *Der Spiegel*, 24 January, p. 24.

Bollmann, Ralph (2001), 'Der Zweck heiligt die Mittel; Als Teile eines Verfassungsorgans werden Fraktionen vom Staat finanziert. Parteien müssen als Zusammenschlüsse von Bürgern ihr Geld selbst verdienen', *Die Tageszeitung*, 8 May.

Bond, Matthew (2007), 'Elite Social Relations and Corporate Political Donations in Britain', *Political Studies* 55(1): 59–85.

Boothby, Daniel and Drewes, Torben (2006), 'Postsecondary Education in Canada: Returns of University, College and Trades Education', *Canadian Public Policy* 32(1): 1–22.

Borland, Jeff (1996), 'Education and the Structure of Earnings in Australia', *Economic Record* 72(219): 370–80.

Brown, W. (1999), 'Party funding and other touchy political issues', *Courier Mail*, Perspectives, 5 February, p. 17.

Budge, Ian and Klingemann, Hans-Dieter (2001), 'Finally! Comparative Over-Time Mapping of Party Policy Movement', in Ian Budge, Hans-Dieter Klingemann, Andrea Volkens, Judith Bora, and Eric Tanenbaum (eds.), *Mapping Policy Preferences: Estimates for Parties, Electors, and Governments, 1945–1998* (Oxford: Oxford University Press), pp. 19–50.

Burris, Val (2001), 'The Two Faces of Capital: Corporations and Individual Capitalists as Political Actors', *American Sociological Review* 66(3): 361–81.

Byfield, Joanne (2003), 'More central control: Chrétien's campaign finance bill further erodes public influence in federal politics', *Citizens Centre Report Magazine*, 30(10).

Cadegan, Ernest (2000), 'Tories don't interest us: media is obsessed with PCs, who barely register on our minds', *The Halifax Daily News*, 28 September, p. 21.

Cairns, Alan C. (1994), 'An Election to Be Remembered: Canada 1993', *Canadian Public Policy* 20(3): 219–34.

Canadian Press Newswire (1995), 'Former premier says NDP should call inquiry into fundraising group', *Canadian Press Newswire*, 14 October.

Canberra Times (2007), 'Political bribery rampant analysis', *Canberra Times*, 2 February.

Carlisle, Tamsin (1988), 'Turner hurts Albert fund raising', *The Financial Post*, 24 August, p. 12.

Carney, Shaun (1994), 'Flogging the wrong horse', *The Age*, Late Edition, News, 24 May, p. 17.

Carpentier, Cécile, L'Her, Jean-François, and Suret, Jean-Marc (2010), 'Stock Exchanges and Markets for New Ventures', *Journal of Business Venturing* 25(4): 403–22.

Carroll, William (2007), 'From Canadian Corporate Elite to Transnational Capitalist Class: Transitions in the Organization of Corporate Power', *Canadian Review of Sociology and Anthropology* 44(1): 265–88.

Carty, R. Kenneth (2002), 'The Politics of Tecumseh Corners: Canadian Political Parties as Franchise Organizations', *Canadian Journal of Political Science* 35(4): 723–45.

Carty, R. Kenneth (2003), 'Canada's Nineteenth Century Cadre Parties at the Millennium', in Paul Webb, David Farrell, and Ian Holliday (eds.), *Political Parties in Advanced Industrial Democracies* (Oxford: Oxford University Press), pp. 345–78.

Casas-Zamora, Kevin (2005), *Paying For Democracy: Political Finance and State Funding for Political Parties* (Colchester: European Consortium for Political Research Press).

Casper, Steven (2001), 'The Legal Framework for Corporate Governance: The Influence of Contract Law on Company Strategies in Germany and the United States', in Peter Hall and David Soskice (eds.), *Varieties of Capitalism: The Institutional Foundations of Comparative Advantage* (Oxford: Oxford University Press), pp. 387–416.

Casper, Steven, Lehrer, Mark, and Soskice, David (2009), 'Can High-Technology Industries Prosper in Germany? Institutional Frameworks and the Evolution of the German Software and Biotechnology Industries', in Bob Hancké (ed.), *Debating Varieties of Capitalism: A Reader* (Oxford: Oxford University Press), pp. 200–20.

Castello, Renato (2008), '$1100 to meet ALP business shells out for 'exclusive access' dinners', *Sunday Mail*, News, 27 April, p. 12.

Center for Responsive Politics (2011a), *Heavy Hitters: AT&T Inc.* http://www.opensecrets.org/orgs/summary.php?id=D000000076

Center for Responsive Politics (2011b), *111th Congress Earmarks*. http://www.opensecrets.org/earmarks/index.php

Cepeda Ulloa, Fernando (2005), 'Financing Politics in Colombia', in Carlos Malamud and Eduardo Posada-Carbó (eds.), *The Financing of Politics: Latin American and European Perspectives* (London: Institute for the Study of the Americas).

Chamberlin, Paul (1995), 'MP access fund-raiser defended', *The Age*, Late Edition, News, 24 October, p. 5.

Chaples, Ernest A. (1994), 'Developments in Australian Political Finance', in Herbert Alexander and Rei Shiratori (eds.), *Comparative Political Finance among the Democracies* (Oxford: Westview Press), pp. 29–40.

Chapman, Bruce, Rodrigues, Mark, and Ryan, Chris (2008), 'An Analysis of FEE-HELP in the Vocational Education and Training Sector', *Australian Economic Review* 41(1): 1–14.

Charlton, P. (1992), 'The race for hearts and minds (...and votes)', *Courier Mail*, 5 December.

Chester, Lynne (2011), 'Another variety of capitalism? The Australian mode of *régulation*'. Paper presented at the Conference of the Association for Heterodox Economics, Nottingham, 6–9 July.

Chrétien, Jean (2007), *My Years as Prime Minister* (Toronto: Alfred Knopf).

Clark, Campbell and Mackie, Richard (2003), 'Bay Street forks out over €2.7 million for Martin', *The Globe and Mail*, 10 December, p. A1.

Clark, Marc (1986), 'P.S. send money', *Maclean's*, 8 September.

Clark, Pilita and Glendinning, Lee (2001), 'Party leaders pledge end to donation rorts', *Sydney Morning Herald*, News and Features, 14 June, p. 1.

Clawson, Dan and Neustadtl, Alan (1989), 'Interlocks, PACs, and Corporate Conservatism', *American Journal of Sociology* 94: 749–73.

Clawson, Dan, Neustadtl, Alan, and Weller, Mark (1998), *Dollars and Votes: How Business Campaign Contributions Subvert Democracy* (Philadelphia: Temple University Press).

Clemens, Clay (2000), 'A Legacy Reassessed: Helmut Kohl and the German Party Finance Affair', *German Politics* 9(2): 25–50.

Clennell, Andrew (2007a), 'Politicians sup at the table with hoteliers', *Sydney Morning Herald*, First Edition, News and Features, 13 February, p. 1.

Clennell, Andrew (2007b), 'Odds fall on new casino for NSW', *Sydney Morning Herald*, First Edition, News and Features, 20 August, p. 1.

Clennell, Andrew (2007c), '$10,000 secures a Iemma Christmas invite', *Sydney Morning Herald*, First Edition, News and Features, 13 November, p. 3.

Clennell, Andrew (2008), 'Anger at Iemma's lopsided war chest', *Sydney Morning Herald*, First Edition, News and Features, 28 January, p. 1.

Clennell, Andrew, Smith, Alexandra, and Robins, Brian (2008), 'MP took year to declare $65,000', *Sydney Morning Herald*, First Edition, 5 March, p. 2.

Coen, David (1997), 'The Evolution of the Large Firm as a Political Actor in the European Union', *Journal of European Public Policy* 4(1): 91–108.

Coen, David and Grant, Wyn (2006), 'Managing Business and Government Relations', in David Coen and Wyn Grant (eds.), *Business and Government: Methods and Practice* (Opladen: Barbara Budrich), pp. 13–22.

Cohen, David (2007), 'The strife of Brian: Focus—WA politics', *The Age*, First Edition, News, 28 February, p. 11.

Cohn, Martin (1987), 'Fundraising curbs urged by Quebec tory MPs', *The Toronto Star*, 9 February, p. A1.

Colebatch, Tim (2000), 'Donations go coalition's way', *The Age*, Late Edition, 2 February, p. 2.

Colebatch, Tim (2007), 'Politics, a rule-free zone', *The Age*, First Edition, News, 13 March, p. 11.

Colebatch, Tim and Austin, Paul (2007), 'Where to draw the line?', *The Age*, First Edition, Insight, 17 March, p. 1.

Conradt, David (1996), *The German Polity*, 6th edn. (White Plains, NY: Longman).

Coorey, Philip (2008), 'Disclosure level to be slashed: party donations—ALP in crisis', *Sydney Morning Herald*, First Edition, p. 5.

Corcoran, Terence (1993), 'Save democracy—halt corporate funding', *The Globe and Mail*, 24 July.

Costar, Brian (2011), Submission to the Joint Standing Committee on Electoral Matters, 13 February. http://aph.gov.au/house/committee/em/elect10/subs/Sub036.pdf

Coultan, Mark and Sexton, Elisabeth (2004), 'Politics at a price', *Sydney Morning Herald*, Late Edition, News Review, 7 February, p. 40.

Courier Mail (2004), 'Integrity an issue in fund raising', *Courier Mail*, Features, 20 May, p. 14.

CP (1983), 'PC contributions €14 million in 1983', *The Globe and Mail*, 7 July.

CP (1988), 'Turner's stand on agreement worries donor, Liberal says', *The Globe and Mail*, 23 February.

CP (1991), 'Tories suffer slip in donations, figures show. NDP, Liberals, reform improve fundraising, Elections Canada says', *The Globe and Mail*, 5 July.

Crabb, Annabel and Rollins, Adrian (2001), 'Party donation revelations spark claims of shady deals', *The Age*, 2 February, p. 2.

Crouch, Colin (1994), *Industrial Relations and European State Traditions* (Oxford: Oxford University Press).

Culpepper, Pepper D. (2001), 'Employers, Public Policy, and the Politics of Decentralized Cooperation in Germany and France', in Peter Hall and David Soskice (eds.), *Varieties of Capitalism: The Institutional Foundations of Comparative Advantage* (Oxford: Oxford University Press), pp. 275–306.

Culpepper, Pepper D. (2007), 'Small States and Skill Specificity: Austria, Switzerland, and Interemployer Cleavages in Coordinated Capitalism', *Comparative Political Studies* 40 (6): 611–37.

Cumming, Douglas J. and MacIntosh, Jeffrey G. (2006), 'Crowding Out Private Equity: Canadian Evidence', *Journal of Business Venturing* 21(5): 569–609.

Cumming, F. (1992), 'Poll rethink after fightback', *Sydney Herald Sun*, 20 December.

Cunningham, Jim, Derworiz, Collette, Stewart, Monte, and Henton, Darcy (1999), 'Storm on the right', *Calgary Herald*, 6 September, p. A10.

Curtis, Jenefer (1999), 'Duelling for dollars. As the fundraising knights of the right joust for corporate donations, Canada's CEOs wonder what to do: play a favourite or hedge their bets', *The National Post Business Magazine*, 1 December, p. 56.

Dahl, Robert A. (1998), *On Democracy* (New Haven, CT: Yale University Press).

Daily Telegraph (1997), 'The believers desert Labor', *The Daily Telegraph*, Local, 16 April, p. 4.

Dalley-Trim, Leanne, Alloway, Nola, and Walker, Karen (2008), 'Secondary School Students' Perceptions of, and the Factors Influencing Their Decision-Making in Relation to VET in Schools', *Australian Educational Researcher* 35(2): 55–69.

Damgaard, Erik (2003), 'Denmark: Delegation and Accountability in Minority Situations', in Kaare Strøm, Wolfgang C. Müeller, and Torbjörn Bergman (eds.), *Delegation and Accountability in Parliamentary Democracies* (Oxford: Oxford University Press), pp. 281–300.

Davies, Anne (2006), 'Dull and duller risk a paying audience', *Sydney Morning Herald*, News and Features, 3 April, p. 13.

Davies, Anne and Norrie, Justin (2006), 'Developer cash keeps parties afloat', *Sydney Morning Herald*, First Edition, News and Features, 1 November, p. 1.

Day, Mark (1995), 'Pollies want a cracker', *The Daily Telegraph Mirror*, 15 July.

Delacourt, Susan (1989), 'Election surplus helps Liberals cut debt', *The Globe and Mail*, 9 January.

Della Porta, Donatella (2004), 'Political Parties and Corruption: Ten Hypotheses on Five Vicious Circles', *Crime, Law and Social Change* 42(1): 35–6.

Douez, Sophie (2001), 'Parties vie for corporate money, beer: election 2001', *The Age*, Late Edition, News, 8 November, p. 10.

Drope, Jeffrey M. and Hansen, Wendy L. (2004), 'Purchasing Protection? The Effect of Political Spending on U.S. Trade Policy', *Political Research Quarterly* 57(1): 27–37.

Dubeki, Larissa and Baker, Richard (2004), 'Gaming, tobacco, developers fill party coffers: political donations', *The Age*, Late Edition, News, 3 February, p. 2.

Duffy, Michael (2000), 'Arrogance struts the corridors of power', *The Daily Telegraph*, 11 November, p. 27.

Dwyre, Diana (1996), 'Spinning Straw into Gold: Soft Money and U.S. House Elections', *Journal of Legislative Studies* 21(3): 409–24.

Dyck, Rand (2004), *Canadian Politics: Critical Approaches*, 4th edn. (Scarborough, Ontario: Nelson).

Eagles, Munro (1992), 'The Political Ecology of Campaign Contributions in Canada: A Constituency-Level Analysis', *Canadian Journal of Political Science* 25(3): 535–55.

Edinger, Lewis J. (1994), 'Pressure Group Politics in West Germany', in Jeremy Richardson (ed.), *Pressure Groups* (Oxford: Oxford University Press), pp. 175–90.

Edwards, Bryce (2007), 'Political finance and inequality in New Zealand'. Paper presented at the joint conference of the Australian Sociological Association and the New Zealand Sociological Association, Auckland, 4–7 December.

Elections Canada (1997), *Thirty-Sixth General Election 1997. Contributions and Expenses of Registered Political Parties and Candidates* (Ottawa: Elections Canada).

Elections Canada (2000), *Thirty-Seventh General Election 2000. Contributions and Expenses of Registered Political Parties and Candidates* (Ottawa: Elections Canada).

Elections New Zealand (2008), *Party Donation Returns 1996–2007*. http://www.elections. org.nz/rules/parties/party-donations/donations-summary.html

Elliott, Geoff (2003), 'Coming to the party', *The Australian*, All-round Country Edition, Features, 12 February, p. 11.

Estevez-Abe, Margarita, Iversen, Torben, and Soskice, David (2001), 'Social Protection and the Formation of Skills: A Reinterpretation of the Welfare State', in Peter A. Hall and David Soskice (eds.), *Varieties of Capitalism: The Institutional Foundation of Comparative Advantage* (Oxford: Oxford University Press), pp. 145–83.

Ewing, Keith D. (2007), *The Cost of Democracy: Party Funding in Modern British Politics* (Oxford: Hart).

Fahrun, Joachim (2005), 'Berliner CDU lebt mit dem Mangel; Strukturelle Defizite bei Organisation und Finanzierung sorgen für große Probleme', *Die Welt*, 23 May.

Farrell, David M. and McAllister, Ian (2006), *The Australian Electoral System: Origins, Variations and Consequences* (Sydney: University of New South Wales Press).

Ferguson, Derek (1988), 'Manitoba crucial to Liberal hopes', *Toronto Star*, 19 September, p. A22.

Ferguson, Jock (1989), 'Liberal backer on inside track in dump stakes', *The Globe and Mail*, 13 March.

Ferguson, Sarah (2008), 'Four corners', Australian Broadcasting Corporation, Programme Transcript, 14 April.

Fischer, Susanne (2000), 'Das Geld sucht seinen Weg', *Der Spiegel*, 31 January, p. 50.

Fisher, Justin (1994), 'Why Do Companies Make Donations to Political Parties?' *Political Studies* 42: 690–9.

Focus (2000a), 'SPENDENAFFAERE; Die 41-Millionen-Mark-Luege', *Focus*, 14 February, pp. 20–30.

Focus (2000b), 'SPENDEN-AFFAERE; Kohls ScheckPott', *Focus*, 13 March.

Focus (2000c), 'BAYERN; Stoiber in der Schuldenfalle', *Focus*, 13 November, pp. 68–70.

Folktinget (2010), *De Politiske Partiers Regnskaber For 2008* (Copenhagen: Danish Parliament).

Free Press Parliamentary Bureau (2001), 'Ridings tapped to aid paying off Liberal party debt', *London Free Press*, 4 November, p. A8.

Frew, Wendy (2008), 'Who cares what the neighbours think', *Sydney Morning Herald*, First Edition, News and Features, 31 May, p. 25.

Frew, Wendy and Besser, Linton (2008), 'Dirty, sexy money', *Sydney Morning Herald*, First Edition, News Review, 23 February, p. 27.

Froehlich, Vera Halla (2002), 'Mehr Transparenz durch ein Wirr-Warr neuer Vorschriften; Lob von CDU und SPD fuer neues Parteiengesetz; Nach grundlegender Reform 1994 jetzt Feinarbeiten', *Associated Press World Stream—German*, 19 April.

Frye, Timothy and Shleifer, Andrei (1997), 'The Invisible Hand and the Grabbing Hand', *American Economic Review* 87(2): 354–8.

Fudge, Judy and Tucker, Eric (2000), 'Pluralism or Fragmentation? The Twentieth-Century Employment Law Regime in Canada', *Labour* 46(3): 251–306.

Funk, Albert (2007), 'Was der Staat beiträgt', *Der Tagesspiegel*, 20 August.

Galloway, Gloria (2000), 'Alliance leader courts Bay Street, but merger may be the key to future donations', *Canadian Press Newswire*, 8 December.

Geddes, John (1990), 'Liberals' woe is how to raise party funding', *The Financial Post*, 11 June.

Geddes, John (1996), 'Memories of Mulroney. Invoking the former prime minister may not cut much ice with typical voters, but the Tories think his record will appeal to business donors', *The Financial Post*, 24 August, p. 13.

Geddes, John (2000), 'The black hole of election money', *Maclean's*, 27 March.

Geddis, Andrew (2007), 'The Funding of New Zealand's Elections: Current Problems and Prospects for Change', Discussion Paper 4/07 (Canberra: Democratic Audit of Australia, Australian National University).

General-Anzeiger (2002a), 'Staatlicher Geldsegen fuer die Parteikasse FINANZEN Die deutschen Parteien finanzieren sich nicht nur aus Spenden und Mitgliedsbeitraegen: Auf jede eingenommene Summe zahlt der Staat noch einmal 50 Prozent drauf...', *General-Anzeiger*, 15 March.

General-Anzeiger (2002b), 'Der Wahlkampf ist ein finanzieller Kraftakt BUNDESTAGS-WAHL Umlageverfahren, Spendenaufrufe und Ruecklagen sind beim Kampf um jede Stimme ebenso gefragt wie die Privatschatulle der Direktkandidaten', *General-Anzeiger*, 17 August.

Gera, Surendra and Songsakul, Thitima (2007), 'Benchmarking Canada's Performance in the Global Competition for Mobile Talent', *Canadian Public Policy* 33(1): 63–84.

Gettler, Leon (2004), 'Can power be bought? Sunday Forum—The Issue: Political donations', *Sunday Age*, Late Edition, News, p. 15.

Gibson, Jano and McClymont, Kate (2008), 'Lunch with a minister only $5100: developer wins Sartor at auction', *Sydney Morning Herald*, First Edition, News and Features, 29 February, p. 1.

Gidlund, Gullan and Koole, Ruud (2001), 'Political Finance in the North of Europe: The Netherlands and Sweden', in Karl-Heinz Nassmacher (ed.), *Foundations for Democracy: Approaches to Comparative Political Finance* (Baden-Baden: Nomos), pp. 112–30.

Gilding, Michael (1999), 'Superwealth in Australia: Entrepreneurs, Accumulation and the Capitalist Class', *Journal of Sociology* 35(2), 169–82.

Gilding, Michael (2004), 'Entrepreneurs, Elites and the Ruling Class: The Changing Structure of Power and Wealth in Australian Society', *Australian Journal of Political Science* 39(1): 127–43.

Gilmore, Heath and Benns, Matthew (2008), 'NRMA faces uproar over $225,000 in political gifts', *The Sun Herald*, First Edition, News, 10 August, p. 15.

Globe and Mail (1980), 'Flesh going unpressed, but mails a bonanza', *The Globe and Mail*, 29 November.

Globe and Mail (1985), 'Dinner "temporarily" cancelled. Fund-raiser follows masse', *The Globe and Mail*, 28 September.

Goar, Carol (1988), 'Why the Liberals are always in the lurch', *Toronto Star*, 5 March, p. D1.

Goerres, Achim and Hoepner, Martin (2011), 'Polarizers or landscape groomers? An empirical analysis of party donations by the 100 largest German companies in 1984–2005', unpublished manuscript (Duisburg: University of Duisburg-Essen).

Gooderham, Mary and Taylor, Paul (1987), 'Province won't probe effects of developers' campaign gifts', *The Globe and Mail*, 18 December.

Gordon, Josh (2004), 'Parties hide donor identities', *The Age*, Late Edition, 2 February, p. 1.

Gordon, Josh (2005), 'Political party donors move to mask their identities', *The Age*, Second Edition, News, 2 February, p. 3.

Gordon, Josh and Carty, Lisa (2008), 'Rudd plans $1m anniversary party: Opposition slams fund-raising hypocrisy', *The Sun Herald*, First Edition, News, 9 November, p. 5.

Gordon, Michael and Ceresa, Maria (1995), 'ALP intimidates business for funds: Libs', *The Weekend Australian*, Saturday Edition, 8 July.

Gordon, Stacy B. (2005), *Campaign Contributions and Legislative Voting* (New York: Routledge).

Grant, Wyn (1993), *Business and Politics in Britain*, 2nd edn. (Basingstoke: Macmillan).

Grant, Wyn, Martinelli, Alberto, and Paterson, William (1989), 'Large Firms as Political Actors: A Comparative Analysis of the Chemical Industry in Britain, Italy and West Germany', *West European Politics* 12(2): 72–90.

Grattan, Michelle (2005), 'Liberals weigh shift in fund-raising', *The Age*, First Edition, News, 25 May, p. 4.

Grattan, Michelle (2008), 'We're going to find out more about who gives what to whom', *The Age*, First Edition, p. 15.

Gray, John (1980), 'Parties richer, but democratic dreams fading. Financing law, six years later', *The Globe and Mail*, 29 November.

Gray, John (1982), 'Think tank set up to define ideology of Conservatives', *The Globe and Mail*, 21 May.

Greenaway, Norma (2003), 'Activists "giddy" about donors: a former aide to Brian Mulroney says corporate Canada would love to finance a new Conservative party', *The Vancouver Sun*, 18 October, p. G11.

Greenwood, Justin and Jacek, Henry (eds.) (2000), *Organized Business and the New Global Order* (Basingstoke: Macmillan).

Griffith, Gareth and Roth, Lenny (2012), 'Banning political donations from third party interest groups: a summary of constitutional issues', *E-Brief*, 1/2012. (Sydney: New South Wales Parliamentary Library Research Service).

Groves, Jason (2010), 'Cash-for-access scandal MPs in line for peerages', *The Daily Mail*, 24 March.

Hacker, Jacob S. and Pierson, Paul (2010), 'Winner-Take-All Politics: Public Policy, Political Organization and the Precipitous Rise of Top Incomes in the United States', *Politics and Society* 38(2): 152–4.

Haddow, Rodney (2002), 'From Corporatism to Associationalism: Linking State and Society, and Deepening Democracy, in the Canadian Polity', *Journal of Canadian Studies* 37(1): 68–88.

Hall, Peter and Gingerich, David W. (2009), 'Varieties of Capitalism and Institutional Complementarities in the Political Economy: An Empirical Analysis', in Bob Hancké (ed.), *Debating Varieties of Capitalism: A Reader* (Oxford: Oxford University Press), pp. 135–79.

Hall, Peter A. and Soskice, David (2001), 'An Introduction to Varieties of Capitalism', in Peter A. Hall and David Soskice (eds.), *Varieties of Capitalism: The Institutional Foundations of Comparative Advantage* (Oxford: Oxford University Press), pp. 1–70.

Hall, Richard (2008), 'The Politics of Industrial Relations in Australia in 2008', *Journal of Industrial Relations* 50(3), 371–82.

Hall, Richard L. and Deardorff, Alan V. (2006), 'Lobbying as Legislative Subsidy', *American Political Science Review* 100: 69–84.

Hall, Richard L. and Wayman, Frank W. (1990), 'Buying Time: Moneyed Interests and the Mobilization of Bias in Congressional Committees', *American Political Science Review* 84: 797–820.

Hamburger Abendblatt (2002), 'Spenden-Sündern droht Haft; PARTEIENGESETZ verschärft—bis zu drei Jahren Gefängnis für illegale Praktiken', *Hamburger Abendblatt*, 20 April.

Hancké, Bob, Rhodes, Martin, and Thatcher, Mark (2009), 'Beyond Varieties of Capitalism', in Bob Hancké (ed.), *Debating Varieties of Capitalism: A Reader* (Oxford: Oxford University Press), pp. 273–300.

Hanna, Jim (2003), 'NSW: Carr defends system of political donations', *AAP Newsfeed*, Domestic News, 6 February.

Hannan, Ewin and Carney, Shaun (2005), 'Pressure on ALP for inquiry into fund-raiser', *The Age*, First Edition, p. 3.

Hansen, Wendy L. and Mitchell, Neil J. (2000), 'Disaggregating and Explaining Corporate Political Activity: Domestic and Foreign Corporations in National Politics', *American Political Science Review* 94(4): 891–903.

Harrigan, Nicholas (2007), 'Political partisanship and corporate donations in Australia', Unpublished paper (Singapore Management University).

Harris, Michael (1983), 'Influence peddling case. Two Liberal fund-raisers fined €25,000', *The Globe and Mail*, 13 May.

Hartcher, Peter (1992a), 'Libs attack donations law', *Sydney Morning Herald*, 10 March, p. 3.

Hartcher, Peter (1992b), 'We have it all—bar the cash; Libs', *Sydney Morning Herald*, Late Edition, News and Features, 4 July, p. 4.

Hayes, Simon (2004), 'Microsoft red-faced on Labor donation', All-round Country Edition, Features, 10 February, p. 30.

Heinz, John, Laumann, Edward, Nelson, Robert, and Salisbury, Robert (1993), *The Hollow Core: Private Interests in National Policy Making* (Cambridge, MA: Harvard University Press).

Henderson, Jennifer (1986), 'Montreal lawyer poised for Liberal presidency', *The Financial Post*, 17 November, p. 10.

Hengst, Björn, Kazim, Hasnain, and Volkery, Carsten (2007), 'Wohltäter ohne Namen', *Der Spiegel Online*, 17 January.

Henker, Julia and Henker, Thomas (2010), Are Retail Investors the Culprits? Evidence from Australian Individual Stock Price Bubbles', *European Journal of Finance* 16(4): 281–304.

Henning, Krumrey (2001), 'FDP; Voll auf die 18', *Focus*, No. 10, pp. 44–6.

Herr, Richard (2002), 'Tasmania:, Political Chronicles, January to June 2002', *Australian Journal of Politics and History* 48(4): 584–9.

Hewett, Jennifer (2003), 'Poor Liberals scratching for corporate scraps', *Sydney Morning Herald*, Late Edition, News and Features, p. 10.

Hillman, Amy, Keim, Gerald, and Schuler, Douglas (2004), 'Corporate Political Activity: A Review and Research Agenda', *Journal of Management* 30(6): 837–57.

Hopkin, Jonathan (1997), 'Political Parties, Corruption and the Economic Theory of Democracy', *Crime Law and Social Change* 27(3–4): 255–74.

Horan, M (1997), 'Libs hypocrites on gifts from gaming, says ALP', *Courier Mail*, 25 March.

Hornig, Frank, Nelles, Roland, Pauly, Christoph, and Schulz, Thomas (2004), 'Lieber rot als tot?', *Der Spiegel*, 26 April.

Howard, Ross (1993), 'Tories face penury as popularity drops. Donations to party may be drying up', *The Globe and Mail*, 22 October.

Howard, Ross (1997a), 'Parties set to spend €100 million. Federal campaign has become a high-stakes business for major contenders, fringe groups', *The Globe and Mail*, 14 April, p. A1.

Howard, Ross (1997b), 'Liberals woo elite in pre-election letter. Access promised in return for €1000', *The Globe and Mail*, 2 May, p. A1.

Huo, Jingjing (2006), 'Comparing Welfare States in Australia and Canada: A Party Competition Theory of Welfare State Development', *Commonwealth and Comparative Politics* 44(2): 167–89.

Impulse (2000), 'PLÄDOYER FÜR HERRN KOHL; Erstmals äußert sich der frühere Bundesverfassungsgerichtspräsident Ernst Benda umfassend zur Parteispendenaffäre: Wie gefährlich die Krise ist, warum es keiner Gesetzesänderungen bedarf und warum die Vorwürfe gegen Kohl weit hergeholt sind', *Impulse*, 1 March, p. 62.

International Institute for Democracy and Electoral Assistance (2002), *Political Finance Database*. http://www.idea.int/parties/finance/db/index.cfm

Ivens, Martin (2009), 'Dirty deals bring an end to the peer show', *The Sunday Times*, 1 February, p. 17.

Iversen, Torben (2005), *Capitalism, Democracy, and Welfare* (Cambridge: Cambridge University Press).

Jacek, Henry (1986), 'Pluralist and Corporatist Intermediation: Activities of Business Interest Associations, and Corporate Profits: Some Evidence from Canada', *Comparative Politics* 18(4): 419–37.

Jackman, Simon (2005), 'Pooling the Polls Over an Election Campaign', *Australian Journal of Political Science* 40: 499–517.

Jacobi, Claus (2000), 'Kohl ist Widder wie Schröder & Bismarck', *Welt am Sonntag*, 19 March.

Jaensch, Dean (1994), *The Liberals* (St Leonard's, NSW: Allen & Unwin).

Janigan, Mary (1987), 'Mulroney's new offensive', *Maclean's*, 23 February, p. 6.

Jayachandran, Seema (2006), 'The Jeffords Effect', *Journal of Law and Economics* 49(2): 397–425.

Jenkinson, Mike (2001), 'Bay-ing of corporate wolves has bite', *Edmonton Sun*, 4 February, p. C17.

Johnston, Damon (2000), 'Big bucks in Labor's name game', *Herald Sun*, 5 June, News, p. 2.

Johnston, Michael (1996), 'The Search for Definitions: The Vitality of Politics and the Issue of Corruption', *International Social Science Journal* 149: 321–35.

Jones, Andrea (1994), 'The legal system is a super, super-dooper ass. It's wicked. It really is', *The Sun Herald*, Late Edition, Tempo, September, p. 143.

Jones, George (2001), 'Betting boss backs Tories with £5m gift', *Daily Telegraph*, 18 January.

Jopson, Debra (2008), 'Money went to party, not me, says Sartor; Donor scandal—special investigation', *Sydney Morning Herald*, First Edition, News and Features, 3 May, p. 10.

Katz, Richard and Mair, Peter (1995), 'Changing Models of Party Organization and Party Democracy: The Emergence of the Cartel Party', *Party Politics* 1(1): 5–27.

Katz, Richard and Mair, Peter (2009), 'The Cartel Party Thesis: A Restatement', *Perspectives on Politics* 7(4): 753–66.

Kaufmann, Daniel, Kraay, Aart, and Zoido-Lobatón, Pablo (1999), 'Governance Matters', Policy Research Paper no. 2195 (Washington, DC: World Bank).

Kellow, Aynsley (2003), 'Tasmania', in Jeremy Moon and Campbell Sharman (eds.), *Australian Politics and Government: The Commonwealth, The States and The Territories* (Cambridge: Cambridge University Press), pp. 131–53.

Kent, Tom (1990), 'Can the Liberals renew faith in politics? Yes, but only if the party drops its reliance on big business', *Toronto Star*, 14 March.

Kerby, Matthew (2009), 'Worth the Wait: Determinants of Ministerial Appointment in Canada, 1935–2008', *Canadian Journal of Political Science* 42(3): 593–611.

Kidd, Michael and Shannon, Michael (1996), 'The Gender Wage Gap: A Comparison of Australian and Canada', *Industrial and Labor Relations Review* 49(4): 729–46.

Kim, Jin-Hyuk (2008), 'Corporate Lobbying Revisited', *Business and Politics* 10(2): Article 3.

King, Gary, Honaker, James, Joseph, Anne, and Scheve, Kenneth (2001), 'Analyzing Incomplete Political Science Data: An Alternative Algorithm for Multiple Imputation', *American Political Science Review* 95(1): 49–69.

Kitschelt, Herbert (1999), 'European Social Democracy between Political Economy and Electoral Competition', in Herbert Kitschelt, Peter Lange, Gary Marks, and John Stephens (eds.), *Continuity and Change in Contemporary Capitalism* (Cambridge: Cambridge University Press), pp. 317–45.

Kitschelt, Herbert, Lange, Peter, Marks, Gary, and Stephens, John D. (1999), 'Convergence and Divergence in Advanced Capitalist Democracies', in Herbert Kitschelt, Peter Lange, Gary Marks, and John Stephens (eds.), *Continuity and Change in Contemporary Capitalism* (Cambridge: Cambridge University Press), pp. 427–60.

Knight, Brian (2007), 'Are Policy Platforms Capitalized Into Equity Prices? Evidence from the Bush/Gore 2000 Presidential Election', *Journal of Public Economics* 91(1–2): 389–409.

Korporaal, Glenda (1995), 'How parties get business to fork out; Poll '95 The knife-edge election', *Sydney Morning Herald*, Late Edition, News and Features, 11 March, p. 1.

Koss, Michael (2011), *The Politics of Party Funding: State Funding to Political Parties and Party Competition in Western Europe* (Oxford: Oxford University Press).

Koutsoukis, Jason and Schubert, Misha (2004), 'Political donors put money where a mouth is', *Sunday Age*, First Edition, News, 1 August, p. 8.

Krozner, Randall and Stratmann, Thomas (2005), 'Corporate Campaign Contributions, Repeat Giving, and the Rewards to Legislator Reputation.' *Journal of Law and Economics* 48(1): 41–65.

Landfried, Christine (1994), 'Political Finance in West Germany', in Herbert Alexander and Rei Shiratori (eds.), *Comparative Political Finance among the Democracies* (Oxford: Westview Press), pp. 133–44.

Landfried, Christine (2000), 'Anreiz zum Sparen', *Die Tageszeitung*, 24 January, p. 10.

Lau, James, Sinnadurai, Philip, and Wright, Sue (2009), 'Corporate Governance and Chief Executive Officer Dismissal Following Poor Performance: Australian Evidence', *Accounting and Finance* 49(1): 161–82.

Laver, Ross and Wallace, Bruce (1988), 'Turner's private trusts', *Maclean's*, 12 September, p. 10.

Lee, Wang-Sheng and Coelli, Michael B. (2010), 'The Labour Market Effects of Vocational Education and Training in Australia', *Australian Economic Review* 43(4): 389–408.

Lersch, Paul and Palmer, Hartmut (1999), 'Die gepflegte Landschaft', *Der Spiegel*, 13 December, p. 36.

Li, Yun Daisy, Iscan, Talan B., and Xu, Kuan (2010), 'The Impact of Monetary Policy Shocks on Stock Prices: Evidence from Canada and the United States', *Journal of International Money and Finance* 29(5): 870–96.

Lijphart, Arend (1999), *Patterns of Democracy: Government Forms and Performance in Thirty-Six Countries* (New Haven, CT: Yale University Press).

Lindblom, Charles (1977), *Politics and Markets: The World's Political-Economic Systems* (New York: Basic Books).

Liptak, Adam (2010), 'Justices, 5–4, reject corporate spending limit', *The New York Times*, 22 January, p. A1.

Lösche, Peter (1993), 'Problems of Party and Campaign Financing in Germany and the United States—Some Comparative Reflections', in Arthur B. Gunlicks (ed.), *Campaign and Party Finance in North America and Western Europe* (Oxford: Westview Press), pp. 219–30.

Luzstig, Michael (1995), 'Federalism and Institutional Design: The Perils and Politics of a Triple-E Senate in Canada', *Publius* 25(1): 35–50.

Luzstig, Michael (1996), *Risking Free Trade: The Politics of Free Trade in Britain, Canada, Mexico, and the United States* (Pittsburgh: University of Pittsburgh Press).

Luzstig, Michael (2004), *The Limits of Protectionism: Building Coalitions for Free Trade.* (Pittsburgh: University of Pittsburgh Press).

McAllister, Ian (2002), 'Political Parties in Australia: Party Stability in a Utilitarian Society', in Paul Webb, David Farrell, and Ian Holliday (eds.), *Political Parties in Advanced Industrial Democracies* (Oxford: Oxford University Press), pp. 379–408.

McCarthy, Shawn (2003), 'PM's donation bill to cost €110 million', *The Globe and Mail*, 30 January, p. A1.

MacDermid, Robert (2000), 'Buying Back Our Political Parties', *Canadian Dimension* 34(6): 32–6.

McFarland, Janet (2000), 'Corporate funds fuel election campaigns', *The Globe and Mail*, 4 November, p. B1.

McIlroy, Anne and Thanh Ha, Tu (1997), 'Mounties seized Grit records. Federal party worker alleged to have sought "donations" from companies in line for grants', *The Globe and Mail*, 9 October, p. A1.

McIntosh, Andrew (1986), 'Architects hired for Quebec prison helped PCs', *The Globe and Mail*, 29 October, p. A1.

MacKenzie, Hilary (1988), 'Debt and dissension', *Maclean's*, 21 March, p. 14.

McLaren, Christine (1988), 'Grits charge €200 to meet Ontario ministers, Tories say', *The Globe and Mail*, 5 October.

Maclean's (1989), 'Dinner for 2,000', *Maclean's*, 9 October.

McMenamin, Iain (2002), 'Poland's Business Associations: Flattened Civil Society or Super Lobbies?', *Business and Politics* 4(3): 299–315.

McMenamin, Iain (2004), 'Parties, Promiscuity and Politicisation: Business–Political Networks in Poland', *European Journal of Political Research* 43(4): 657–76.

McMenamin, Iain (2008), 'Business, Politics and Money in Australia: Testing Economic, Political and Ideological Explanations', *Australian Journal of Political Science* 43(4): 377–93.

McMenamin, Iain (2009), 'The Four Logics of Business, Money and Political Parties', in Conor McGrath (ed.), *Interest Groups and Lobbying in the United States and Comparative Perspectives* (Lampeter: Edwin Mellen Press), pp. 207–23.

McMenamin, Iain (2011), 'Liberal Market Economies, Business, and Political Finance: Britain under New Labour', *West European Politics* 34(5): 1021–43.

McMenamin, Iain (2012a), 'If Money Talks, What Does It Say? Varieties of Capitalism and Business Financing of Parties', *World Politics* 64(1): 1–38.

McMenamin, Iain (2012b), 'Business Financing of Politics in Ireland: Theory, Evidence and Reform', *Irish Political Studies* (forthcoming).

McMenamin, Iain and Schoenman, Roger (2007), 'Together Forever? Explaining Exclusivity in Party–Firm Relations', *Political Studies* 55(1): 153–73.

McMullin, Ross (1991), *The Light on the Hill: The Australian Labor Party 1891–1991* (Melbourne: Oxford University Press).

McNish, Jacquie and Laghi, Brian (2002), 'Bay Street dismisses new look Alliance. Corporate leaders insist on united right before opening the money spigot', *The Globe and Mail*, 22 March, p. A1.

McQuaig, Linda (1988a), 'Fund-raising solution ignored. Liberals' money crisis avoidable, critics say', *The Globe and Mail*, 24 May.

McQuaig, Linda (1988b), 'Turner, Peterson not invited. Toronto's elite pay €1,500 each for birthday party with DelZotto', *The Globe and Mail*, 15 July.

McQueen, Rod (1995), 'Corporate executives send message to Quebec: "We care deeply": As the referendum approaches, more businesspeople need to speak up', *The Financial Post*, 30 September, p. 19.

Magleby, David B. and Smith, E. A. (2003), 'Party Soft Money in the 2000 Congressional Elections', in David B Magleby (ed.), *The Other Campaign: Soft Money and Issue Advocacy in the 2000 Congressional Elections* (Oxford: Rowman & Littlefield), pp. 27–50.

Manning, Haydon (2002), 'South Australia: Political Chronicle, January to June 2002', *Australian Journal of Politics and History* 48(4): 576–83.

Maron, Thomas (2010), 'Spender dürfen keinerlei Gegenleistung erwarten', *Stuttgarter Zeitung*, 20 January, p. 4.

Martin, Cathie-Jo (2000), *Stuck in Neutral: Business and the Politics of Human Capital Investment* (Princeton, NJ: Princeton University Press).

Martin, Cathie-Jo (2005), 'Corporatism from the Firm Perspective', *British Journal of Political Science* 35(1): 127–48.

Martin, Cathie-Jo (2006), 'Consider the Source! Determinants of Corporate Preferences for Public Policy', in David Coen and Wyn Grant (eds.), *Business and Government: Methods and Practice* (Opladen: Barbara Budrich), pp. 51–78.

Martin, Don (2003), 'Chrétien a scary lame duck', *Calgary Herald*, 23 January, p. A3.

Matas, Robert (1987), 'Top defence firms deny donations to PCs linked with federal contracts', *The Globe and Mail*, 8 August.

Matas, Robert (1994), 'How politics turns a profit. Thanks to the public, the parties strike gold when the nation votes', *The Globe and Mail*, 29 October, p. A1.

Matas, Robert (1995), 'Raising money. Anatomy of a fundraiser. History is filled with tales linking political contributions to government kickbacks. But many would argue that raising money when visiting politicians come to town is the very stuff of democracy', *The Globe and Mail*, 29 April.

Metherell, Mark (2005), 'High-profile Libs call for tighter rules on funding', *Sydney Morning Herald*, First Edition, News and Features, 24 May, p. 5.

Meyer, Peter (2000), 'Aufstand gegen Schäuble', *Hamburger Adendblatt*, 16 February.

Millar, Royce (2008a), 'Political donations linked to developers, contractors; Investigation', *The Age*, Second Edition, News, 7 July, p. 1.

Millar, Royce (2008b), 'With strings attached? Politics', *The Age*, First Edition, News, 7 July, p. 11.

Millar, Royce (2008c), 'Party donations good for democracy, says Premier; Money and Politics', *The Age*, First Edition, News, 9 July, p. 5.

Millar, Royce (2008d), 'A little bit of give and take; Politics', *The Age*, First Edition, News, 11 July, p. 15.

Millar, Royce (2009), 'Big property developers help line the pockets of ALP', *The Age*, First Edition, 3 February, p. 6.

Mills, C. Wright (1959), *The Power Elite* (New York: Oxford University Press).

Milne, Glenn (2008), 'No party is ready to stop mainlining cash', *The Australian*, Features, 18 August, p. 26.

Milyo, Jeffrey (2002), 'Bribes and Fruit Baskets: What Does the Link between PAC Contributions and Lobbying Mean?', *Business and Politics* 4(2): 157–9.

Mitchell, Alex (2006), 'ALP sets price for post-poll "dialogue"', *The Sun Herald*, First Edition, News, 2 July, p. 10.

Mittelstaedt, Martin (1993), 'Liberal campaign hits a bump. Grits accused of selling access to leader at €1,000-a-person affair', *The Globe and Mail*, 7 October.

Moise, Edwin (2008), *Modern China: A History*, 3rd edn. (Harlow: Pearson).

Molm, Linda (2000), 'Theories of Social Exchange and Exchange Networks', in George Ritzer and Barry Smart (eds.), *The Handbook of Social Theory* (New York: Sage), pp. 260–72.

Moon, Jeremy and Sharman, Campbell (eds.) (2003), *Australian Politics and Government* (Cambridge: Cambridge University Press).

Munger, Michael (1988), 'On the Political Participation of the Firm in the Electoral Process', *Public Choice* 56(3): 295–8.

Nassmacher, Karl-Heinz (ed.) (2001), *Foundations for Democracy: Approaches to Comparative Political Finance* (Baden-Baden: Nomos Verlagsgesellschaft).

Nassmacher, Karl-Heinz (2001), 'Political Finance in West Central Europe (Austria, Germany, Switzerland)', in Karl-Heinz Nassmacher (ed.), *Foundations for Democracy: Approaches to Comparative Political Finance* (Baden-Baden: Nomos Verlagsgesellschaft), pp. 92–111.

Nassmacher, Karl-Heinz (2010), *The Funding of Party Competition: Political Finance in 25 Democracies* (Baden-Baden: Nomos Verlagsgesellschaft).

Naumetz, Tim (1986a), 'Opposition grumbles as Tory club collars PM for private fall session', *The Globe and Mail*, 16 August, p. A3.

Naumetz, Tim (1986b), 'Liberals court corporations, wealthy to wipe out debts', *The Globe and Mail*, 13 September, p. A6.

Naumetz, Tim (2000), 'Alliance event raises eyebrows', *Sudbury Star*, 1 September, p. A6.

Newcastle Herald (2004), 'Political funding; Old Dart doctors', *Newcastle Herald*, News, 3 February, p. 8.

Nölke, Andreas and Vliegenthart, Arjan (2009), 'Enlarging the Varieties of Capitalism: The Emergence of Dependent Market Economies in East Central Europe', *World Politics* 61 (4): 670–702.

O'Keefe, N. (1992), 'When "free speech" is costly', *Herald Sun*, 7 September.

O'Malley, Eoin (2007), 'The Power of Prime Ministers: Results of an Expert Survey', *International Political Science Review* 28(1): 7–28.

O'Malley, Kady (1999), 'UA hunts for political donations. No plans to officially register as a party', *Hill Times*, 9 August.

O'Neil, Peter (2001), 'Canadian Alliance strategists find more weaknesses than strengths', *Vancouver Sun*, 19 January, p. A4.

Offe, Claus (1985), *Disorganized Capitalism* (Cambridge: Polity Press).

Olson, Mancur (1971), *The Logic of Collective Action: Public Goods and the Theory of Groups* (Cambridge, MA: Harvard University Press).

Olson, Mancur (2000), *Power and Prosperity: Outgrowing Communist and Capitalist Dictatorships* (New York: Basic Books).

Orr, Graeme (2006), 'Political Finance Law in Australia', in Kenneth D. Ewing and Samuel Issacharoff (eds.), *Party Funding and Campaign Financing in International Perspective* (Oxford: Hart), pp. 99–122.

Orr, Graeme (2007), 'Electoral Law in Australia: Lackadaisical Law', *Election Law Journal*, 6: 72–88.

Orr, Graeme, Mercurio, Bryan, and Williams, George (2003), 'Australian Electoral Law: A Stocktake', *Election Law Journal* 2(3): 383–402.

Ovenden, Norm (2000), 'Corporate Canada digs deep to dine with Day: Alliance fund-raiser could bring in €2m', *Edmonton Journal*, 13 October, p. A1.

Padgett, Stephen (1999), *Organizing Democracy in Eastern Germany: Interest Groups in Post-Communist Society* (Cambridge: Cambridge University Press).

Padgett, Stephen (2003), 'Germany: Modernising the Left by Stealth', *Parliamentary Affairs* 56(1): 38–57.

Palango, Paul (1978), 'Fund-raiser finds job tougher', *The Globe and Mail*, 14 July.

Palmer, Anna and Phillip, Abby (2012), 'Corporations don't pony up for super PACs', *Politico*, 3 March. http://www.politico.com/news/stories/0312/73804.html

Paltiel, Khayyam Z. (1970), *Political Party Financing in Canada* (Toronto: McGraw-Hill Ryerson).

Parkin, Andrew (2003), 'South Australia', in Jeremy Moon and Campbell Sharman (eds.), *Australian Politics and Government: The Commonwealth, The States and The Territories* (Cambridge: Cambridge University Press, 2003), pp. 104–30.

Paun, Akash and Hazell, Robert (2010), 'Hung Parliaments and the Challenges for Westminster and Whitehall: How to Make Minority and Multiparty Governance Work', *The Political Quarterly* 81(2): 213–27.

Peake, Ross (2003), 'Ex-minister caught up in laundering row; Senior Labor MP donated money from Filipino fugitive in his own name, says Abbott', *Canberra Times*, Late Edition, 24 June, p. 3.

Pedersen, Rick (2001), 'Deep money troubles prompted latest crisis: Defiant to the end', *Edmonton Journal*, 10 July, p. A1.

Persily, Nathan (2006), 'The Law of American Party Finance', in Keith D. Ewing and Samuel Issacharoff (eds.), *Party Funding and Campaign Finance in International Perspective* (Oxford: Hart), pp. 213–40.

Pinto-Duschinsky, Michael (2002), 'Financing Politics: A Global View', *Journal of Democracy* 13(4): 69–86.

Poguntke, Thomas (1994), 'Parties in a Legalistic Culture: The Case of Germany', in Richard S. Katz and Peter Mair (eds.), *How Parties Organize: Change and Adaptation in Party Organizations in Western Democracies* (London: Sage), pp. 185–215.

Poirier, Patricia (1987), 'MPs want retirement of bagmen in Quebec', *The Globe and Mail*, 13 November.

Pontusson, Jonas and Rueda, David (2008), 'Inequality as a Source of Political Polarization: A Comparative Analysis of Twelve OECD Countries', in Christopher Anderson and

Pablo Beramendi (eds.), *Democracy, Inequality, and Represenation: A Comparative Perspective* (New York: Russell Sage Foundation).

Poschardt, Ulf (2010), 'Krisengipfel; FDP-Generalsekretär warnt vor Schwarz-Grün', *Welt Online*, 7 February.

Pridham, Geoffrey (1977), *Christian Democracy in Western Germany: The CDU/CSU in Government and Opposition, 1945–76* (London: Croom Helm).

Pulzer, Peter (1995), *German Politics 1945–95* (Oxford: Oxford University Press).

Queensland (2011), 'Electoral Reform and Accountability Amendment Act 2011', Act No. 14 of 2011.

Rademacher, Ludwig (1994), 'Zuschesse; Bangen um den satten Geldregen', *Focus*, 18 April, pp. 82–3.

Ramsay, Ian, Stapledon, Geof, and Vernon, Joel (2002), 'Political Donations by Australian Companies', *Federal Law Review* 29: 179–218.

Ramsey, Alan (1998), 'Nobody dares throw stones', *Sydney Morning Herald*, 4 April, p. 47.

Reitz, U., Barrey, K., and Oschwald, H. (1993), 'International; Die ungebremste Gier nach Spenden', 4 October, pp. 210–11.

Richter, Christine (2007), 'Landowsky jetzt vorbestraft; Berliner Landgericht verurteilt den früheren CDU-Politiker im Bankenprozess zu 16 Monaten Haft auf Bewährung/Auch mehrere Manager für schuldig befunden', *Berliner Zeitung*, 22 March.

Rollins, Adrian (2001a), 'Packer gift dogs Premier', *The Age*, Late Edition, News, 6 February, p. 2.

Rollins, Adrian (2001b), 'Bracks sees read over teacher threat', *The Age*, Late Edition, News, 17 May, p. 4.

Ronit, Karsten and Schneider, Volker (1998), 'The Strange Case of Regulating Lobbying in Germany', *Parliamentary Affairs* 51(4): 559–67.

Rose-Ackerman, Susan (1999), *Corruption and Government: Causes, Consequences, and Reform* (Cambridge: Cambridge University Press).

Ross, Shane (2009), *The Bankers: How the Banks Brought Ireland to its Knees* (Dublin: Penguin).

Rueda, David and Pontusson, Jonas (2000), 'Wage Inequality and Varieties of Capitalism', *World Politics* 52: 350–83.

Rush, Michael (1998), 'The Canadian Experience: The Lobbyists Registration Act', *Parliamentary Affairs* 51(4): 516–23.

Saalfeld, Thomas (2000), 'Court and Parties: Political Funding in Germany', in Robert Williams (ed.), *Party Finance and Political Corruption* (Basingstoke: Macmillan), pp. 89–122.

Salisbury, Robert (1984), 'Interest Representation: The Dominance of Institutions', *American Political Science Review* 78(1): 64–76.

Sallot, Jeff (1983), 'Tory delegates won't know who's bankrolling candidates', *The Globe and Mail*, 2 April.

Sallot, Jeff (1986), 'Liberal convention '86. Cheque presentation is cancelled over red ink', *The Globe and Mail*, 28 November, p. A4.

Savoie, Donald (1999a), *Governing from the Centre: The Concentration of Power in Canadian Politics* (Toronto: University of Toronto Press).

Savoie, Donald (1999b), 'The Rise of Court Government in Canada', *Canadian Journal of Political Science* 32(4): 635–64.

Scarrow, Susan E. (2002), 'Party Decline in the Parties State? The Changing Environment of German Politics', in Paul Webb, David Farrell, and Ian Holliday (eds.), *Political Parties in Advanced Industrial Democracies* (Oxford: Oxford University Press), pp. 77–106.

Scarrow, Susan E. (2006), 'Money, politics, and the balance of power: comparing official stories'. Paper presented at the annual meeting of the American Political Science Association, Philadelphia.

Scarrow, Susan E. (2007), 'Political Finance in Comparative Perspective', *Annual Review of Political Science* 10: 193–210.

Scheinpflug, Günter (2010), 'Keiner schafft 50-Prozent-Hürde', *Stuttgarter Zeitung*, 8 February.

Scherer, Peter (2004), 'Kanther kommt doch vor Gericht; OLG lässt Anklage wegen Finanzaffäre in hessischer CDU zu', *Die Welt*, 14 January.

Schmale, Holger (2010), 'Vorwurf der Parteilichkeit gegen Lammert Gabriel kritisiert Untätigkeit bei Sponsoring', *Berliner Zeitung*, 5 March, p. 5.

Schmidt, Wolf and Wyputta, Andreas (2010), 'Mieten Sie Rüttgers!; SYSTEM RÜTT-GERS Das Gebaren der NRW-CDU ging weit über die bei allen Parteien gängige—und problematische—Praxis hinaus', *Die Tagzeitung*, 25 February, p. 3.

Schmitter, Philippe C. and Streeck, Wolfgang (1981), 'The Organization of Business Interests: A Research Design to Study the Associative Action of Business in the Advanced Industrial Societies of Western Europe' (Berlin: International Institute of Management).

Schneider, Volker (2006), 'Business in Policy Networks: Estimating the Relative Import-ance of Corporate Direct Lobbying and Representation by Trade Associations', in David Coen and Wyn Grant (eds.), *Business and Government: Methods and Practice* (Opladen: Barbara Budrich), pp. 109–27.

Schöll, Torsten (2005), 'SPD: CDU-Finanzierung durch Verlag 'stinkt'; Auch Sozialde-mokraten wittern verdeckte Parteienspenden—Grüne halten Konstrukt für fragwürdig', *Stuttgarter Nachrichten*, 4 January.

Schubert, Misha (2006), 'Party incomes hit record high as donors dig deep; Wheat scandal', *The Age*, First Edition, News, 2 February, p. 8.

Schubert, Misha and Rood, David (2008), 'MP bought seat for $280,000: Lib; Political parties set record for donations as Labor pledges to tighten disclosure rules', *The Age*, First Edition, 2 February, p. 12.

Schunder, Josef (2004), 'Mitglieder und Spender bezahlen für Materialschlacht; Kreisvor-sitzende schreiben Bettelbriefe—Kosten gehen in die hunderttausende', *Stuttgarter Nachrichten*, 22 October.

Sexton, Elisabeth (2005), 'Dead ends in money maze', *Sydney Morning Herald*, First Edition, News and Features, 26 February, p. 33.

Sexton, Elisabeth (2006a), 'Law has holes you could drive a truck through', *Sydney Morning Herald*, First Edition, p. 2.

Sexton, Elisabeth (2006b), 'Greasing the wheels', *Sydney Morning Herald*, First Edition, News Review, p. 32.

Sharman, Campbell and Moon, Jeremy (2003), 'One System or Nine?' in Jeremy Moon and Campbell Sharman (eds.), *Australian Politics and Government: The Commonwealth, the States, and the Territories* (Cambridge: Cambridge University Press), pp. 239–62.

Shecter, Barbara (2002), 'Risks outweigh rewards in political donations: survey', *National Post*, 11 March, p. FP2.

Sheppard, Robert (1980), 'Who's who of political donors unveiled', *The Globe and Mail*, 11 July.

Sheppard, Robert (1984), 'Slightly more than three-quarters of the declared contributions to Peter Lougheed's Conservative Party come from firms or professional groups that do business with the Alberta Government', *The Globe and Mail*, 13 November.

Shonfield, Andrew (1969), *Modern Capitalism: The Changing Balance of Public and Private Power*, 2nd edn. (Oxford: Oxford University Press).

Simeon, Richard (2004), 'Canada: Federalism, Language, and Regional Conflict', in Ugo Amoretti and Nancy Bermeo (eds.), *Federalism and Territorial Cleavages* (Baltimore: Johns Hopkins University Press), pp. 93–122.

Simpson, Jeffrey (1978), 'Bagmen stalk the land as political parties hunt for cash', *The Globe and Mail*, 15 November.

Skelsey, Mark (2003), 'Pubs' late shout for ALP election battle', *The Daily Telegraph*, Local, 1 August, p. 3.

Skelton, Russell (2008), 'Power and dirty, sexy money; Political donations', *The Age*, First Edition, Insight, 22 March, p. 21.

Smilov, Daniel and Toplak, Jurij (eds.) (2007), *Political Finance and Corruption in Eastern Europe: The Transition Period* (Aldershot: Ashgate).

Smith, Alexandra (2008), 'Iemma injects a little honesty into donations; Labor in disarray', *Sydney Morning Herald*, Third Edition, 29 February, p. 4.

Smith, Bradley (2008), 'Outlook: Obama and the End of Fundraising Limits', *Washington Post*. http://www.washingtonpost.com/wp-dyn/content/discussion/2008/10/24/DI2008102402766.html

Smith, Gordon (1982), *Democracy in Western Germany: Parties and Politics in the Federal Republic*, 2nd edn. (London: Heinemann).

Sorauf, Frank J. (1992), *Inside Campaign Finance: Myths and Realities*. (New Haven, CT: Yale University Press).

Soroka, Stuart, Penner, Erin, and Blidook, Kelly (2009), 'Constituency Influence in Parliament', *Canadian Journal of Political Science* 42(3): 563–91.

Soskice, David (1999), 'Divergent Production Regimes: Coordinated and Uncoordinated Market Economies in the 1980s and 1990s', in Herbert Kitschelt, Peter Lange, Gary Marks, and John Stephens (eds.), *Continuity and Change in Contemporary Capitalism* (Cambridge: Cambridge University Press), pp. 101–34.

Stanbury, William T. (1993), *Money in Politics: Financing Federal Parties and Candidates in Canada* (Toronto: Dundurn Press).

Statistics Norway (2010a), http://www.ssb.no/english/subjects/07/02/10/partifin_en/tab-2010-09-08-02-en.html

Statistics Norway (2010b), http://www.partifinansiering.no/

Stead, Sylvia (1980), 'Ontario Liberals lag far behind in campaign funds', *The Globe and Mail*, 5 August.

Stigler, George J. (1971), 'The Theory of Economic Regulation', *Bell Journal of Economics and Management Science* 2(1): 3–21.

Stock, Jenny Tilby (2002), 'The South Australian Election of 9 February 2002', *Australian Journal of Political Science* 37(3): 537–46.

Stratmann, Thomas (2005), 'Some Talk: Money in Politics—A (Partial) Review of the Literature', *Public Choice* 124: 135–56.

Streeck, Wolfgang (1983), 'Between Pluralism and Corporatism: German Business Associations and the State', *Journal of Public Policy* 3(3): 265–84.

Streeck, Wolfgang (1992), 'Productive Constraints: On the Institutional Conditions of Diversified Quality Production', in Wolfgang Streeck, *Social Institutions and Economic Performance: Studies of Industrial Relations in Advanced Capitalist Economies* (London: Sage), pp. 1–40.

Streeck, Wolfgang (1997), 'Germany Capitalism: Existence and Survival', in Colin Crouch and Wolfgang Streeck (eds.), *Political Economy of Modern Capitalism: Mapping Convergence and Diversity* (London: Sage), pp. 33–54.

Strøm, Kaare and Narud, Hanne Marthe (2003), 'Norway: Virtual Parliamentarism', in Kaare Strøm, Wolfgang C. Müeller, and Torbjörn Bergman (eds.), *Delegation and Accountability in Parliamentary Democracies* (Oxford: Oxford University Press), pp. 523–51.

Stuttgarter Nachrichten (2007), 'Nur die FDP schreibt rote Zahlen; Industriellen-Familie Quandt wichtigster Einzelspender für die CDU', *Stuttgarter Nachrichten*, 23 May.

Stuttgarter Zeitung (2002), 'Wahlkampf köchelt auf kleiner Flamme; Die Parteien verfügen über einen Etat von rund 1000 Euro—Kandidaten bezahlen Inserate selbst', *Stuttgarter Zeitung*, 12 May.

Sundberg, Jan (2003), 'The Scandinavian Party Model at the Crossroads', in Paul Webb, David Farrell, and Ian Holliday (eds.), *Political Parties in Advanced Industrial Democracies* (Oxford: Oxford University Press), pp. 181–216.

Syal, Rajeev, Wintour, Patrick, and Meikle, James (2012), 'Cash-for-access: Cameron meetings with donor to remain private', *The Guardian*, 26 March.

Sydney Morning Herald (2005), 'He who pays the piper . . . ', *Sydney Morning Herald*, First Edition, News and Features, 15 February, p. 12.

Tadros, Edmund and Jopson, Debra (2008), 'Candidates forced to hand over funds; special investigation—donor scandal', *Sydney Morning Herald*, First Edition, News and Features, p. 11.

Tagesspiegel Der (2008), 'Spendenabend für Tempelhof: Geld geht an die Landes-CDU', *Der Tagesspiegel*, 20 January.

Taylor, Graham and Baskerville, Peter (1994), *A Concise History of Business in Canada* (Toronto: Oxford University Press).

Tham, Joo-Cheong (2003), 'Campaign Finance Reform in Australia: Some Reasons for Reform', in Graeme Orr, Bryan Mercurio, and George Williams (eds.), *Realising Democracy: Electoral Law in Australia* (New South Wales: The Federation Press), pp. 114–29.

Tham, Joo-Cheong (2005), 'Donor threshold over the top', *Sydney Morning Herald*, First Edition, News and Features, 30 May, p. 21.

Tham, Joo-Cheong (2006), 'Party funds threaten democracy', *The Age*, News, 26 May, p. 15.

Thomas, Paul G. (2009), 'Parliament Scrutiny of Government Performance in Australia', *Australian Journal of Public Administration* 68(4): 373–98.

Tillack, Hans-Martin (2004), 'Mehr Geld, weniger Kontrolle; Eine Studie belegt: Europas PARTEIEN können sich in Brüssel künftig auf eine Weise finanzieren, die in Deutschland verboten ware', *Stern*, 7 October, p. 220.

Tingle, Laura (1996), 'ALP to rethink poll challenges', *The Age*, Late Edition, News, 30 November, p. 9.

Tingle, Laura and Cookes, Thom (1997), 'Business millions flow to Liberals', *The Age*, Late Edition, News, 4 February, p. 1.

Totaro, Paola and Wainwright, Robert (2002), 'High price of joining Club Labor', *Sydney Morning Herald*, Late Edition, News and Features, 9 August, p. 4.

Toulin, Alan (1997), 'CEOs say unity top election issue. Poll: Tax cuts should be government's second priority, they say, ahead of deficit reduction', *The Financial Post*, 24 May, p. 5.

Transparency International (2009), *Corruption Perceptions Index 2009*. http://www.transparency.org/policy_research/surveys_indices/cpi/2009/cpi_2009_table

Tretbar, Christian (2010), 'Das Gesetz der Parteien; Eine Spende aus dem Hotelgewerbe bringt die FDP in Erklärungszwang. Funktionieren die Regeln noch?', *Der Tagesspiegel*, 19 January.

Trueman, Mary (1978), 'Only one voter in 150 gives to a federal party', *The Globe and Mail*, 10 July.

Trueman, Mary (1979), 'Liberal support grows only slightly. Individual contributions to Tories up sharply', *The Globe and Mail*, 4 July.

Trumbull, Robert (1975), Untitled, *New York Times*, 17 August, p. 16.

Tullock, Gordon (1972), 'The Purchase of Politicians', *Western Economic Journal* 10: 354–5.

Useem, Michael (1984), *The Inner Circle: Large Corporations and the Rise of Business Political Actors* (New York: Oxford University Press).

Vancouver Sun (1997), 'Evening the odds in the electoral ring', *The Vancouver Sun*, 8 July, p. A9.

Verrender, Ian (2001), 'The tide of pokie money that threatens to engulf Joe Tripodi; Power of the pokies—A Herald Investigation', *Sydney Morning Herald*, Late Edition, News and Features, 11 April, p. 1.

Vitols, Sigurt (2001), 'Varieties of Corporate Governance: Comparing Germany and the UK', in Peter Hall and David Soskice (eds.), *Varieties of Capitalism: The Institutional Foundations of Comparative Advantage* (Oxford: Oxford University Press), pp. 337–60.

Vogel, David (1996), *Kindred Strangers: The Uneasy Relationship between Politics and Business in America* (Princeton, NJ: Princeton University Press).

von Armin, Hans Herbert (1993), 'Campaign and Party Finance in Germany', in Arthur B. Gunlicks (ed.), *Party Finance in North America and Western Europe* (Oxford: Westview Press), pp. 201–18.

von Bartsch, Matthias (2004), 'Ursprung des Schwarzgelds bleibt ominös; Kanther-Prozess: Schwarze Kassen der CDU wohl von Spenden-Waschanlagen gefüllt—doch es fehlen Beweise', *Frankfurter Rundschau*, 2 November.

von Heimeier, Katharina (2006a), 'Ein Bestecher, aber kein Bestochener; JUSTIZ: Ab Mittwoch steht Hans Kremendahl wieder vor Gericht. Nachdem der Bundesgerichtshof das Urteil gegen den früheren Wuppertaler OB und den Baulöwen Uwe Clees aufgehoben hat, wird nun in Dortmund beraten', *General-Anzeiger*, 6 February, p. 5.

von Heimeier, Katharina (2006b), 'Wieder geht es um die Rotweinrunde; JUSTIZ: Der ehemalige Wuppertaler Oberbürgermeister Kremendahl beteuert bei der Neuauflage seines Prozesses erneut seine Unschuld', *General-Anzeiger*, 9 February, p. 5.

von Irion, Christoph (2001), 'Frösche im Spenden-Sumpf; Das Geld der Parteien und die Transparenz', *Berliner Morgenpost*, 3 February.

von Jungholt, Thorsten and Marx, Iris (2007), 'Griff in die Staatskasse; Weil SPD und Union Wähler und zahlende Mitglieder verlieren, wollen sie mehr Steuergeld—Grüne und FDP protestieren', *Die Welt*, 20 August.

von Nowak, Nikolaus (2000), 'Der Griff in die iberische Mottenkiste; Spanien und Portugal können nicht verstehen, was ihre Vergangenheit mit der CDU-Spendenaffäre zu tun haben soll', *Berliner Morgenpost*, 4 February.

von Ulla, Thiede (2010), 'Jeder kehre vor seiner Tür', *General Anzeiger*, 5 March, p. 2.

Wailes, Nick, Ramia, Gaby, and Lansbury, Russell (2003), 'Interests, Institutions and Industrial Relations', *British Journal of Industrial Relations* 41(4): 617–37.

Wainwright, Robert (1992), 'Criminal probes on three ex-premiers', *The Advertiser*, 21 October.

Wainwright, Robert (2003), 'Labor leads with a $10m party punch'; Decision 03 Where the money is coming from', *Sydney Morning Herald*, Late Edition, Supplement, 1 March, p. 26.

Walker, William (1987), 'Tories trying to get back on feet. Leadership, philosophy loom large at Ontario party conference', *Toronto Star*, 21 November, p. D6.

Walkom, Thomas (1988), 'Pressed flesh and passed hats', *The Globe and Mail*, 6 October.

Walters, Joan (1998), 'Drive for funds divides the right: Tories fume as united alternative goes after corporate donations', *The Ottawa Citizen*, 5 December, p. A3.

Walther, Rudolf (2004), 'Die Sache mit dem Nummernkonto; In seiner Familiengeschichte der Flicks weiß Thomas Ramge nichts wirklich Neues zu berichten', *Frankfurter Rundschau*, 30 August.

Wanna, John (2003), 'Queensland', in Jeremy Moon and Campbell Sharman (eds.), *Australian Politics and Government: The Commonwealth, the States and the Territories* (Cambridge: Cambridge University Press, 2003), pp. 74–103.

Warhurst, John (1998), 'Locating the Target: Regulating Lobbying in Australia', *Parliamentary Affairs* 51(4): 538–50.

Watt, Nicholas (2009), 'Erminegate: Police Called to Examine Corruption Allegations in the House of Lords', *The Guardian*, 26 January, p. 3.

Weller, Patrick and Fleming, Jenny (2003), 'The Commonwealth', in Jeremy Moon and Campbell Sharman (eds.), *Australian Politics and Government* (Cambridge: Cambridge University Press), pp. 12–40.

Welt, Die (2002), '"Strafe gefährdet Wahlkampf nicht"; CDU-General Meyer: Partei wird Rechtsmittel gegen Spenden-Urteil einlegen', *Die Welt*, 14 June.

Wesley, Jared (2007), 'Canadian provincial party systems: toward a new comparative framework'. Paper presented to the Annual Meeting of the Canadian Political Science Association, Saskatoon, Saskatchewan, 1 June.

Western Report (1996), 'Oh, that €2.5m account. Saskatchewan political parties are wedded to unreported slush funds', *Western Report*, 24 June, p. v11.

Whitaker, Reginald (1977), *The Government Party: Organizing and Financing the Liberal Party of Canada* (Toronto: University of Toronto Press).

The White House, Office of the Press Secretary (2010), 'Statement from the President on Today's Supreme Court Decision', 21 January.

Wiegrefe, Klaus (2001), 'Kampf gegen die Sozis', *Der Spiegel*, 20 August, p. 52.

Wilkinson, Marian (1996), 'The Fixer', *The Age*, Late Edition, News, 10 February, p. 21.

Williams, Robert (ed.) (2000), *Party Finance and Political Corruption* (Basingstoke: Macmillan).

Willis, Andrew (2003), 'United right win's Street's hearts, wallets', *The Globe and Mail*, 17 October, p. B1.

Wilson, Graham (1990), 'Corporate Political Strategies', *British Journal of Political Science* 20(2): 281–8.

Winsor, Hugh (1984), 'Forget paranoia and govern, Turner tells PCs in fiery attack', *The Globe and Mail*, 6 December.

Winsor, Hugh (1987), 'Liberals take steps to slash spending', *The Globe and Mail*, 19 January.

Winsor, Hugh (2001), 'Yond White looks lean and hungry', *The Globe and Mail*, 13 June, p. A13.

Winsor, Hugh (2003), 'Arrogance breeds cynicism about politics', *The Globe and Mail*, 17 February, p. A5.

Wood, Stewart (2001), 'Business, Government, and Patterns of Labor Market Policy in Britain and the Federal Republic of Germany', in Peter Hall and David Soskice (eds.), *Varieties of Capitalism: The Institutional Foundations of Comparative Advantage* (Oxford: Oxford University Press), pp. 247–74.

Woodside, Kenneth (1989), 'The Canada–US Free Trade Agreement', *Canadian Journal of Political Science* 22(1): 155–70.

Yaffe, Barbara (1980), 'Got extra funds as N.S. Liberal leader. Regan named in RCMP papers', *The Globe and Mail*, 19 March.

Yaffe, Barbara (2002), 'Selling access to cabinet is plain wrong', *Vancouver Sun*, 13 August, p. A14.

Young, Sally and Tham, Joo-Cheong (2006), *Political Finance in Australia: A Skewed and Secret System* (Canberra: Australian National University).

Zeytinoglu, Isik and Cooke, Gordon B. (2009), 'On-the-Job Training in Canada: Associations with Information Technology, Innovation and Competition', *Journal of Industrial Relations* 51(1): 95–112.

Index

Index